The
OXFORD
Children's Encyclopedia of
Our World

OXFORD
UNIVERSITY PRESS

OXFORD
UNIVERSITY PRESS

Great Clarendon Street, Oxford OX2 6DP

Oxford University Press is a department of the University of Oxford.
It furthers the University's objective of excellence in research, scholarship,
and education by publishing worldwide in

Oxford New York

Auckland Bangkok Buenos Aires Cape Town Chennai
Dar es Salaam Delhi Hong Kong Istanbul Karachi Kolkata
Kuala Lumpur Madrid Melbourne Mexico City Mumbai Nairobi
São Paulo Shanghai Taipei Tokyo Toronto

Oxford is a registered trade mark of Oxford University Press
in the UK and in certain other countries

British Library Cataloguing in Publication Data

Data available

ISBN 0-19-910775-0

3 5 7 9 10 8 6 4

Typeset by Oxford Designers and Illustrators
Typeset in Photina and Rotis
Printed in China

Contents

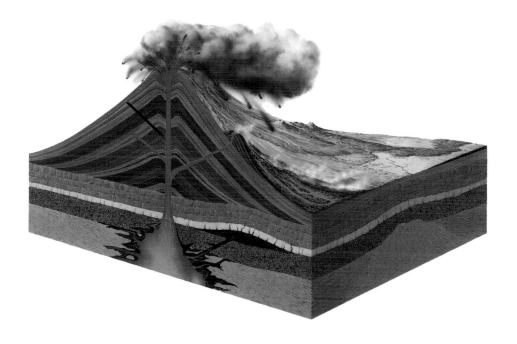

Contributors

Editor
Ben Dupré

Coordinating editors
Ian Crofton
Joanna Harris

Proofreaders
Helen Maxey
Susan Mushin

Indexer
Ann Barrett

Design
Jo Cameron
Oxford Designers and Illustrators

Art editor
Hilary Wright

Assistant art editor
Jo Samways

Cover design
Jo Cameron

Photographic research
Charlotte Lippmann

Consultants
Professor Adrian Brockett
John R. Brown
Stuart Corbridge
Frank Eckardt
Professor David Harris
Vivien McKay
Colin Mills
Joyce Pope
Judy Ridgway
Alisdair Rogers
Elspeth Scott
Michael Scott
Peter Teed
Bob Unwin
Patrick Wiegand
Elizabeth Williamson

Authors
Dr R. E. Allen
Jill Bailey
Professor Adrian Brockett
Gerald Butt
Arthur Swift Butterfield
Ian Crofton
Tony Drake
Frank Eckardt
David Glover
Gib Goodfellow
Susan Goodman
Dr Terry Jennings
Susan Keeler
Keith Lye
Dr Nick Middleton
Dr Jacqueline Mitton
Judy Ridgway
Dr Alisdair Rogers
Stewart Ross
Theodore Rowland-Entwistle
Nigel Smith
Andrew Solway
Imogen Stewart
Peter Teed
Teresa Thornhill
Patrick Wiegand
Elizabeth Williamson
Jill A. Wright

Acknowledgments

Key t top; b bottom; c centre; r right; l left
NHPA = Natural History Photographic Agency; NGIC = National Geographic Image Collection; RH = Robert Harding; SPL = Science Photo Library

Photos are reproduced by kind permission of:
Front cover Corbis/Getty Images. 7 NGIC, George F. Mobley. 8b NHPA, Jonathan Chester. 9b B & C Alexander. 11t RH, Thomas Laird. 11br RH, Duncan Maxwell. 11bl RH, Nevada Wier. 14t RH, Nigel Gomm. 14b RH, David Lomax. 15t Image Bank, Andre Gallant. 16t NHPA, John Shaw. 16b RH, John Miller. 17t RH, Fred Friberg. 19t RH, Nigel Gomm. 20t RH, T. Megarry. 20b RH, Gavin Hellier. 22t Images of Africa, David Keith Jones. 23t RH, Nigel Temple. 26t Image Bank, Jurgen Vogt. 26b Irish Embassy. 27t NHPA, Anthony Bannister. 27cl RH, Robert Francis. 28t Images of Africa, David Keith Jones. 29t Image Bank, Carlos Navajas. 30tr Oxford Scientific Films, Hjalmar R. Bardarson. 31t Planet Earth Pictures. 31b SPL, NASA. 32t Topham, Y. Shimbun. 35tr RH. 36b Getty Images, Hans Peter Merten. 38b Topham, G. Marinovich. 39t Getty Images, Kevin Horan. 39b Images of Africa, David Keith Jones. 40t RSPCA. 40b Getty Images, Mitch Kezar. 41tr Images of Africa, David Keith Jones. 41tl Getty Images, Gary Braasch. 42b Getty Images, Ian Murphy. 44t NHPA, Rod Plank. 46t RH, David Martyn Hughes. 46b Image Bank, Peter and Georgina Bowater. 48t RH, Gavin Hellier. 49t NHPA, John Shaw. 49b NHPA, Christophe Ratier. 50b Greenpeace, Sims. 52t Images of Africa, Johann Van Tonder. 52b Woodfall Wild Images; Nigel Hicks 53t SPL, Pekka Parviaien. 53b NGIC, Medford Taylor. 54br Images of India. 55tr Link Picture Library, Eric Meacher. 55cl Images of India, Roderick Johnson. 55b Images of India. 56t RH, Nigel Gomm. 56b Image Bank, HMS Images. 57t Images of India, Michael Ravinder. 58b RH, Roy Rainford. 59t SPL. 60t SPL, Douglas Faulkner. 61b Image Bank, Marc Romanelli. 62b NGIC, David A. Harvey. 65b SPL, M-SAT Ltd. 66b NGIC. 67b Getty Images, Nabeel Turner. 68t Colorific, Ian Bradshaw. 70t NHPA, David Woodfall. 70b NHPA, Michael Leach. 72t Getty Images, Oldrich Karasek. 72b SPL, W. Bacon. 73b RH, Julian Pottage. 74t RH, D. Maryk. 74b David Keith Jones. 76t Image Bank, Eric Meola. 76b Image Bank, Stuart Dee. 77t RH, David Lomax. 78b Electric de France, Michel Brigaud. 80b RH. 81tr SPL, NOAA. 81br Image Bank, Yiu Chun Ma. 81bl Topham, Kurt Adams. 83t RH, J. H. C. Wilson. 83b Getty Images, Christopher Arneseh. 85t RH, Philip Craven. 85b SPL. 86, 87t, b Geo Science Features/Dr B. Booth. 88t Image Bank, P. & G. Bogwater. 88b Getty Images, Natalie Fobes. 89b Image Bank, Harald Sund. 90b Getty Images. 91b RH, Rolf Richardson. 92t Getty Images, Arnulf Husmo. 93t RH, Thomas Laird. 93b NGIC, Stephanie Maze. 94t SPL, National Snow and Ice Data Centre. 94b Image Bank, Steve Dunwell. 95t Sainsbury's Archives. 96b RH, T. Waltham. 97b, 98t, b South American Pictures. 99b Colorific, Raghubir Singh. 100bl South American Pictures. 101b NHPA, David Woodfall. 102t Getty Images, Jon Riley. 102b Getty Images, Lorne Hesnick. 103t Image Bank, Erik Simonsen. 103b RH, John Miller. 104t RH, Robert Francis. 104b Image Bank, Steve Allen. 105b Jersey Tourism. 107t Image Bank, John P. Kelly. 107b Image Bank; Foto World. 108b RH, Lorraine Wilson. 109t Rex Features/SIPA; Arthur Pengelly. 113t SPL/NASA. 115t RH, Financial Times. 115b NHPA, John Shaw. 116tl NHPA, Stephen Krasemann. 116b NHPA, Dr. Ivan Polunin. 116r NHPA; Dr.Ivan Polunin. 117t NGIC. 117b Image Bank, Steve Proehl. 118t Telegraph Colour Library, Masterfile.

Illustrations are by:
Baker, Julian: 22cl, 63b, 79t, 82t, 92b, 100br, 118b
Barber, John: 44b
Cottam, Martin: 29b
Gecko Ltd: 63t
Hawken, Nick: 50t
Hinks, Gary: 18t, 23b, 24b, 28b, 30b, 48b, 60b, 71t, 78t, 84, 86, 95b, 108tr, 109b, 111, 114b
Milne, Sean: 43
Oxford Illustrators: 12, 24t, 59b
Polley, Robbie: 51
Raynor Design: 101t
Sanders, Martin: 113b
Sneddon, James: 32b, 33t, 34, 42t, 69, 110b, 112
Visscher, Peter: 36t
Woods, Michael: 18b
All maps are by Olive Pearson and Phoenix Mapping.
All flags courtesy of the Flag Institute.

Yo5911

Finding your way around

The *Oxford Children's Encyclopedia of Our World* has many useful features that will help you find the information you need quickly and easily.

The articles in the encyclopedia are arranged in alphabetical order from Africa to Wool. When you want to find out about a particular topic, the first step is to see whether there is an **article** on it in the A–Z sequence. If there is no article, there are two things you can do.

First of all you can look at the **footers** at the bottom of the page.

These may include the topic you want, and give you the name of the article where you can find out about it. If there is no footer, the next thing to do is to look the topic up in the alphabetical **index** at the back of the book. This will tell you which page or pages you can look at to find out what you want to know.

The **header** tells you what articles are on the page, for quick reference.

Articles are arranged alphabetically, so that they are easy to find.

The **opening paragraph** gives a friendly introduction to the topic.

The **main text** gives an account of the topic in a continuous and readable way. Key terms are picked out in *italic text*.

Detailed **maps** illustrate geographical and historical articles.

Locator maps place countries and continents on the globe.

Margin notes provide nuggets of extra information and amazing facts.

The **find out more panel** points you to other articles related to the topic.

Captions not only describe the photographs and illustrations but give additional information on the topic.

Colourful illustrations and **photographs** bring the topic to life.

Mediterranean

The Mediterranean Sea stretches over 3000 kilometres from west to east. When we talk about the Mediterranean, we often mean both the sea and the shores surrounding it, where more than 100 million people live.

The Mediterranean region has mild, wet winters and hot, dry summers. The eastern Mediterranean is drier than the west. The coast of North Africa, especially Libya, is desert. It can be very hot here, as it is also in the far south of Italy.

The mountains are wetter and cooler than the coastal plains. In summer, a dry dusty wind often blows from the Sahara. This is the sirocco. In winter comes the mistral, an icy wind from northern Europe, bringing with it a sudden chill.

Shipping and ports

The Mediterranean has been an important sea route since before the civilizations of Greece and Rome. Today, ocean-going tankers bring oil through the Suez Canal and luxury liners take tourists cruising through the islands. Marseille is the largest Mediterranean trading port.

• Over 30 million tourists visit the Mediterranean each year. The Spanish coasts of the Costa del Sol, Costa Brava and Costa Blanca are especially crowded. So too are the Riviera coasts of France and Italy, the Greek islands and Tunisia in North Africa.

find out more
Africa
Europe
Middle East
Oceans and seas

Mexico

Mexico is the most northerly country of the Spanish-speaking Americas. Its landscape changes from dry deserts in the north, through ranges of high mountains and volcanoes, to low tropical jungle in the south-east.

The capital, Mexico City, is 2200 metres above sea level, and although it is usually warm during the day it can be cold at night. Down at sea level in the south-east of Mexico it is warm all the year round. The peninsula known as the Yucatán is very flat and hot and has some fine beaches of white coral sand.

Large oil deposits have been discovered off Mexico's east coast. But Mexico has not become as rich as some oil-producing countries because oil prices fell and foreign debts took most of the money. Today many Mexicans are still very poor. Millions of Mexicans have journeyed to the USA in the 20th century to find better-paid jobs.

— FLASHBACK —

Modern Mexico dates from the 16th century, when the Spaniards conquered the Aztecs. The Mexicans gained their independence in 1821, after 11 years of war. For a century after that, dictators ruled the country. The present republic emerged after a civil war lasting from 1911 to 1940.

▼ More than 18 million people live in Mexico City, one of the largest cities on Earth. Beyond Mexico City you can see two of Mexico's highest volcanoes, which are both over 5000 metres high. Their names come from old Aztec words: Iztaccíhuatl and Popocatépetl.

• Central and southern Mexico has been the home of a number of ancient civilizations, such as the Maya, the Aztecs and the Olmecs. Today many remains of their buildings and even complete cities can still be seen.

find out more
North America
See also Countries and flags section, page 124

The **footer** provides a short cut to topics that do not have their own articles.

Africa

Africa is the world's second largest continent, covering one-fifth of the Earth's land area. It sits squarely on the Equator, extending almost the same distance to the north and south. Apart from the narrow strip of land at Suez which joins it to Asia, it is completely surrounded by sea.

Almost all of Africa is warm or hot. The countries which lie on the Equator are wet all year round. North and south of the Equator there are two seasons, a wet season and a dry one. The driest parts of Africa are the Sahara, Namib and Kalahari deserts, where it is hot all year and there is hardly any rainfall. The Mediterranean shores and the tip of South Africa have warm, wet winters and hot, dry summers.

• All the independent countries of Africa have entries in the Countries and flags section on pages 122–125.

◆	capital city	
■	large city	
	country boundary	
▲	highest peaks (height in metres)	

land height in metres

- 2000–5000
- 1000–2000
- 500–1000
- 200–500
- sea level
- less than 200
- land below sea level

Aborigines *see* Australia • **Agriculture** *see* Farming • **Air** *see* Atmosphere *and* Pollution

Landscapes

Africa's chunky shape gives it far less coastline than western Europe and there are few natural harbours. Much of the south and east of Africa is high plateau country. Among the more dramatic highlands are the Ruwenzori range in east Central Africa, and the Drakensberg range along the south-eastern coast. Mount Kilimanjaro in Tanzania is the highest mountain.

The north and west of Africa are in general lower. The area around Lake Chad is an inland basin, and rivers empty themselves into the lake. The Sahara Desert, the largest desert in the world, is also in the north.

The heart of the continent is tropical rainforest. Away from the forest stretches the savannah – lands of tall grass dotted with trees. Most of the large African wildlife live in the savannah.

Africa has four of the world's greatest rivers: the Nile, the Congo, the Niger and the Zambezi. The River Nile is the longest river in the world. Africa also has some of the world's largest freshwater lakes, the largest of which is Lake Victoria.

People and languages

Much of the population of Africa is concentrated in just a few areas. The coast of West Africa, the Nile Valley and the area around Lake Victoria are crowded.

Over 1000 different languages are spoken in Africa, and very many Africans speak more than one language. In North Africa most people speak Arabic. In West Africa, Hausa, Yoruba, Akan and Malinke are important languages. Most East Africans can speak Kiswahili. South of the Equator people speak one or other of a number of languages known collectively as Bantu.

In the late 19th century, several European nations ruled most of Africa. French, Portuguese and English are still spoken by many Africans.

Religion

The Arabic-speaking people of the north are Muslims, as are the majority of the people of Mali, Sudan and northern Nigeria. About half of all Africans are Muslims and the numbers are growing. Christian Churches are strong, too. As well as Roman Catholics and Anglicans, there are many independent African Churches. Traditional African religions have their own rituals. Africans worship with dance and music, and these are important art forms throughout the continent.

▶ FLASHBACK ◀

Scientists believe that human beings evolved in Africa and spread out to other parts of the world. Very little is known of Africa in prehistoric times, but from about 4000 BC powerful empires grew up beside the River Nile. The most famous was ancient Egypt.

From the 5th century AD trading empires arose in West Africa, using camels to cross the Sahara Desert with gold, salt and slaves. Many of their kings adopted the Muslim religion. Other states grew up in the forest areas nearer to the coast. City states on the east coast sent ivory, gold, copper and gum by sea to Arabia, India and China. The gold came from the powerful inland state of Zimbabwe.

The slave trade had long existed in Africa, but in the 16th to 18th centuries it grew enormously. This was because Europeans took huge numbers of Africans to be sold into slavery abroad. By the late 19th century much of Africa was conquered and divided up between European nations who created countries with artificial frontiers, separating people who spoke the same language.

From 1956 onwards, one by one the states of Africa achieved their independence. The new countries kept the artificial boundaries that the Europeans had drawn, and this has been the cause of terrible conflicts in some parts of Africa. Difficult climates, fast-growing populations, lack of resources, and local wars have caused widespread famine and unrest.

▲ In the hot desert lands of North Africa, camels have always played an important role. Camel markets, such as this one in Sudan, do a busy trade.

• The first Europeans to reach East Africa were the Portuguese. During the 15th century Portuguese sea captains such as Bartolomeu Dias and Vasco da Gama opened up a sea route to India around the African coast.

find out more
Deserts
Grasslands
Nigeria
South Africa
Valleys

Antarctica

Antarctica is the Earth's fifth largest continent – and the coldest. Nearly all of its huge area is covered with ice over 3 kilometres thick. There is very little wildlife, and for thousands of years there were no people. But since the early 20th century, human activity in Antarctica has steadily grown.

The Antarctic ice-cap has built up over millions of years. The sheet of ice spreads out onto the sea, where huge pieces break off to make icebergs. Geologists who study the rocky areas that are not under ice have discovered coal and the fossils of plants and animals. These finds show that Antarctica once had a warm climate. It began to get cold about 150 million years ago. The climate is made worse by very strong, icy winds. Except in summer, the sea around the continent is full of ice.

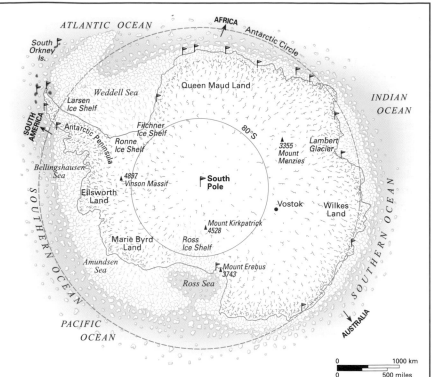

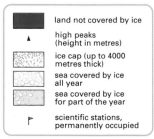

	land not covered by ice
▲	high peaks (height in metres)
	ice cap (up to 4000 metres thick)
	sea covered by ice all year
	sea covered by ice for part of the year
⚑	scientific stations, permanently occupied

Exploration

One of the first explorers to sight Antarctica may have been the British naval captain, James Cook, who sailed south in 1774. The first people to set foot on the continent were probably seal hunters in about 1820. But the extreme cold and the ice made exploration difficult. By 1895 people were keen to find out what Antarctica was like. Members of a Belgian party that sailed in 1897 were the first people to spend a winter on the ice.

Between 1901 and 1904 Captain Robert F. Scott led an unsuccessful British expedition to the South Pole. In 1910 Scott began a second attempt, and soon afterwards a Norwegian explorer, Roald Amundsen, also set out for the Pole. Amundsen arrived first, on 14 December 1911, and returned home successfully. Scott and his companions reached the Pole a month later, but died on the return journey.

A continent for research

Since the early 20th century, many countries have sent scientific expeditions to Antarctica, and have set up permanent stations where scientists can live and work. Most scientific research is done in the summer. In recent years, there has also been a small amount of tourism in the summer months.

In 1959 the USA, Russia and 10 other countries signed an Antarctic Treaty, in which they agreed not to make rival claims to territory but to use the Antarctic only for peaceful research. Many more countries have since accepted the treaty, and in 1991 a 50-year mining ban was agreed.

◀ Whole mountain ranges are buried under the Antarctic ice. Just the very tops poke through. The tallest peak is called the Vinson Massif and is 4897 m high.

find out more
Arctic
Continents
Glaciers
Ice
Rain and snow

Arabia *see* Middle East • **Arabs** *see* Middle East

Arctic

The Arctic is the area inside the Arctic Circle around the North Pole. It is a huge frozen ocean, surrounded by islands and by the northern coasts of Asia, Europe and North America.

The Arctic is cold all year round. In winter the Sun never comes above the horizon, and the sea is frozen over. In summer, temperatures creep above freezing, the edge of the Arctic Ocean melts, and for weeks the Sun never sets. The Arctic Ocean is rich in plankton and fish. These are food for millions of sea birds, which nest in the Arctic in summer, and for seals, whales and other sea creatures.

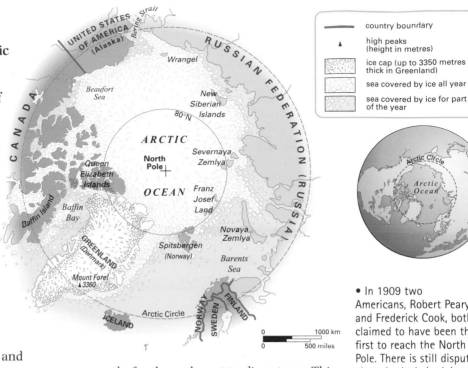

Tundra

The land around the Arctic Ocean is flat and treeless. It is called the tundra, which means 'treeless'. The tundra is only free from snow and ice for a few months of the year.

Lichens, mosses, grasses and sedges are the main plants of the tundra. But there are also a few flowering plants and small shrubs that can withstand the winter cold and flower in the short summer. Animals that live in the tundra all year include voles, shrews and lemmings. In winter they tunnel beneath the snow and dig up plant roots for food. Arctic foxes also stay all year, but polar bears wander more widely, hunting seals and walruses on the ice sheets. Musk oxen are pony-sized animals, related to sheep. They are found in Canada and Greenland, and have long woolly coats and massive horns. They protect themselves from wolves by bunching themselves in a circle, horns outwards.

When summer arrives, animals from further south come to the tundra to benefit from the rich food that is briefly available. Huge herds of reindeer (caribou) wander north, followed by packs of hungry wolves. Many birds such as geese, swans and wading birds also come to the tundra in summer to breed.

People

The Arctic region is one of the most sparsely populated areas in the world. The Inuit (Eskimo) have survived in the Arctic lands of Greenland, Canada and Alaska for thousands of years, feeding themselves by hunting and fishing. Nowadays they are able to buy what they cannot get or make for themselves at trading stores. This includes guns, metal tools and clothes made in factories. But the clothes that Inuit women make from animal skins are often more suitable for Arctic life.

Most Inuit live in villages or small towns on the coasts. In the past they would move from one place to another throughout the year, living in tents or igloos. They walked, rode on sledges pulled by dogs, or paddled boats.

Although some Inuit still make their living from the land and its animals, the development of towns has led to an increase in the number of people doing modern jobs. The discovery of oil has also brought people from further south to work in the Arctic.

• In 1909 two Americans, Robert Peary and Frederick Cook, both claimed to have been the first to reach the North Pole. There is still dispute about both their claims.

find out more
Antarctica
Ice

▼ The traditional way of life of the Inuit people of the Arctic is gradually changing with the introduction of new technology. This Inuit man uses a skidoo (motorized sledge) to get about.

Asia

The continent of Asia is the largest in the world, covering one-third of the Earth's land surface. It also has the most people. About two-thirds of the world's population live in Asia. Most of them live in the densely populated southern part of the continent, which is separated from the sparsely populated lands of central and northern Asia by the Himalaya Mountains.

Asia is so large that some parts are more than 2500 kilometres from the sea. This far inland, the climate is very hot in summer, but extremely cold in winter. At this time the land lies under a great cushion of cold heavy air. Cold dry winds blow out from the centre of the continent. In summer the land heats quickly and warms the air, which rises. Wet winds blow in from the sea, bringing heavy monsoon rains to the south. However, the barrier of the Himalayas stops the wet winds from reaching the continent's interior.

• Asia's border with Europe is formed by the Ural Mountains in Russia. The Middle East is usually counted as part of Asia.

◆ capital city
■ large city
●—● Trans-Siberian Railway with major stations
— country boundary
ㅆㅆ ice cap
▲ highest peaks (height in metres)

land height in metres
more than 5000
2000–5000
1000–2000
500–1000
200–500
less than 200
sea level
land below sea level

0 ——— 1000 km
0 ——— 500 miles

• All the independent countries of Asia have entries in the Countries and flags section on pages 122–125.

keeping central Asia, western China and Mongolia dry.

Landscapes

Flat frozen plains of mosses and lichens cover much of the far north. Further south is a band of coniferous forest called the taiga, stretching right across the continent. The steppes of western Asia are grasslands, with rich, black soils that are excellent for agriculture. Much of central Asia, from the Red Sea to Mongolia, is desert. The largest is the bare, rocky Gobi Desert.

The Himalayas separate central Asia from the tropical lands of southern and South-east Asia. They curve in a great arc from Pakistan in the west to Tibet in the east. They form the largest mountain system in the world. The huge peaks reach heights of over 8000 metres, while in some places rivers have cut gorges nearly 5000 metres deep. The rivers that drain the Himalayas, such as the Ganges, the Indus and the Brahmaputra, carry silt and mud to the flood plains to the south, forming rich, fertile soils.

People

The largest number of Asians live in India, Bangladesh and the eastern half of China. Other great centres of population are Japan, Indonesia and Pakistan. The most crowded areas are on the coasts and along the flood plains of rivers in China, India and Bangladesh.

There are also vast areas where few people live. In most of Mongolia, the western half of China and Siberia in Russia the average number of people per square kilometre is less than one.

The majority of Asians live in the country and make their living from some kind of farming.

▼ Rice is the most important crop in large parts of southern and eastern Asia. The seeds are sown in special seed beds, then transferred to a flooded field, or paddy, after 25 to 50 days. This Vietnamese woman is moving some seedlings that are ready for transplanting.

▲ Despite the difficult terrain, there are many kinds of farming and industry in the Himalayas. Rice, sugar cane and other crops are grown; sheep, goats and yaks (above) are reared. About one-third of the Himalayas is forest, used mainly for paper and firewood. The mountains also contain valuable minerals, iron ore and coal.

Rice is the main crop in most of India, China and South-east Asia; wheat is the main crop in Russia and Kazakhstan; and the plains of central Asia are grazed by herds of cattle, goats or yaks. However, in southern and South-east Asia, more and more people are moving to cities. Seoul, Bangkok, Jakarta, Mumbai (Bombay), Calcutta and several Chinese cities now have more than 5 million inhabitants. Many of these cities have tremendous overcrowding problems.

Asia has some of the world's poorest countries as well as some of its richest. South Asian countries have fewer doctors per person than anywhere else, and many people do not have a balanced diet. The average life expectancy in Laos, for example, is about 50 years, whereas people in Japan usually live to be nearer 80. The death rate for infants is higher in Cambodia than in any other country in the world.

▶ Calcutta, India's second largest and most important city, has problems such as overcrowding caused by poverty and rapid growth. The city is polluted, the streets are mostly narrow and in poor repair, and about a third of the people live in crowded slum housing. Many people have no house at all, and make their home on the pavement.

find out more

Arctic
Bangladesh
China
Continents
Deserts
Forests
Grasslands
India
Indonesia
Japan
Middle East
Mountains
Pakistan
Russia

Atmosphere

The atmosphere makes it possible for us to live on the Earth. It consists of layers of air that surround our planet. They are wrapped around the Earth rather like orange peel is wrapped around the fruit inside. The air itself is a mixture of gases, mainly nitrogen and oxygen.

The weight of the atmosphere is quite considerable. Every cubic metre of the air around us contains more than 1 kilogram of air. The weight of all this air above pushing down on us is called atmospheric pressure. It is like having 1 kilogram pressing on every square centimetre of our bodies.

The different layers of the atmosphere merge into one another, so it is difficult to give their exact heights. They vary depending on the time of year, the latitude, and activities of the Sun, such as sunspots and solar flares. We live in the *troposphere*, the lowest layer. It contains 90 per cent of the air in the atmosphere. As you move up through the troposphere, the temperature drops, and on high mountains there is not enough oxygen to breathe easily. The air in the layer above the troposphere, the *stratosphere*, is much thinner, and the temperature rises. The stratosphere contains a gas called ozone, which is a type of oxygen. It absorbs much of the harmful ultraviolet radiation from the Sun.

Above the stratosphere, the temperature drops rapidly. Higher up, in the *ionosphere*, there are layers of particles called ions which carry electrical charges. These layers are very important in bouncing radio signals around our planet. The *exosphere* is where the Earth's atmosphere really becomes part of space. In this layer temperatures can be as high as 1000 °C.

Auroras

High up in the atmosphere, between 80 and 600 kilometres above the ground, huge patches of glowing coloured lights sometimes appear in the night sky. Scientists call this display the aurora. The pattern of lights can look like rays from a searchlight, twisting flames, shooting streamers or shimmering curtains. In the northern hemisphere, the popular name for this display is the 'northern lights'. We are more likely to see an aurora when there are big sunspots on the Sun. Atomic particles from the Sun collide with atoms in our atmosphere, giving off the different coloured lights.

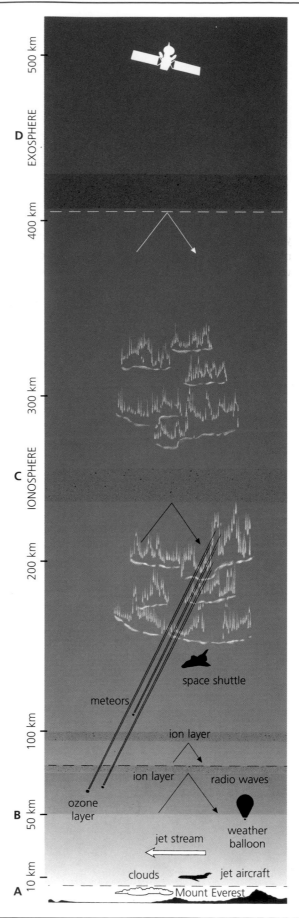

find out more
Earth
Greenhouse effect
Pollution
Weather

D The highest layer, the **exosphere**, contains hardly any gas, only a few molecules of hydrogen and helium.

C Radio signals from Earth bounce off the **ionosphere** before returning to Earth hundreds of kilometres from where they started.

A and **B** Weather balloons carrying instruments are sent up through the **troposphere (A)**. Clouds form in this layer. In the lower part of the next layer, the **stratosphere (B)**, long-distance aircraft take advantage of the lack of air resistance, helped by high-speed 'jet-stream' winds.

Diagram labels:
500 km — EXOSPHERE — D
ion layer
400 km — radio signals
300 km — aurora (glowing gas)
IONOSPHERE — C — ion layer
200 km
space shuttle
meteors
100 km — ion layer
ion layer — radio waves
50 km — B — ozone layer — weather balloon
jet stream
10 km — A — clouds — jet aircraft — Mount Everest

Australia

Australia is a large country of great natural beauty. Australian society is varied, combining the culture of its Aboriginal population with the traditions of more recent settlers from all parts of the world.

The Australian landmass has been stable for over 300 million years. There have been no major periods of earthquakes, volcanic activity or mountain-building. This means that wind and water have worn down the land and made it flat.

Landscape

Most of Australia, between the Great Dividing Range in the east and the western coast, is known as the 'outback'. The western half of the country is mostly desert. Few people live there, and plants and animals must adapt to the high temperatures and lack of rain. The central lowlands are also dry and flat, but there is water trapped under the surface, which can be reached by digging wells.

The Great Dividing Range separate a narrow coastal strip from the dry interior. Because the rainfall here is higher and the soils are more fertile, this is where most Australians live.

People and cities

Eighty per cent of Australians live in cities and towns along the coasts. The largest city is Sydney, where one in five of the population lives. Outside Australia's south-eastern corner there are a few isolated cities, such as Perth on the south-west coast and Darwin in the tropical north. In the interior there is just one major town – Alice Springs.

Rich resources

European settlers brought many new crops and farm animals to Australia. Where there is enough rainfall, farmers grow wheat, fruit and sugar cane. In drier areas, there are huge sheep and cattle ranches. Australia is also very rich in minerals and metals.

▶ FLASHBACK ◀

The Aborigines arrived in Australia at least 45,000 years ago. In 1770 Captain James Cook landed in Australia and claimed it for Britain. Many British settlers arrived during the 19th century, and occupied more and more of the land of the Aborigines. In 1901 Australia became a self-governing country. In the last 50 years people from all parts of the world have come to live in Australia.

- Australia is the main landmass of the continent of Oceania, which includes New Zealand, Papua New Guinea and the many islands of the central and southern Pacific.

- Australia was separated from other continental landmasses 65 million years ago. Because of this long isolation, the country has many animals found nowhere else. Echidnas and duck-billed platypuses are unique mammals that lay eggs. Kangaroos, koalas and wombats belong to a group of mammals called marsupials, which keep their young in pouches.

find out more
Continents
Pacific Islands
See also Countries and flags section, page 122

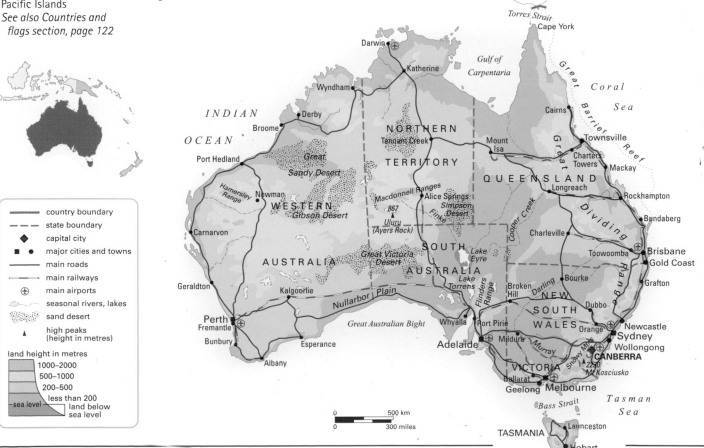

Bangladesh

Bangladesh is a flat country in southern Asia formed by the deltas of the Ganges, Brahmaputra and Meghna rivers. Nearly 120 million people live there, making it one of the most crowded countries in the world.

The climate of Bangladesh is hot and wet. Much of the country receives over 2000 millimetres of rain each year, most of it during the monsoon season, between June and September. Monsoon rains can cause devastating floods, as in 1988, when floods killed thousands of people and left over 30 million homeless. From November to May, tropical cyclones (hurricanes) sweeping in from the Bay of Bengal can also cause great destruction.

People

Most Bangladeshis are farmers and live in villages. The low-lying land and abundant water are ideal for rice, which is the country's main crop. Many farmers also grow jute, a plant used to make rope, sacks and carpet backing. The land is criss-crossed by waterways, so boats are the main form of transport.

Bangladeshis are mostly Muslims. Usually the men work the fields, while the women work in and near the home. The typical Bangladeshi household includes several generations of extended family.

▶ FLASHBACK ◀

The modern nation of Bangladesh was founded in 1971. It had been part of British India until 1947. Then the subcontinent was split into India and Pakistan. Pakistan itself was made up of two parts, separated by Indian territory. To the west was West Pakistan (today's Pakistan) and to the east was East Pakistan. In 1971 East Pakistan became Bangladesh after a terrible war in which more than a million people were killed.

◀ Rope-making in Bangladesh. Jute used to be the main fibre used for ropes, but nylon and other synthetic fibres are now often used.

find out more
Asia
India
Pakistan
See also Countries and flags section, page 122

Brazil

Brazil is the biggest country in South America and covers nearly half the continent. It stretches from the foothills of the Andes mountains in the west to the Atlantic Ocean in the east.

The north-eastern corner of Brazil is a vast, harsh, very dry region made up mostly of thorny scrub. In the south the climate is good for crops. Brazil is one of the biggest producers of coffee in the world and also grows sugar cane, tobacco, rice, soya beans, maize (corn) and many fruits.

The rainforest around Brazil's Amazon River is the largest in the world. It has a richer plant life than anywhere else on Earth. However, the forest is being cleared for cattle ranches and farms. As well as adding to global warming, this destruction is robbing many Native Americans of their forest homes.

Brazil is one of the 10 biggest industrial nations in the world. There are deposits of iron ore and other minerals. Much of the ore is used for steel-making, and the steel is used to make motor cars, locomotives, ships and other goods.

▶ FLASHBACK ◀

The Portuguese were the first Europeans to colonize Brazil in 1500. That is why Brazilians are the only South Americans whose language is Portuguese. In 1825 Brazil became independent under Emperor Pedro I. Brazil became a republic in 1889. As well as the original native peoples, Portuguese colonists, and African slaves, many other nationalities have emigrated to Brazil from Europe, the Middle East and the Far East.

◀ In Brazil the few very wealthy people live in luxury, while the millions who are poor live in shanty towns like this one in São Paulo.

find out more
Forests
Rivers and streams
South America
See also Countries and flags section, page 122

Canada

Canada is the world's second largest country. It stretches 5000 kilometres from the Pacific Ocean to the Atlantic Ocean and almost the same distance from near the North Pole to half-way to the Equator.

Even though Canada is so vast, most people live in the south-east, near the border with the USA. Much of the rest of Canada is unpopulated. The north is covered in snow and ice, the high Rocky Mountains, though tree-covered, are mostly home to wildlife, and the interior plains where wheat is grown are sparsely inhabited by ranchers.

Settlement

Three out of every four Canadians live in cities. Along the Atlantic and Pacific coasts, cities with safe harbours flourish. The largest of these on the

▲ Snowploughs and trucks clear the roads in snow-bound Ottawa, Canada.

Atlantic, Halifax, began as a British naval base. Vancouver on the Pacific grew as the port at the western end of Canada's first continental railroad.

Between the coasts, cities are strung along railroads, highways and the Great Lakes–St Lawrence Seaway in the south. Half of Canada's population and most of its large cities are found along this water system. ◗

• Snow covers much of Canada from November until April. Sometimes a midwinter warm spell melts the snow, but then more replaces it. In the country people ski and skate and travel over frozen lakes on snowmobiles, a Canadian invention similar to a motorcycle. Summers are generally warm.

Legend:
- country boundary
- province boundary
- ◆ capital city
- ■ ● major cities and towns
- main roads
- main railways
- ⊕ main airports
- ice cap
- ▲ high peaks (height in metres)

land height in metres
- 2000–5000
- 1000–2000
- 500–1000
- 200–500
- sea level — less than 200

Resources

Canada is very rich in farmland, forest and minerals, and has one of the world's largest developments of hydroelectricity. It exports wheat and other grains, timber and paper, and zinc, gold, nickel and platinum. There are huge deposits of oil, natural gas and coal.

Canada's forest-product industries employ many thousands of workers; and it manufactures aluminium products for the North American aircraft industry. It is also known worldwide for its electrical and telecommunications products.

People and culture

Most Canadians speak one of Canada's two official languages, French or English. Most of Canada's 500,000 native people speak one of 11 native languages and English or French, which they learn in school. Canadians who are half French and half Native American are known as métis, and have separate lands and a separate culture. Both English and French are widely used, French especially in Québec Province. However, there are tensions between the two cultures. Many French Canadians want

Québec to leave Canada and become an independent country.

▶ FLASHBACK ◀

The first Native Americans came to Canada from Asia at least 25,000 years ago. The Inuit (Eskimo) of the Arctic regions arrived 4000 years ago. From the 17th century many French and British people came to settle in Canada. After the British defeated the French in 1759, the whole of Canada was ruled by Britain. In 1867 Canada became a self-governing country.

▲ Peyto Lake, on the eastern slopes of the Rocky Mountains in Alberta, Canada.

find out more
Arctic
North America
United States of America
See also Countries and flags section, page 122

Caribbean

The Caribbean Sea stretches over 3000 kilometres from the coast of Central America to Trinidad and Barbados. The Caribbean also includes all the islands around the sea, the Caribbean coastlands of Central and South America, and the countries of Guyana, Suriname and French Guiana. These do not touch the Caribbean Sea but have links with the island chain.

Some of the islands are very large. Cuba, the largest, is over 1100 kilometres long, and has a population of over 10 million. There are more than 20 independent or self-governing countries in the region, and hundreds of smaller islands, many of which are so small

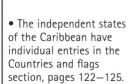

• The independent states of the Caribbean have individual entries in the Countries and flags section, pages 122–125.

find out more
Africa
South America

that no one lives on them. Some islands are built up from coral reefs, and are so flat that they hardly rise above the sea. Others have steep-sided mountains, 2000–3000 metres high, covered with thick rainforest. Many of these mountains are volcanoes, some of which are still active.

Climate

The Caribbean has a warm, tropical climate, but the islands

▲ The land on Antigua, one of the Leeward Islands, is not so good for farming, but there are beautiful sandy beaches. More than 100,000 tourists visit the island every year.

and coasts are cooled by breezes from the sea. In the mountains it is quite cool. Rainfall is heavy, but comes in short, violent showers, so there is plenty of sunshine too. Most rain falls from June to November. From February to April, it can be very dry. There is much more rainfall

in the mountains than on the coast. Occasionally, during the rainy season, there is a violent storm known as a hurricane. Hurricanes can cause very serious damage.

Life and work

Many tropical crops thrive in the Caribbean climate. Sugar cane, bananas, coffee, spices and cocoa are all grown for export. There are few minerals or energy resources, except for some bauxite and a little oil and natural gas. (Bauxite, from which aluminium is made, is mined in some islands.) Many factories have been set up and farming has been modernized. Tourism and banking are important in many places.

There is now a strong North American influence on the Caribbean way of life. Many people have relatives in the USA and Canada, travel there to study or on holiday, and watch American TV programmes. However, many people in the Caribbean are also now placing much more emphasis on their own culture and identity.

▶ FLASHBACK ◀

Five hundred years ago there were two groups of Native Americans in the Caribbean, the Arawaks and the Caribs. In 1492 Christopher Columbus sailed into the Caribbean and claimed the islands he found for Spain. The Spanish built up an empire in the Caribbean and the Americas. Many of the Arawaks and Caribs died in fighting, or from European diseases.

In the 17th and 18th centuries the French, Dutch and English fought the Spanish and each other over possession of many of the islands. At this time about 5 million Africans were brought to the Caribbean as slaves to work on the sugar and tobacco plantations. The African traditions they brought with them gradually combined with the ways of the Europeans. After the abolition of slavery in the 19th century, the British and Dutch hired workers from India. Their descendants still live on the islands.

Most of the former British colonies are now independent countries, but the French islands are governed as if they were districts of France. Puerto Rico, once a Spanish colony, is linked to the USA. Many West Indians have emigrated to the USA, Canada and Europe.

▲ Grenada, St Vincent, St Lucia and Dominica are known as the Windward Islands. Bananas have been an important export crop on these islands for a long time. The workers at this banana plantation are washing and sorting banana bunches.

▼ The islands of the Caribbean are sometimes called the West Indies.

Caves

find out more
Erosion
Rocks and minerals

The most spectacular caves in the world are found in areas with lots of limestone, such as the Carlsbad Caverns in New Mexico, USA. Impressive stalactites and stalagmites form in many of these limestone caves. Caves also occur in seashore cliffs and in volcanic areas.

Limestone rock is made up mainly of calcium carbonate, which dissolves in rainwater. Water seeps through cracks and joints in limestone rock, which is permeable (lets water through easily). Gradually the water widens the cracks and joints. Sometimes it makes a deep tunnel down through the permeable rock, called a swallow hole. Underground rivers also wear the limestone away, leaving large caves and sometimes lakes.

Caves can occur in rocks such as basalt (cooled lava from volcanoes). When the surface of the liquid lava cools and hardens, a cave may be left when the lava below stops flowing. Sea caves are formed by waves hurling stones and rocks at the cliffs, and by the force of the waves themselves.

Stalactites and stalagmites

Stalactites hang down from the ceiling of a cave as thin stone columns. Stalagmites rise from the floor as pillars of stone. Sometimes they join together to form a whole column of rock. Every time a drip of water forms on the cave roof, some of the water evaporates leaving a tiny deposit of calcium carbonate. These deposits grow very, very slowly to form stalactites, while deposits pile up on the cave floor to form stalagmites.

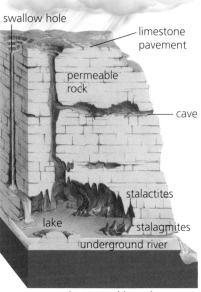

▼ A cross-section of an underground cave system.

swallow hole
limestone pavement
permeable rock
cave
stalactites
lake
stalagmites
underground river
impermeable rock

Cereals

find out more
Farming
Food

One of the most important kinds of food we eat is made from the seed of a type of grass. Since prehistoric times people have grown plants of the grass family, called cereals. The most common cereals are rice, wheat, maize (corn), oats, rye, barley and millet.

The seeds of cereal plants are called grains. They are quite large and full of carbohydrates, which are filling and provide the body with a quick source of energy. The grains also contain some protein, vitamins and minerals, and have plenty of fibre. Most of the fibre is found in the bran, the grain's outer layer.

Cereal grains can be eaten whole or processed. Ready-to-eat cereals are made mainly from maize, rice and wheat. Some breakfast cereals use the whole grain and they are more nutritious than those that do not. Cereal grains can also be ground into flour to make bread, pasta, porridge and puddings.

rice

oats
wheat
barley

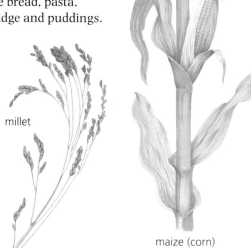

millet
rye
maize (corn)

China

China has the world's largest population: over 1.2 billion people live there. It is also the third largest country in the world by area.

• To control floods and generate electricity, China is building a huge dam on the Chang Jiang river, in an area called the Three Gorges. It will create a lake nearly 1000 km long, and over a million people will lose their homes.

China has over 4000 years of written history. For most of this time it has been ruled by a series of emperors, but since 1949 it has been led by the Chinese Communist Party.

Landscape

The most isolated and barren part of China is the Tibetan plateau in the west. Two rivers, the Huang He and the Chang Jiang (Yangtze), flow from the plateau towards the sea in the east. The Huang He carries large amounts of fine yellow silt called loess. When the river

floods, the loess is left behind, producing very rich soils.

Bamboo forests across much of central China are home to the giant panda and other rare animals. The south is tropical, hot and humid. It often has typhoons (hurricanes), but the climate is good enough to grow three crops of rice a year. ◗

▲ A Tibetan woman milking a yak. Yaks are natural inhabitants of the Tibetan plateau that have been domesticated. Tibetans make use of their milk, hair and meat.

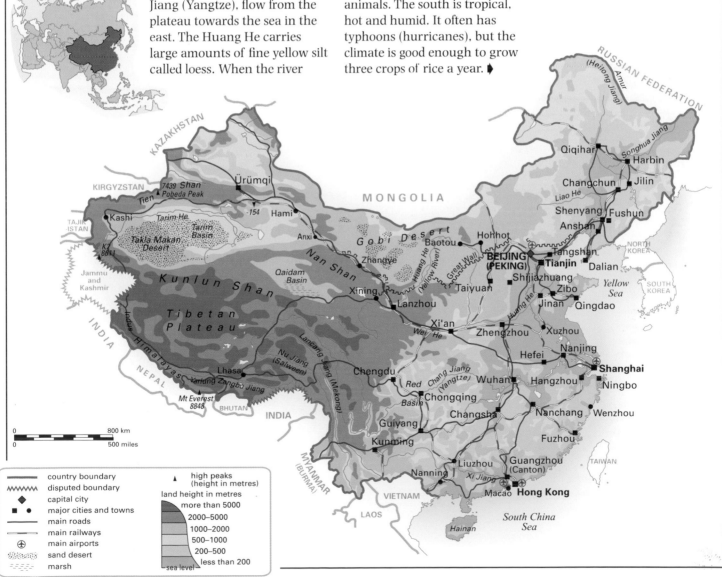

Legend
- country boundary
- disputed boundary
- ◆ capital city
- ■ ● major cities and towns
- main roads
- main railways
- ⊕ main airports
- sand desert
- marsh
- ▲ high peaks (height in metres)
- land height in metres
  - more than 5000
  - 2000–5000
  - 1000–2000
  - 500–1000
  - 200–500
  - less than 200
  - sea level

China

▲ The Huang He used to be called the Yellow River because of the yellow colour given to it by the loess (silt).

• In 1989 many democracy campaigners were killed during a demonstration in Tiananmen Square in Beijing. There was an international outcry over this massacre.

People

Ninety per cent of China's population belong to a people called the Han, but they speak many different dialects of Chinese. There are also over 50 non-Han minority groups with their own languages and traditions. The largest group is the Zhuang, who live in the centre of the country.

Most Chinese live in the countryside and work the land. In the north they grow mostly wheat and potatoes. Rice is more common in the south, where it is warmer and wetter. There is not enough suitable land for animals such as cattle, so farmers keep pigs, ducks and chickens. Many fruits come from China, such as apricots, tangerines and lychees.

Villages and cities

Village life is very traditional, but in recent years there have been changes. Couples have been encouraged to have fewer children, to help control population growth. Small factories and workshops have been set up to provide alternatives to farming and to stop country people moving to the cities.

For most of the 20th century China was a poor country, but in the past 20 years its economy has boomed. Chinese factories now make half the world's toys. They also produce steel, textiles, shoes, ships and cars. These new industries have changed the cities. Shanghai is building a huge new office district and new shopping malls. People in cities can now afford colour television sets, although the countryside remains quite poor.

Much of the investment in cities and factories has come from Hong Kong. Hong Kong was a British colony from 1842 until 1997, when it once more became part of China. Its key position and its natural harbour have made it a thriving trading centre.

► FLASHBACK ◄

Chinese civilization is one of the oldest in the world. From before 2000 BC until the 20th century China was ruled by a series of emperors. In 1911 a revolution overthrew the last emperor.

In 1949, after many years of civil war, the communist leader Mao Zedong set up the People's Republic of China. Since Mao's death in 1976 China has encouraged private enterprise, and this has created a lot of wealth. However, political opposition is still not allowed.

find out more
Asia
See also Countries and flags section, page 122

► A road junction in the Chinese city of Kunming. Bicycles are a much more important form of transport in China than cars, buses or lorries.

Climate

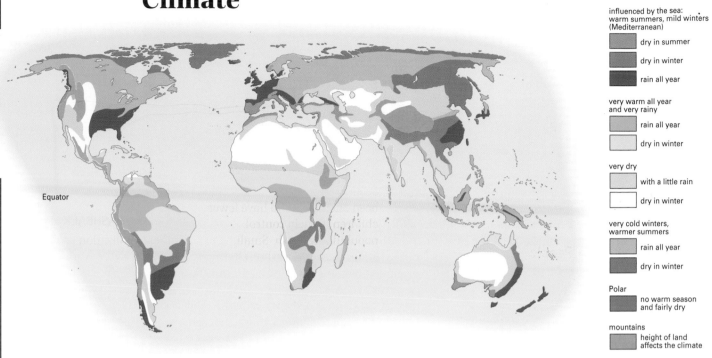

influenced by the sea:
warm summers, mild winters
(Mediterranean)

- dry in summer
- dry in winter
- rain all year

very warm all year and very rainy

- rain all year
- dry in winter

very dry

- with a little rain
- dry in winter

very cold winters, warmer summers

- rain all year
- dry in winter

Polar

- no warm season and fairly dry

mountains

- height of land affects the climate

Equator

▲ This map of the world shows the different types of climate, and where they occur on Earth.

Climate and weather are not the same thing. The weather may change from day to day – it may be warm and dry one day, and cool and rainy the next. The climate of a place is the pattern of its weather over a long period of time. Climate is often described in terms of temperature and rainfall.

Every place on Earth has its own climate, which may be similar to the climate of other places faraway. For example, the Mediterranean region has a similar climate to California, in the USA, and to south-eastern Australia. The main factors that affect climate are: latitude (distance from the Equator), altitude (height above sea level), distance from the sea, and type of wind.

Latitude

The latitude of a place affects how much heat it receives from the Sun's rays. At the North and South Poles, which are at high latitudes, the Sun's rays fall at a very low angle. Much of their heat is absorbed as they pass through a thick layer of the Earth's atmosphere. As a result, the *polar* climate is cold, with short summers and long dark winters.

The areas around the Equator are the tropical areas, or tropics, where the Sun is almost overhead at noon for much of the year, and the hours of daylight are the same month after month. The tropics receive more sunlight than

anywhere else in the world. The *tropical* climate is warm all year round, usually with marked dry seasons and wet seasons.

In the mid-latitudes (between the polar regions and the tropics) are the *temperate* regions, which have four distinct seasons. Here the Sun is low in the sky in winter, and high in summer, resulting in long summer days and short winter ones.

Altitude and distance from sea

The height of a place above sea level affects its temperature – the higher you go, the cooler it becomes. Mountainous regions are generally cooler than lowland areas. Some mountains, for example Mount Kilimanjaro in tropical Africa, may have snow all year round. This type of climate is a *montane* (mountain) climate.

In general, water warms up and cools down much more slowly than land. As a result, in winter the sea is often warmer than the land, and in summer it is often cooler. Coastal areas and islands in temperate regions such as northern Europe tend to have less extreme variations in temperature when compared with areas such as the central USA and eastern Europe, which are further away from the sea. So places near the sea have a *maritime* climate, which is milder than the *continental* climate of places further inland. ▶

- Mountain ranges may produce an effect called a *rain shadow*. As moist air passes over a mountain, it rises and water vapour condenses to form rain clouds. Rain falls on the mountainside facing the wind, but the other side is drier because no moisture is left in the air. The vast Tibetan plateau lies in the rain shadow of the Himalayas.

find out more
Atmosphere
Clouds
Deserts
Greenhouse effect
Maps
Rain and snow
Seasons
Weather
Wind

Climate

Winds

Winds carry moisture in clouds and as water vapour. They may also be dry, as well as hot or cold. Winds tend to blow in particular directions in different parts of the world.

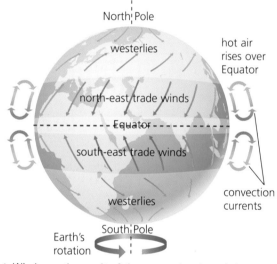

▲ Winds are the result of the uneven heating of air masses around the Earth, and they are also influenced by the rotation of the Earth. They move around the world in a series of wind belts.

In the tropics, the land surface is hot and so heats the air above. The hot air rises, cools and sheds its water content, producing the heavy rainfall that is typical of a tropical climate. Cooler air from places to the north and south of the Equator replaces the rising hot air. These are called *trade winds*. As the air rising from the Equator moves from the tropics towards the Poles, it becomes cooler and more dense, so it descends towards the Earth. It has already shed its water content as rain, so the regions beyond the trade winds contain many deserts, for example the Sahara Desert and the central Australian desert.

Climate change

The world's climate is changing slowly over many hundreds or thousands of years. For example, we know from fossils that the Sahara Desert was home to flowing rivers with crocodiles only 5000 years ago. Ice ages are the most important climate changes that temperate areas like northern Europe have experienced. Only 18,000 years ago northern Europe and North America were covered by an ice-sheet.

Scientists believe that there are many natural reasons for climate change. These include long-term changes in the Earth's orbit around the Sun, and variations in the amount of the Sun's heat that reaches the Earth's surface. Recently it has been suggested that our climate is also affected by human activity. By burning large amounts of fossil fuels such as coal and oil, we are releasing increased amounts of carbon dioxide and other gases into the atmosphere. Higher levels of these so-called greenhouse gases may be responsible for increasing the greenhouse effect. This increase may result in *global warming* – a rise in the world's temperatures.

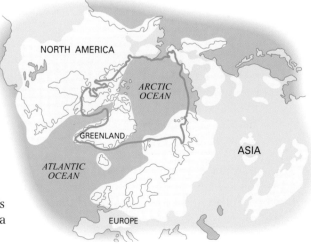

- Major volcanic eruptions are a possible cause of climate change. They send large amounts of ash and gases into the upper atmosphere. The ash reduces the amount of heat from the Sun that reaches the Earth.

- Scientists predict that the Earth's average temperature will increase by between 1 °C and 3.5 °C in the 21st century.

◄ The last ice age began about 1.8 million years ago and ended around 11,000 years ago. The climate was much colder than today, and much of the northern hemisphere was covered in ice. During this ice age there were at least 17 periods called 'glacials' when ice-sheets were expanding. These were interrupted by warmer periods when the ice melted.

◯ present-day limit of permanent ice

▢ approximate extent of glaciers

Clouds

Clouds form in different shapes and appearances at varying heights in the sky. Thin wispy cirrus clouds may form up to 15 kilometres above the ground, while low-lying stratus clouds can suddenly appear on high ground, creating problems for hikers and climbers.

The Earth's atmosphere contains lots of water vapour. But since the temperature in the air is not always the same everywhere, the water vapour sometimes changes back to a liquid by condensation. Clouds are formed when water vapour condenses to become small droplets in the air. These droplets are so small they are not heavy enough to fall to the ground as rain. They stay in the air and come together to form clouds.

Thunderstorms

Thunderstorms come from cumulonimbus clouds, the biggest in the sky. They bring heavy rain, thunder and lightning. Thunderstorm clouds have electrical charges. At the top the charge is positive, while at the bottom the charge is negative. The ground below a thunderstorm is also positive. When all these charges build up, there is a lightning flash which very briefly lights up the sky. Thunder is the noise we hear when the air in front of a stroke of lightning expands rapidly because of the great heat. Thunderclouds have bigger droplets than other clouds. Very big drops are too heavy to stay in the cloud and fall as rain. When the air in the cloud is very cold, the raindrops freeze and fall as hailstones.

▲ Low-lying nimbostratus clouds give us most of our heavy rain. They are dark grey and threatening.

find out more
Atmosphere
Climate
Rain and snow
Weather

1 Cirrus clouds consist of ice because they occur at heights where the temperature is always below freezing-point.
2 Cirrocumulus is often seen when fair weather approaches after a depression. A 'mackerel sky' (a form of cirrocumulus) means that rain is on the way.
3 In summer, layers of **altocumulus** clouds can be seen in late evening or early morning.
4 A veil of even, grey **altostratus** cloud is an almost certain sign of rain.
5 Cumulonimbus is the thundercloud of hot, still summer weather.
6 Stratus cloud often appears suddenly over high ground. It may thicken and turn to fog, drizzle or rain.
7 Heavy, cauliflower-shaped **cumulus** clouds are formed by currents of warm rising air.

height
−9 km
−8 km
−7 km
−6 km
−5 km
−4 km
−3 km
−2 km
−1 km

Coal

• In places such as Ireland and Scotland, peat is dug up, dried and burned as fuel. It is rather smoky.

• Highly compressed peat produces anthracite, a hard black coal which burns slowly with very little smoke.

find out more
Fossils
Geology
Greenhouse effect
Mining
Rocks and minerals

The coal we are most familiar with – bituminous coal – is hard, black and shiny. It is the most common kind of coal and burns easily. Another kind of coal, called lignite, is soft and brown. All coal is the fossilized remains of plants. These plants grew with the help of the Sun's energy millions of years ago.

Some coal is simply burned as fuel, not only in household fires but also in power stations, to produce electricity. Much coal is also turned into coke, by baking it rather than burning it. Coke is a valuable smokeless fuel, and is also used in making iron from iron ore. When coke is made, coal tar and ammonia are also formed.

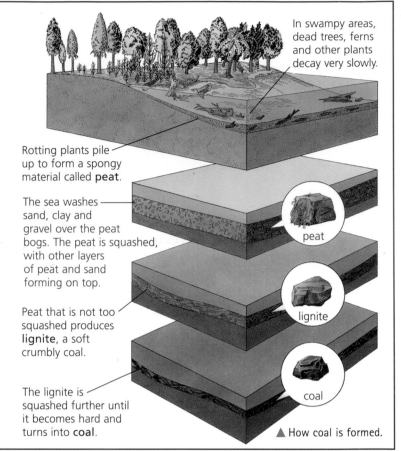

In swampy areas, dead trees, ferns and other plants decay very slowly.

Rotting plants pile up to form a spongy material called **peat**.

The sea washes sand, clay and gravel over the peat bogs. The peat is squashed, with other layers of peat and sand forming on top.

Peat that is not too squashed produces **lignite**, a soft crumbly coal.

The lignite is squashed further until it becomes hard and turns into **coal**.

peat

lignite

coal

▲ How coal is formed.

Coasts

• Where a river drops a lot of sand or mud as it enters the sea, it may build out the coast to form a huge fan-shaped delta, such as the Mississippi or Nile delta.

find out more
Caves
Climate
Erosion
Greenhouse effect
Oceans and seas
Rivers and streams
Seashore

A coast is the boundary where land meets sea. The world has about 312,000 kilometres of coastline. Many of the world's major cities, such as New York, Sydney, Shanghai and Rio de Janeiro, lie on the coast. Fertile plains along low-lying coasts, such as those in Bangladesh, are home to millions of people.

The pattern of coastlines is constantly changing as some coasts are worn away by the sea and others are built up by mud and sand. Waves are amazingly powerful forces that can wear away cliffs and carve out caves. They pound the worn-away rock into smaller and smaller pieces that are swept along the coast, helping to wear away more rocks. In the process these pebbles are worn down to sand and deposited as beaches. Each year, billions of tonnes of sand and silt are carried to the oceans by rivers. This material is then washed in by breaking waves to build up the beach.

Some stretches of coastline are fast disappearing under the waves, for example along the east coast of England. In many parts of the world there are natural sea defences such as salt marshes, sand dunes and mangrove swamps, which absorb the impact of the waves. However, many of these natural barriers are gradually being destroyed by human activities.

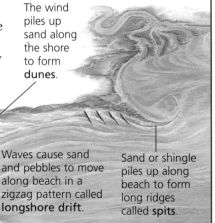

The wind piles up sand along the shore to form **dunes**.

The sea wears away cliffs to produce rocks and sand.

Waves cause sand and pebbles to move along beach in a zigzag pattern called **longshore drift**.

Sand or shingle piles up along beach to form long ridges called **spits**.

Breaking waves carry sand and shingle up the beach.

Continents

The large masses of land on the Earth's surface are called continents. They cover 29 per cent of the total surface area. Millions of years ago, all the continents were joined together in one giant landmass, called Pangaea. Gradually this supercontinent broke up into smaller pieces to form the seven continents we know today.

plate boundaries
—— moving apart
---- moving together
—— passive

▲ This map shows the present-day position of the world's continents, as well as the names and the boundaries of the rocky plates that make up the Earth's crust.

• Liquid rock is pushing up through a deep crack in the middle of the floor of the Atlantic Ocean. As the two halves of the ocean floor are forced apart, the continent of Africa is moving gradually to the east and South America to the west.

Europe is the smallest continent. Some people insist that it is really part of Asia because there is no clear division between the two. (The Ural Mountains and the Ural river are usually taken to be the boundary.) Oceania is counted as a continent although it is made up of Australia, New Zealand and other Pacific islands.

The heart of each continent is a flat slab or 'shield' of ancient rock. Around this lie regions on which are piled great thicknesses of sedimentary rocks. At the edges are mountains. Continents are generally 30–40 kilometres thick. Continental rocks are much older than the rocks which lie under the oceans.

Moving plates

• The Earth's plates are all moving in different directions. North America will eventually reach Russia to the west. Africa may move northwards, closing off the Mediterranean Sea.

The rocky surface of the Earth is divided up into several large plates. These great rafts of rock 'float' on top of the liquid rocks of the mantle, the Earth's main inner layer. The plates move slowly over the Earth's surface. Over millions of years this movement, although only a few centimetres each year, has caused continents to split apart and collide.

The explanation of these plate movements is called *plate tectonics*. On some parts of the ocean floor, plates pull apart. New crust forms when hot, liquid rocks (magma) from undersea volcanoes rise to plug the gap. The magma rises

through weak areas of the Earth's crust to form underwater mountains (mid-oceanic ridges), rift valleys, and volcanic mountains or islands. Deep-sea trenches form where one part of the ocean floor is pushed under another.

At other plate boundaries, when one plate edge is forced under another, earthquakes can occur. Great mountain ranges such as the Himalayas and the Andes form where one plate pushes against another.

Continental drift

We can find evidence of how the continents gradually drifted to their present-day positions when we see how well the coastlines of different continents match up. For example, Africa and South America fit neatly together. Identical fossils of ferns and reptiles have been found in South America, Africa, India, Antarctica and Australia. These plants and animals could not have crossed the oceans, so they must have lived on the same landmass at some time in the past.

▼ About 200 million years ago, Pangaea began to split into the supercontinents of Laurasia and Gondwanaland. These landmasses broke up further to become the continents we know today.

250 million years ago   175 million years ago   present day

Coral islands *see* Islands • **Corn** *see* Cereals • **Costume** *see* Dress and costume

Cotton

Fibres from the cotton plant are used to make clothing fabric which is cool and comfortable to wear. Cotton fabric absorbs moisture and lets it out, so your skin can breathe. Cotton fibres are also made into towelling, cheesecloth, curtaining, furniture fabric and heavy-duty industrial fabrics.

Cotton grows in tropical and subtropical areas. Each plant produces seed pods (bolls) which contain about 30 seeds. The ripened bolls burst open to reveal a fluffy mass of fibres. When the fluffy mass is separated from the seeds, it is known as cotton lint, which is what is used to make fabrics. The cotton seeds are not thrown away. The fat is extracted to produce an edible oil, and the seeds are then processed into cattle cake and fertilizer.

Machinery is used on the largest cotton plantations for almost all jobs, from sowing to picking. On the smaller plantations in poorer countries, the cotton worker uses teams of

oxen or buffalo and picks the cotton by hand. Although harvesting by machine is quicker, hand-picking is often better because the cotton pickers pick only the really ripe bolls.

Cotton fibres vary in length between about 2 and 4 centimetres. Short and medium-length fibres account for about 90 per cent of world production of cotton fabric. The finest fabrics are made from long fibres. Cotton fabric is easily dyed and printed. It can be treated so that it is waterproof. Also, it is not affected by static electricity in the atmosphere and therefore stays clean much longer than other materials. It is now frequently reinforced with other fibres, such as polyester and Acrilan.

◀ Cotton-harvesting by machine in California, USA.

find out more
Textiles

• Cotton is grown on a commercial basis in more than 75 countries. The largest producers are the USA, China and Uzbekistan, followed by India and Pakistan.

• A cotton worker can pick 110 kg of seed cotton by hand a day. A machine can pick the same amount in just one hour.

Countries

A country is a territory (land) with its own people. Some countries are self-governing. We call them *sovereign countries*. The government of a sovereign country has the right to make laws for its own people. It can also print currencies, sign treaties with other sovereign countries, and even declare war. Most sovereign countries are members of the United Nations, which at present brings together over 180 countries.

Territories that are not fully self-governing but are ruled by another country are called *colonies* or *dependent territories*. There are around 60 such territories in the world, most of them very small. For example, Anguilla, in the Caribbean, is a dependency (dependent territory) of the United Kingdom. Many sovereign countries today, particularly in Africa and Asia, used to be colonies ruled by European countries. Most of these colonies became independent countries in the second half of the 20th century.

If a country has a head of state who is born to the position, like a king or queen, it is a

▼▶ To enter another country or to re-enter your own country you usually need a *passport*. Sometimes your passport is stamped (below) when you enter and leave a country. To enter some countries you need to obtain a special *visa*.

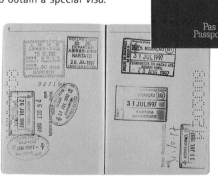

monarchy; if it does not, it is a *republic*. The head of state of a republic is usually called a *president*. The Netherlands is a monarchy, but France and the USA are republics. Most countries are democracies, which means that they have elected governments. A few, such as Bhutan, are ruled directly by monarchs, while others, such as North Korea, are run by unelected dictators.

find out more
Continents
Economics
European Union
See also Countries and flags section on pages 122–125

Country records
Largest country
– by area
Russia
17,075,400 sq km
– by population
China 1,215,293,000
Smallest country by area and by population
Vatican City
0.44 sq km,
population 1000

Deserts

A desert is a large, extremely dry area of land. Geographers say that a 'true' desert receives less than 250 millimetres of rain in an average year. Yet rainfall in the desert can vary a great deal from year to year, and is difficult to predict. A desert may have heavy rains in one year, followed by several years with no rain at all. To survive in the desert, the people and wildlife living there have to adapt to the changing conditions.

• In coastal deserts, such as the Namib Desert in south-western Africa, fog may be the most reliable source of water for many smaller animals and plants.

▼ Cracked mud lies on the surface of the Atacama Desert in Chile. The longest period of drought ever recorded occurred in the Atacama. It lasted for 400 years, ending in 1971 when rain finally fell.

The map below shows that most deserts are near the tropics of Cancer and Capricorn. These are the *hot deserts*, where the Sun shines constantly from cloudless skies. During the night, the clear skies allow heat to escape, and it can become surprisingly cold. In coastal areas, fog may roll into the desert at night and dew sometimes forms at dawn.

The deserts of central Asia are not near the tropics. They are far inland, where the winds are dry. Deserts such as the Gobi are hot in summer and bitterly cold in winter. The polar regions, including Antarctica and Greenland, also receive very little rain, sometimes only up to 130 millimetres a year. These areas are known as the *cold* or *polar deserts*.

Desert landscapes

Sand covers only a small area of most hot deserts. Only about one-tenth of the Sahara Desert, for example, is sandy, and most other

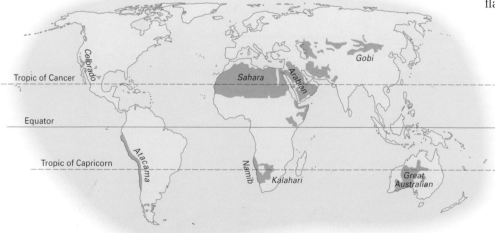

▲ A gemsbok (oryx) stands before sand dunes in Africa's Namib Desert. During a long period of drought, large animals such as this often move to other areas where there is more rain.

hot deserts have even less sand. The remaining desert areas consist mainly of vast flat expanses of gravel and boulders, and some mountainous regions. In places, wind has carried the sand over long distances and piled it up to form *dunes*. These sand dunes are constantly moving as sand is blown up one side of the dune and then rolls down the steep face on the other side.

The landscape in some older desert areas has been eroded (worn away) by wind and water for thousands of years. Wind-blown sand acts like sandpaper, wearing away the softer layers of rock. Mountains have been eroded, often by the wind, to form strange shapes, such as the flat-topped mesas (tablelands) of Arizona, USA. Water is also important in shaping the desert. When storms occur, they sweep down the wadis (dry valleys) and flood over the land. The water wears away the rocky surfaces to produce steep-sided gorges and great spreads of rock and gravel.

Spreading deserts

In some parts of the world, particularly around the Sahara, the desert areas are expanding, and destroying the fertile lands that

▼ The world's principal deserts.

Colorado

Tropic of Cancer

Sahara

Arabian

Gobi

Equator

Tropic of Capricorn

Atacama

Namib

Kalahari

Great Australian

surround them. We call this process *desertification*. Its main causes are overgrazing by livestock, the cutting-down of trees, mainly for firewood, and changes in the climate, which have resulted in longer periods of drought. Once the grass has been eaten and the trees have been removed, the desert soils become dry and dusty, leading to increased erosion of the land.

To reclaim some of the newly created desert areas, trees are planted to reduce the damaging effects of the wind. New methods of farming are also being introduced, and farmers are being encouraged to reduce the size of livestock herds.

Desert peoples

At one time, the only permanent settlements in hot desert areas were in oases and in the valleys of rivers like the Nile, which flows through the desert. Today, there are probably more people than ever living in the deserts. New settlements have grown up where deposits of oil and valuable minerals such as uranium are found. Water for these settlements can be extracted from deep wells or brought in by pipelines or lorries.

Many traditional desert inhabitants are *nomads*, who move around in search of fresh grazing land for their animals. Nomads live in tents or build new shelters each time they stop. In the deserts of Arabia and in the Sahara, the Bedouin peoples graze their herds of camels, sheep and goats, which they sell. The nomadic Bushmen of the Kalahari and the Aborigines in Australia have special skills for finding water, and can survive by eating desert plants and animals.

▲ A Turkana woman waters her livestock in a dried-up river-bed in the desert region of northern Kenya.

Desert wildlife

Desert plants and animals face similar challenges in order to survive in the harsh hot desert conditions. Many animals avoid the heat by sleeping during the day and coming out to find food at night. Insects and other small animals shelter in the sand, while larger animals keep cool by seeking shade under a tree or a rockface.

Desert wildlife also has to survive with little or no water for long periods of time. Camels can live for several weeks without a drink. They store fat in their humps, and their bodies produce water by breaking down this stored fat. Many desert plants store water in their stems, leaves or roots. Some have a thick waxy coating that reduces the amount of water lost through their leaves.

find out more
Africa
Asia
Australia
Climate
Erosion
Nomads
North America
South America
Wells and springs

● Places in the desert where water lies at or close to the surface are called *oases*. The soil here may be quite fertile, and trees, shrubs and crops can all flourish because their roots can reach water.

Desert records

Largest hot desert
Sahara Desert,
8.4 million sq km

Highest temperature
58 °C, recorded in
Libya in 1922

Longest drought
400 years, in the
Atacama Desert, Chile

Highest sand dunes
430 m high, in eastern
Algeria

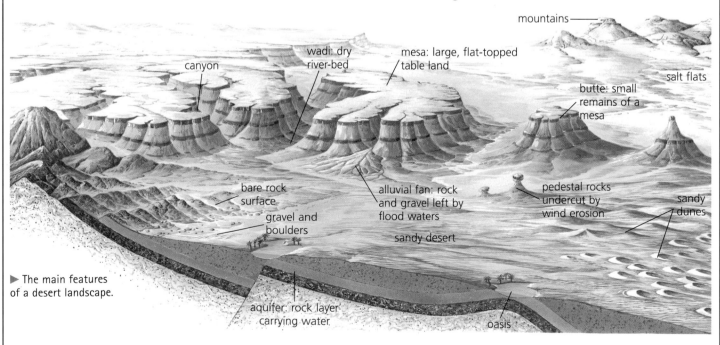

mountains
canyon
wadi: dry river-bed
mesa: large, flat-topped table land
salt flats
butte: small remains of a mesa
bare rock surface
gravel and boulders
alluvial fan: rock and gravel left by flood waters
sandy desert
pedestal rocks undercut by wind erosion
sandy dunes
▶ The main features of a desert landscape.
aquifer: rock layer carrying water
oasis

Dress and costume

People choose to wear certain clothing – to have a particular style of dress – for many different reasons, practical, cultural and personal. In many parts of the world, people wear clothing that protects them from the climate. Some people like to wear bright, distinctive clothes for decoration or to identify with a particular group.

Climate has the most basic influence on the choice of clothing. When it is hot, light-coloured clothes and hats are usually preferred as they deflect the Sun's rays. This type of clothing is worn all year round in hotter regions of the world. In colder regions, clothing is usually woollen and multi-layered for warmth.

• Sports players wear special clothing for their sport. Athletes, for example, wear leotards or shorts and vests to allow complete freedom of movement. American footballers wear elaborate helmets and special padding on their bodies to guard against injury.

find out more
Textiles

▼ Across the world, clothing has been influenced by such factors as climate and cultural values. The Inuit man, for example, wears animal skins to keep warm. The Bedouin woman wears a dress that covers her entire body, because in her society women are not supposed to show bare skin.

▶ This woman from Rajasthan in India wears the traditional dress of her region: a brightly coloured long skirt and blouse.

Traditional dress

In some countries many people wear the same style of dress as each other. This style is handed down from generation to generation. One country may have several different styles of traditional dress. In India, for instance, Rajasthani women wear brightly coloured long skirts and blouses. Further north in the Punjab they wear *shalwar* (loose trousers) and *kamiz* (a long shirt). In the south and east the sari is the normal dress for women, though it can be tied in different ways. All over India traditional clothes are worn for everyday work as well as for special occasions.

In European countries hardly anyone now wears traditional styles of dress for everyday use. But in some regions people wear national dress (sometimes called folk costume) for festivals, weddings and other celebrations.

Dress for work

The work that people do can dictate what they wear. People in the police force and nursing, for example, have to wear uniforms so that members of the public will recognize them. Other workers, such as fire-fighters, need to wear special clothes for their own protection.

India

20th-century China

Japan

Bedouin, Negev Desert, Israel

Berber, Atlas Mountains, Morocco

Cameroon

Bella, Mali

Masai, Kenya

Native American, Andes, South America

Inuit, Canada

Earth

The Earth is one of the nine planets in the Solar System. It is a huge rocky ball whose surface is two-thirds water and one-third land. The layers of air that surround the Earth make up its atmosphere. The atmosphere contains oxygen, which is essential to living things. The Earth is tiny compared with some of the other planets, or with the Sun. Jupiter and Saturn are hundreds of times bigger than Earth, and the Sun is over a million times bigger.

The Earth is constantly moving. It spins round in space like a top, and at the same time it travels around the Sun in an orbit (path) that takes one year to complete. Satellite photographs taken from space

▲ An eruption of Krafla, a large, active volcano in Iceland. Since the year 1500, about one-third of the Earth's total lava flow has come from Iceland's volcanoes.

show the Earth as a blue ball covered with masses of swirling cloud. Closer views can show its surface features, such as the shapes of the continents, the oceans, the great snow-covered mountain ranges, and even large rivers and cities.

Inside the Earth

We live on the outer part of the Earth, which is called the *crust*. It is made up of hard rocks and is covered with water in places. The crust is about 5 kilometres thick under the oceans and up to 30 kilometres thick under the land.

Beneath the crust lies a ball of hot rock and metals. The inside of the Earth is extremely hot, and below about 70 kilometres the rocks are molten (melted). This molten rock comes to the surface when a volcano erupts. The deeper below the surface, the hotter and denser (thicker) the rock becomes. The main inner layer of molten rock, immediately below the crust, is called the *mantle*. It surrounds the hot

metallic centre, which is called the core. The core is partly solid and partly liquid metal.

How the Earth developed

The Sun, like other stars, developed from huge spinning clouds of gas, called nebulas. The Sun is thought to have formed about 5000 million years ago. When it first formed, a broad disc of dust and gas swirled around the Sun. Some of the dust and gas collected together to form larger lumps of material, which became the planets of the Solar System. One of these planets was Earth.

When it was first formed, about 4600 million years ago, the Earth is thought to have been a ball of molten rock. The surface was probably as hot as 4000 °C. It took many millions of years for the surface to cool down enough for a solid crust to form.

▼ A cross-section of the Earth shows the different layers beneath the outer layer, or crust. Scientists find out about the inside of the Earth by measuring the speed at which the waves from earthquakes travel through the layers.

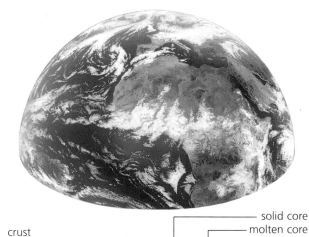

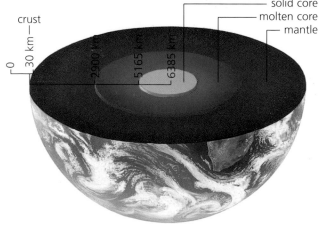

crust
30 km
0
2900 km
5165 km
6385 km

solid core
molten core
mantle

Average distance from Sun
149,600,000 kilometres
Surface area
510 million square kilometres
Distance from surface to centre (average)
6385 kilometres
Distance around Equator
40,075 kilometres
Area of land
149 million square kilometres (29%)
Area of oceans and seas
361 million square kilometres (71%)
Volume
1,083,230 million cubic kilometres
Weight
76 million million million tonnes
Greatest height
8848 m Mount Everest
Greatest depth
11,035 m Marianas Trench
Age
4600 million years (cooled to 1000 °C and first rains, 4300 million years ago)
First living things
about 3500 million years ago
Temperature at core
5000 °C

At first, the Earth had no atmosphere, just like most of the other planets today. However, volcanic eruptions all over the surface produced enough gases to create a primitive atmosphere. This early atmosphere had no oxygen, and the first forms of life on Earth survived without oxygen. They are believed to date from 3500 million years ago. Oxygen, which is mainly produced by plants, came later, when plants started to develop and spread across the Earth.

No rocks on Earth are as old as the Earth itself. The oldest

rocks are a little less than 4000 million years old. But by the time these rocks were formed, the earliest rocks had already been worn down to sediments and used to form new rocks. The earliest evidence of life is found in rocks from about 3500 million years ago. These contain fossils of tiny creatures called blue-green algae. Fossils of a few other primitive animals appear in rocks about 1000 million years old. Then there is a sudden explosion of life in rocks from about 550 million years ago. The first mammals developed 200 million years ago, and the dinosaurs are thought to have become extinct 65 million years ago. The first human beings probably arrived only about 2 million years ago.

Remote sensing

Satellite photography of the Earth is called remote sensing because scientists can observe or 'sense' major features of the Earth from a distance. Remote sensing allows weather forecasters to see the large-scale patterns of clouds, which can be used to predict the weather.

It provides information about climate and agriculture, for example crop yields, and helps geologists to find valuable minerals. Remote sensing also enables scientists to assess the effects of human activities on forests, deserts and waterways. Today, the quality of the photographs is so good that houses and even cars can sometimes be identified.

▲ Below the surface of the world's oceans are long mountain chains called oceanic ridges. Here, hot lava from below the surface pushes up to form a new ocean crust. The 'black smokers' in the picture are hydrothermal vents, where water heated to over 300 °C escapes from the hot rocks.

▶ This photograph of the Earth taken from space shows Egypt and the Sinai peninsula. The Red Sea is in the bottom-left corner of the photo; the dark band across the centre is the River Nile, which opens out into the Nile Delta, where it meets the Mediterranean. The Suez Canal runs between the Mediterranean and the top-left fork of the Red Sea.

find out more
Atmosphere
Climate
Continents
Earthquakes
Geology
Mountains
Oceans and seas
Rocks and minerals
Seasons
Volcanoes
Weather

Earthquakes

Earthquakes happen when the surface of the Earth moves. A small earthquake feels like a distant rumble, but the most serious ones can destroy whole buildings, rip apart roads and bridges, and destroy electricity and gas services. Often fires break out and great floods occur. Many people may be killed as buildings collapse on top of them.

The Earth's crust is divided into great plates which are moving extremely slowly all the time. The edges of these plates mark lines of weakness in the crust. When two plates can no longer move easily against each other, pressure builds up under the surface until suddenly it becomes too great. Then the plates jerk against each other and an earthquake happens. The city of San Francisco, USA, has experienced numerous earthquakes. It lies on the San Andreas Fault, which marks the boundary between two plates.

The earthquake's *focus* (the place where the violent movement begins) is usually no more than 100 kilometres below the surface. The point on the Earth's surface directly above this is the *epicentre*, although the destructive power of the earthquake may not be greatest at this point. During the 1985 earthquake in Mexico City, the epicentre was some distance from the city. Earthquakes also happen out at sea, often deep down in ocean trenches. They cause huge waves called *tsunamis* to form, often travelling towards the shore at up to 800 kilometres an hour.

▼ This section of highway collapsed as a result of the powerful earthquake that devastated the Japanese city of Kobe in 1995.

• The size of every earthquake is measured on a scale from 1 (tiny) to 10 (total devastation). The scale, known as the Richter scale, measures the forces involved.

• *Seismologists* (people who study earthquakes) map where faults are and monitor slight movements in the surface, but they are unable to forecast accurately when and where an earthquake will happen, or how powerful it will be.

find out more
Continents
Earth
Volcanoes

Eclipses

We see an eclipse when the Earth, the Moon and the Sun line up in space. If the Moon moves between the Earth and the Sun, there is an eclipse of the Sun. If the Earth is between the Sun and the Moon, we see an eclipse of the Moon.

The Moon goes round the Earth once a month, but it only goes directly in front of the Sun a few times each year. Although the Sun is very much bigger than the Moon, it is also a lot further away. By chance, the Moon and the Sun look about the same size as seen from Earth, so the Moon sometimes just covers the Sun to make a total eclipse. When this happens, the sky goes dark and the Sun's corona, a faint halo of glowing gas, can be seen around the black disc of the Moon. Even then, a total eclipse can be seen only from places along a narrow strip of the Earth's surface, just a few kilometres wide. In any one place, total eclipses of the Sun are rare. Partial eclipses, when the Moon covers just part of the Sun, are seen much more frequently.

Eclipses of the Moon are easier to see because they are visible from all the places where the Moon has risen. During an eclipse, the Moon looks a lot darker and reddish, but it does not disappear completely.

Total eclipses of the Moon
9 January 2001
16 May 2003
9 November 2003
4 May 2004

Total eclipses of the Sun
21 June 2001
4 December 2002
23 November 2003
8 April 2005

▼ Eclipses of the Moon last for several hours while the Moon passes through the Earth's shadow.

Sun

Earth

Moon's orbit around the Earth

Moon passes into Earth's shadow

▼ Total eclipses of the Sun last for a few minutes while the Moon covers the Sun.

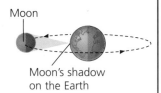

Sun

Moon

Moon's shadow on the Earth

Economics and development

We are all consumers, buying the goods and services we need. Most people are also producers, working to make goods or provide services. Economics is all about how we produce the things people need and want and about how those goods and services are shared out.

There are many economic problems in the world. People's wants are endless, but resources – things we need for production – are limited. In poor countries people have very little, whilst in better-off countries people often have more than they need. Many countries also suffer from inflation, when prices keep going up and up, and unemployment, when people cannot find jobs.

Capitalism and communism

In communist countries, the government decides what things people need and arranges for them to be produced. In capitalist countries people are free to set up businesses producing what they think consumers might want to buy.

Countries that use elements of both systems are called *mixed economies*. In a mixed economy, most businesses belong to private individuals and shareholders, but the government provides some services and tries to manage the economy.

find out more
Industry
Trade

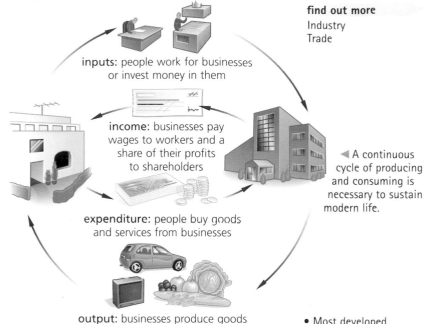

inputs: people work for businesses or invest money in them

income: businesses pay wages to workers and a share of their profits to shareholders

expenditure: people buy goods and services from businesses

output: businesses produce goods and services for sale to people

◀ A continuous cycle of producing and consuming is necessary to sustain modern life.

Developed and developing countries

Countries are also often described as either developed or developing. Development is the process by which the people living in a country become generally richer, healthier and more educated. As a country becomes developed, it builds better communications such as roads. And it tends to have more industries, shops, banks, schools and hospitals.

• Most developed countries are in the northern hemisphere, while most of the countries in the southern hemisphere are developing countries. The developing countries are sometimes called the 'Third World'.

▼ This world map uses a scale that compares the wealth rather than the physical size of different countries. It measures 'gross domestic product' (GDP) (the value of all the goods and services produced within a country in a year).

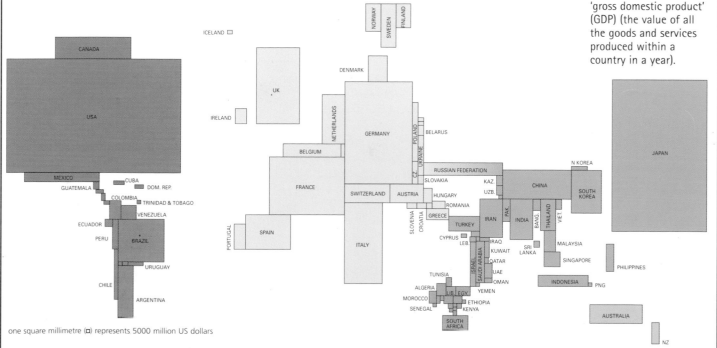

one square millimetre (▫) represents 5000 million US dollars

33

Energy

Our bodies depend on energy, as do our homes, vehicles and factories. On Earth, the Sun is the source of nearly all of our energy. Without energy, nothing would live, move or change.

If something has energy, it means that it is capable of doing work. To scientists, work is done whenever a force makes something move.

Energy from fuels

More than 80 per cent of the energy that industrial societies use comes from burning coal, oil and natural gas. These are called *fossil fuels*, because they formed from the remains of plants and tiny sea creatures that lived on Earth many millions of years ago. Most large power stations burn fossil fuels.

There are two main problems with burning fossil fuels. First, their waste gases pollute the atmosphere. Second, fossil fuels cannot be replaced. Supplies will eventually run out, so we must find alternatives.

Nuclear fuel, used in nuclear power stations, does not burn. Instead, its energy is released as heat by nuclear reactions. Nuclear power stations produce no waste gases, but they are expensive to build, and produce dangerous radioactive waste.

For many people in developing countries, wood is the main fuel. Although new trees can be grown, at present not enough trees are being planted to replace those that are cut down.

Alternative energy

To reduce our use of fossil and nuclear fuels, alternative energy sources are needed. There are many possibilities.

The energy that radiates from the Sun's surface as heat and light is the source of almost all the energy we use.

Solar panels use the energy from the Sun to heat water. Solar cells use sunlight to produce small amounts of electricity.

We get energy from the food we eat. The food may be from plants or from animals that feed on plants.

Green plants use the energy in sunlight falling on their leaves to produce their own food from water and carbon dioxide.

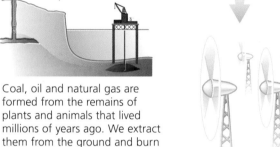

Coal, oil and natural gas are formed from the remains of plants and animals that lived millions of years ago. We extract them from the ground and burn them to get energy. This energy is used to power engines, to make electricity and for heating.

Weather systems are driven by heat radiated from the Sun. Hot air rising above the Equator causes belts of wind around the Earth. Heat and wind lift water vapour from the oceans and so bring rain and snow.

For centuries people have been using the power of the wind to move ships, pump water and grind corn. Today, huge wind turbines are used to turn electrical generators.

▲ How the Sun provides the Earth's energy.

Hydroelectric schemes generate electricity using the flow of water from a lake behind a dam. *Solar panels* use the Sun's energy to heat water, while *solar cells* use it to generate electricity. In *wind farms*, generators are turned by giant wind turbines (windmills). *Biofuels* are made from plant or animal matter. Gases from sewage, dung and rotting waste can be used as fuels, and some power stations burn rubbish as their fuel.

All of these alternative energy sources are renewable, but none can be used without affecting the environment in some way. Also, none of these sources can yet provide enough energy to meet our present demands. For these reasons, many people think that we should find ways of being less wasteful with our energy.

find out more
Coal
Greenhouse effect
Industry
Oceans and seas
Oil
Pollution
Tides
Transport
Waste disposal
Wind

England

• The other parts of the United Kingdom are Scotland, Wales and Nothern Ireland.

England forms the largest part of the United Kingdom, a country in north-west Europe.

England is a cool, moist region. The surrounding sea stops the land from becoming too hot or cold. The weather is very variable, and it is mostly affected by depressions (areas of low pressure) which move eastwards across the Atlantic Ocean, bringing cloud and rain.

Landscape

The landscape varies across the country. The mountains of the Lake District and the Pennines are in the north. There is much high moorland in the south-west peninsula of Cornwall and Devon, where the coastline is rugged.

Much of the rest of England is lowland, with several long ridges of low hills. These include the Cotswolds, the Chilterns and the North and South Downs. Many southern hills are made of chalk, and their soil is very thin. East Anglia is flat and low, and parts of the East Anglian Fens are below sea level. Much of the eastern and southern coastline of England is smooth, with long beaches of sand or shingle.

▶ A view from Buckden Pike in the Yorkshire Dales, North Yorkshire. North Yorkshire is the largest county in England, and the most rural.

Cities

England contains some of the most crowded regions in the world. A great chain of cities stretches from London to Liverpool. The industrial cities of the north grew rapidly in the 19th century. Nearby coal provided the energy for their factories.

Today there are still contrasts between the north and the south. In the north there is higher unemployment because the older industries have declined. In the south, particularly in and around London, houses are more expensive because more and more people want to live there. London is one of the world's oldest capital cities, and it is the world's sixth largest city. It is a focal point for modern manufacturing industry and tourism, and is also an important financial centre.

find out more
Europe
Northern Ireland
Scotland
United Kingdom
Wales

───	national boundary
◆	capital city
■ ●	major cities and towns
───	main roads
───	main railways
⊕	main airports
▲	high peaks (height in metres)

land height in metres
500–1000
200–500
100–200
less than 100
sea level
land below sea level

Erosion

find out more
Glaciers
Ice
Rivers and streams
Rocks and minerals
Soil
Valleys

• 'Erosion' comes from the Latin word meaning 'to gnaw'.

• Soft rocks are eroded more quickly than hard ones. Hard rocks may lead to the formation of a waterfall along a river or headlands at the seaside.

All around us, the rocky surface of the Earth is being slowly worn away by the action of water, wind and sun. Tiny pieces of rock are then carried away by water and wind and deposited in other places, especially in the sea. This process is called erosion.

Erosion is the work of moving water, ice or wind. It is usually a slow process. But during storms, water and wind are much more powerful. They carry bigger fragments of rock and erode the land more quickly. Rivers are deepening and widening their valleys all the time, but a river in flood can erode more land in a few hours than it would normally do over many years.

The breaking-down of rocks by snow and frost, sun and rain is called *weathering*. When rocks are exposed to the atmosphere, they are affected by the weather. Constant heating and cooling can split some rocks. When water in these split rocks freezes and then expands, it cracks them. Rainwater is a weak acid and can dissolve or change the chemicals in rocks. Weathering can be speeded up by plant roots and burrowing animals.

The rock pieces that have been broken up by weathering are moved away by water, ice and wind. Although weathering and erosion are different, they both work together to reshape the landscape.

▲ The pounding action of sea waves has worn away the cliff to form a cave.

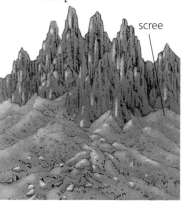

scree

▲ Scree (piles of rock fragments) forms around the base of mountains as a result of ice erosion.

Europe

Europe is the smallest continent, yet it is the most crowded, with about one-eighth of all the world's people. Over the past 500 years Europeans have settled in every other continent, and today European languages can be heard all over the world.

There is no clear boundary between eastern Europe and western Asia. The Ural Mountains in Russia make a convenient line on the map, so Russia is partly in Europe but mainly in Asia. The countries between the Black and Caspian seas are usually counted as part of Europe. But many people consider Azerbaijan and Armenia to be Asian. Turkey is usually counted as part of western Asia.

Landscapes

Europe is a continent of peninsulas and islands. In fact, it is really a westward extension of Asia. There are two main sea inlets: the Baltic Sea to the north and the Mediterranean Sea to the south. The main mountains are the Alps, a line of jagged, snow-capped peaks stretching between France and Austria. The Pyrenees, between Spain and France, and the mountains of Scandinavia, Greece and the Balkans are not so high. The North European plain, from Brittany in France to Russia, is low and mainly flat.

Climate

Most winds in Europe come from the west. They are wet because they have crossed the Atlantic

◀ The Rhine in western Germany, one of Europe's busiest waterways. Other great rivers used for transporting goods include the Rhône in France and the Danube in central and eastern Europe.

Europe

Ocean. Depressions move over Europe all the time, bringing quick changes in the weather. In winter, warm Atlantic ocean currents keep the coasts free from ice. Far from the sea, though, winters can be calm, clear and very cold. The Mediterranean region has warm, wet winters and hot, dry summers. There are long periods of sunshine and clear, blue skies in summer.

Countries and languages

The borders of European states have changed many times in the 20th century. Norway, Finland and Albania were made countries before World War I. Poland, Czechoslovakia, Hungary, Yugoslavia, Iceland and Ireland won independence shortly afterwards. The Baltic states of Estonia, Latvia and Lithuania became independent states in 1920, but in 1940 they were forced to join the USSR. In 1991 they became independent again. Malta and Cyprus date from the 1960s.

Some new states have changed again. Czechoslovakia divided into the Czech Republic and Slovakia in 1993. Croatia, Slovenia, Macedonia, and Bosnia and Herzegovina split from Yugoslavia after 1991.

The languages spoken in Europe can tell us something of the early history of the continent. German, Dutch, Danish, Swedish and English are all Germanic languages. Polish, Bulgarian, Czech, Slovak and Serbo-Croat are Slavonic languages related to Russian. Italian, Spanish, Romanian and French developed out of the Latin language which was spoken all over the Roman empire.

▶ FLASHBACK ◀

From the 1940s until the end of the 1980s, the countries of eastern Europe had communist governments controlled by the USSR. Then communism collapsed, and democracy was introduced. In 1991 the USSR itself split into a number of new countries.

find out more
England
European Union
France
Germany
Ireland, Republic of
Italy
Northern Ireland
Russia
Scandinavia
Scotland
Spain
United Kingdom
Wales
See also Countries and flags section, pages 122–125

European Union

find out more
Europe

European Union member

associate member

0   1000 km
0   600 miles

The European Union consists of a number of countries in Europe which have agreed to work more closely with each other. They hope that by working together they can maintain a peaceful and prosperous Europe.

In 1957 six countries – Belgium, France, West Germany, Italy, Luxembourg and the Netherlands – signed the Treaty of Rome to form the European Economic Community. By 1998 the Community had grown into a European Union (EU) of 15 countries.

In 1993 a single market was created within the countries of the Union, allowing money, goods, services and people to move freely without customs

◀ Member countries of the European Union in 1998.

and other controls at frontiers. In 1998 the member countries were still working towards the use of a single currency, called the Euro. A single currency should make it even easier for European businesses to trade with each other.

Institutions of the Union

The European Union is run by the Council of Ministers and the Commission. The Council of Ministers, made up of ministers from each country's government, has the final say on Union policies. The Commissioners take routine decisions and propose new laws. The members of the European Parliament are elected by voters in each member state. Euro MPs comment on the Commissioners' proposals. The Court of Justice has the power to enforce European Union law on member states.

Famine

• In 1845 the Great Famine began in Ireland, after the failure of the potato cròp, the country's staple food. By 1849 1 million people had either died from starvation or disease, or emigrated to North America.

• In 1974 Bangladesh suffered famine after disastrous floods destroyed the rice harvests. About 300,000 people died of starvation, either through food shortages or because they could not afford to buy the food that was available.

find out more
Farming
Food
Migration

When a large number of people are starving because they do not have enough to eat, we say there is a famine. Famines have been common throughout human history, from the Bible's account of seven years of famine in ancient Egypt to the African famines of the 20th century.

Famines may be caused by climatic disasters such as drought or flooding, as well as by pests and diseases. A drought can destroy crops that need rainwater to grow properly, and floodwaters can drown crops and sweep them away. Both droughts and floods helped to cause famines in African countries such as Sudan, Ethiopia and Mozambique during the 1980s.

Human action can cause famine or make it worse. There were a number of famines in parts of Europe during World War II. Many famines, in African countries in particular, have occurred during civil wars. The wars disrupt farmers' work and make the distribution of food difficult.

Other causes have been suggested for famine. Sometimes traditional farming methods cannot produce enough food while a population is growing fast. Another basic cause of famine is poverty. People may not have enough money to buy food even when it is available in their markets. In 17th-century Britain, in years of poor harvests, famine occurred because the inhabitants of the fast-growing towns were fed while peasants in the countryside starved.

▲ A young boy at a famine relief centre near Mogadishu in Somalia (1992). During famines, food is distributed from such centres, which are usually run by international aid agencies.

Farming

Most types of farming produce food for people to eat. Farmers make the best use they can of the natural resources available to them (such as soil and climate) to produce crops and rear animals.

▲ In the developed world at harvest time, most farm work is done by machine. Machines like this carrot picker are complicated and very expensive, but they save the farmer a lot of time and hard work.

• Market gardens are small farms where vegetables are grown to be taken straight to the market where they are sold. Tomatoes, lettuces and spring onions are just a few of the crops that need to be sold soon after they are picked. They are best grown close enough to the market to get them there before they go rotten.

Different types of plants and animals need different conditions to grow, so there is a variety of types of farming around the world.

Types of farming

Dairy farming produces milk, butter and cheese from cows that graze in grassy fields. Dairy farms are usually quite close to large cities so that fresh milk can quickly reach people's kitchens.

Arable farming involves ploughing the land and planting seed or small plants to grow crops. The most important arable crops are rice, wheat, maize (corn) and potatoes.

Mixed farming involves both crops and livestock. The main area is the corn belt of the midwest USA. Here farmers grow maize to feed to hogs (pigs) and cattle. Oats and hay are also grown as feed, as well as other crops such as soy beans and wheat. Mixed farming is found in Europe, too, in a region that stretches from northern Portugal and Spain across Britain, France, Germany and Poland and into the Ukraine.

Mediterranean farming is found in areas with a Mediterranean climate, where winters are mild and wet, summers long and dry, and rainfall is quite low. There are areas like this around the Mediterranean Sea, and there are others in California, Chile, South Africa and Australia. Winter crops include wheat, barley and broccoli. Summer crops include peaches, citrus fruits, tomatoes, grapes and olives.

Shifting cultivation is a common type of farming in many tropical countries. It is different from settled farming because shifting cultivators raise crops in a place only for as long as the soil allows the crops to grow well. After a year or so in one place the farmer moves on, chops away the natural vegetation from another area, and leaves the first plot to return to its natural state. After about a decade the old site may be reused. Shifting cultivation is practised in the tropical forests of Central and South America, Africa and South-east Asia. Farmers grow maize, rice, manioc, yams, millet and other food crops.

Farm animals

Sheep, cattle, pigs, chickens and goats are all farm animals. Sheep are kept both for their meat and wool, and are generally left to graze on grasslands. The grasslands usually cannot be used for other types of farming because they are too steep or too dry. Dogs often help to round up the sheep and to protect them and their lambs from wild animals such as wolves and eagles.

Lamb and mutton (from older sheep) are popular meats in many regions of the Middle East. Pigs are not kept on farms in the Middle

▼ Kamba people ploughing with oxen near Emali, Kenya. Soil is ploughed to bury weeds. The earth is then broken up and raked over to make it ready for planting.

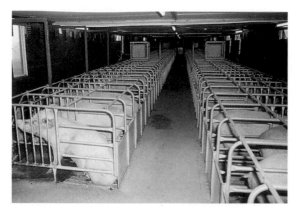

▶ Pregnant sows being kept in stalls. This form of intensive farming was banned in the countries of the European Union in 1998.

East, however, because most people there are Muslims and do not eat pork. Chickens are found on farms in many regions of the world. In western Europe and North America large numbers of chickens are kept indoors in row upon row of small cages, often never seeing the light of day. Farmers feed these 'battery hens' each day and collect their eggs.

Keeping battery hens is an example of *intensive farming*, in which farmers organize their animals and crops to get the maximum food from them. Intensive farming uses lots of machinery to make it more efficient. Tractors are used to plough fields and plant seed, and chemical fertilizers make plants grow stronger, while insecticides kill insect pests and herbicides kill weeds.

Pastures and cattle ranges

Much of the beef in hamburgers eaten in North America comes from cattle that graze in Central and South America. To expand cattle-ranching, tropical forests have been cut down to provide grasslands for 'hamburger cattle'. Cattle also graze on natural grasslands such as the pampas of Argentina.

In countries where intensive farming is practised, some cattle are not only fattened on pastures, they are also given extra food and injected with drugs that make their bodies produce more meat. Where this is not done, the farming is 'extensive' rather than intensive, as quite large areas of grassland are needed to fatten one cow. In parts of East Africa, where grasslands are not good enough to feed cattle all the year round, farmers have to move their herds with the seasons to find new grazing land.

Grain farming

Grain (cereals) is the most important food source for most people in the world. The main types of grain are wheat, maize and rice. Grain can be made into many different kinds of food. Wheat is mainly eaten as pasta in Italy and as bread in North America and elsewhere. The USA, Argentina, Australia and Ukraine are the world's main areas of wheat production. Farming in these countries is mostly intensive. The use of machines, fertilizers, pesticides (insecticides and herbicides) means that the amount of grain produced from a hectare of field (its 'yield') in North America is over four times that produced from a hectare of field in Africa. The USA is the world's biggest exporter of grain. Nearly every African country has to import grain.

Organic farming

There are problems with some modern farming methods. Fertilizers and pesticides cause pollution of soil and water, and they may kill plants and animals that the farmer does not want to kill. Very small traces of the chemicals may also be left in crops, which can make them dangerous to eat.

▶ In North America there are large areas of intensive farming where the wheat or, in this case, ripe barley is harvested with combine harvesters.

▲ Trucks irrigating (watering) crops in the USA. Without such irrigation much of this land would be too dry for crops to grow properly.

▲ A traditional boom-type irrigation system on the River Nile, Egypt. The beam swings like a see-saw to dip the bucket in the water. Irrigation, using simple systems like this or motorized pumps in wealthier countries, is very important to farmers in the drier parts of the world.

Farmers who choose to farm organically do not use artificial chemicals on their land. They use compost and manure from farm animals to fertilize the land, and other plants to control insects. Animals kept on organic farms are allowed to roam in the open air and are not confined for long periods. The number of organic farms in the USA and Europe has grown in recent years. Many people believe that food grown organically tastes better and is safer than food produced by intensive methods.

Farms of the future

Some of the problems of arable farming, including the effects of poor weather or pests, can be solved by breeding new crops. This sort of breeding, using 'plant genetics', has gone on for centuries, but it is likely to become more and more common in farming in the future. In laboratories, scientists take samples of the crops they want to improve and cross them with wild varieties that have a certain quality that is beneficial to the new plant. It is a long and difficult business, and can take many years. This battle will always continue, because although a new plant can be made to resist a disease, it is usually attacked by a different disease just a few years after it is introduced to the fields.

Feeding the world

When people cannot get enough to eat, it seems obvious that farming is not producing enough food. Sometimes this is true, such as when

climatic disasters, like droughts or floods, ruin harvests, but it is not always the case.

The world produces enough food to feed everyone on the planet, but problems arise when food is not in the right place at the right time. In the 1980s in Europe, for example, farmers were encouraged by their governments to produce so much food that excess 'food mountains' were created that cost a lot of money to store. Some of the food could have been sold or given to people who needed it; but this did not always happen.

Agricultural revolutions

The first agricultural revolution of modern times began in Britain in the 18th century. Between 1750 and 1870 there was a huge increase in farm output. Farmers learned how to drain their fields and enclose them in hedges. They found that by alternating crops they could use a field continuously, without having to leave it empty (fallow) for a time. Also, stock breeders developed larger and fatter animals.

In the late 18th and early 19th centuries farm machinery rapidly developed, mostly in the USA. First reapers, then threshers, and then combine harvesters appeared. Steam engines were used to power the traction engines used for ploughing and threshing. This mechanical revolution meant that more food could be grown by fewer people.

The latest agricultural revolution began in the 1960s and is still going on. It is called the 'Green Revolution'. Plant breeders have created new varieties of grains such as rice, wheat and maize that give higher yields. This has helped countries such as India, the Philippines and Mexico that have fast-growing populations.

• Most farmers have different jobs to do at different times of the year. Springtime is when lambs are born, while in winter sheep may have to be protected from harsh weather. Autumn is harvest time for crops such as wheat, and the time to sow the seed for next year's crop. In areas like the steppes (grasslands) of central Asia the harvest must be brought in before the cold winter sets in.

find out more
Cereals
Cotton
Food
Hunter-gatherers
Nomads
Rubber
Soil
Wood
Wool

Fishing

find out more
Oceans and seas

There are two main types of industrial fishing: inshore fishing and deep-sea fishing. Inshore fishing boats stay near the coast and catch fish using rods and lines or small nets. They sail and return the same day.

Most of the world's fish catch comes from the deep oceans, too far from land for ships to catch and return the same day. Deep-sea fishing ships are much bigger than those that fish inshore. They can stay at sea for months. Many trawlers feed their catches into a 'factory ship', where the fish are cleaned, gutted and frozen while at sea.

So many fish have been caught from some oceans that the wild fish stocks are running out.

• In fish 'farms' lakes, rivers and parts of the coast are stocked with fish which are kept in cages or released to be caught and eaten.

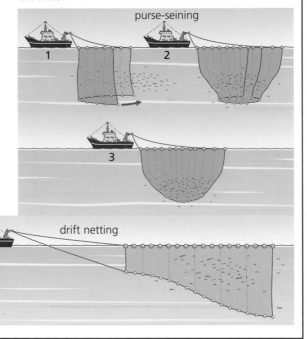

▼ These are the three main types of net used to catch most of the world's fish. Drift and purse-seine nets are used to catch fish near the surface; trawls catch fish near the ocean floor. The nets of some modern ships are too heavy to be dragged on board, so some have great pipes which suck up the catch from the net while it is still in the water.

purse-seining

trawling

drift netting

Food

find out more
Cereals
Famine
Farming
Fishing

In most parts of the world people eat a lot of the foods that grow particularly well in the area where they live. These are known as staple foods.

Staple foods are often cheaper than imported foods, and they can be a good source of energy and body-building materials. Rice is a staple food in parts of India, southern China and South-east Asia. In north-east China noodles and steamed buns made of wheat are more common. Maize (corn) is a staple food in Central and South America. Wheat and potatoes are staple foods in North America and Europe.

Different crops need different climatic conditions and soils. Tropical fruits and vegetables only grow where it is warm or very hot throughout the year. They include groundnuts (peanuts), bananas and plantains, pineapples, mangoes, yams and okra.

North and south of the tropics are the temperate zones. Here quite different fruits and vegetables grow, including olives, grapes, oranges, aubergines and figs. Apples, pears,

▲ These village children in Zambia are preparing flour to make bread – a good staple food.

strawberries, blackberries, potatoes, carrots and wheat grow further north or south of the tropics. In countries bordering the sea, fish form a major part of the diet. In central Europe meat is often preserved and eaten as sausages.

Forests

A forest is a large area of land covered mainly with trees and undergrowth. Some forests, such as the great Amazon rainforest, have existed for thousands of years. Vast areas of forest have been destroyed by human activity, but others have been planted, and a fifth of the world's land is still covered by forest.

Forests create their own special environment. At ground level they are generally shady and cool, because the crowns of the trees shade the forest floor. The air is still, because the trees shield the forest interior from the full force of the wind. The days are cooler and the nights warmer, making the forest a sheltered place for wildlife.

Types of forest

Forests can grow wherever the temperature rises above 10 °C in summer and the annual rainfall exceeds 200 millimetres. Different climates and soils support different kinds of forest.

Rainforests thrive in the humid tropics. The weather is the same all year round – hot and very rainy. The rainforest has such a dense tangle of vegetation that it is often difficult to distinguish the various layers. Plants, including some orchids, even grow perched on the trunks and branches of trees and fallen logs. There are many different kinds of tree: a small patch of forest may contain over 100 different tree species.

Deciduous forests are found in temperate climates, where it is cool in the winter and warm in the summer. There are many fewer different types of tree than in the rainforest. The main trees are deciduous, which means that they shed their leaves in winter (or in the dry season in some regions). The trees also produce flowers, fruits and nuts at particular times of the year. When the trees are leafless in springtime, the forest floor receives plenty of light, so smaller plants may grow and flower.

Coniferous forest is found further north and higher up mountain slopes than any other kind of forest. The main trees are conifers (cone-bearing trees) such as pines. Most are evergreen (they keep their leaves all year), with needle-like leaves coated in wax to reduce water loss. Conifers can survive drought and the freezing of soil water in winter. Their branches slope downwards, so that snow easily slides off. Some conifer forests have arisen naturally, but others

have been planted by people, in order to grow wood for timber, paper and other uses.

The importance of forests

Forests have important functions. Like all green plants, trees absorb carbon dioxide from the air, and release oxygen. So forests are major suppliers of the oxygen humans and all animals need, and they help stop the levels of carbon dioxide in the air from rising too high. This is important because high levels of carbon dioxide in the air cause global warming. ♦

▼ **The structure of a forest**
In the rainforest shown here, the larger trees form an almost continuous *canopy* over the roof of the forest. A few very tall trees, called *emergents*, grow through the canopy into the sunlight above. Below the canopy smaller trees and young saplings form the *understorey*. Below them are shrubs and briars, and on the *forest floor* a layer of smaller shrubs and plants. Each layer of the forest has its own animal communities.

1 harpy eagle
2 macaw
3 spider monkey
4 cock of the rock
5 tree boa
6 sloth
7 ocelot
8 poison frog
9 capybara
10 coral snake

▲ Autumn in a deciduous forest in Utah, USA. As the leaves die, the chemical that makes leaves green is broken down, and they turn many different colours. By shedding their leaves for the winter or during the dry season, the trees are able to save energy and greatly reduce the amount of water they need.

A forest acts like a giant sponge, absorbing rainfall and only gradually releasing it into rivers. By holding the water back, the forest prevents disastrous flooding further downstream. Forest cover also prevents the soil being eroded (worn away) and silting up rivers and lakes.

Forests provide shelter and food for many animals. Leaves, flowers, fruits, seeds and nuts are food for insects, birds and small mammals, such as squirrels and mice, which in turn are food for larger birds and mammals. The moist forest soil has its own community of worms, centipedes, beetles, ants, and the eggs and larvae of many insects.

Forests provide people with an enormous range of important products. For large areas of the world, firewood is the main source of energy, the only source that people can afford. Wood is used for house frames, shipbuilding, papermaking, packaging, fencing and many other purposes. The fruits and nuts of forest trees provide food and spices. Forest trees also provide oils for cooking and industry, syrups, resins, varnishes, dyes, corks, rubber, kapok, insecticides, and medicines such as antibiotics.

Vanishing forests

Every year the world consumes 3 billion cubic metres of wood. In Britain and much of north-west Europe, human beings have cut down most of the trees. In tropical regions, an area of rainforest the size of a football pitch is cut down every second.

Many rainforests grow on very poor soils. Most of the goodness of the land is locked up in the plants. When rainforest is cut down and burned, the remaining soil is often too poor to support crops for long. The soil is easily washed away in the tropical rains, and silts up lakes and reservoirs. The area may even turn to desert.

Forests, especially tropical rainforests, contain a huge variety of plants and animals. If forests are cut down at the present rate, around half the world's remaining rainforests will have vanished by the year 2020, with the loss of around one-tenth of all the species on Earth. Scientists and others are campaigning to stop this destruction of the Earth's resources.

find out more
Deserts
Farming
Greenhouse effect
Wood

▼ **Rot and decay**
When trees die or parts of the tree fall, they quickly rot. Woodpeckers drill holes in soft rotting trunks, and bark beetles excavate tunnels under the bark, allowing fungi to enter. Fungi break down the tree's tissues and absorb the nutrients. When the fungi die, they in turn are broken down by bacteria. The dead plant material gradually crumbles into the soil, and the nutrients it contained escape into the soil, to be taken up by new plants.

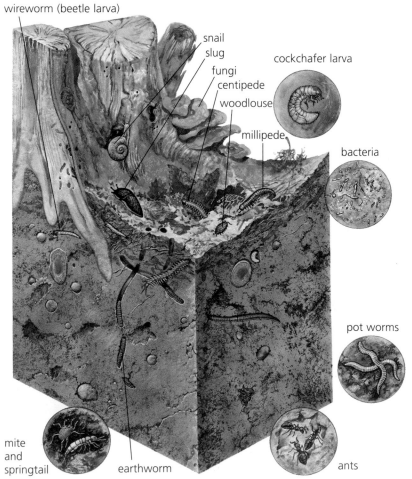

wireworm (beetle larva)
snail
slug
fungi
centipede
woodlouse
millipede
cockchafer larva
bacteria
pot worms
mite and springtail
earthworm
ants

France

France is the largest country in western Europe. It has many different landscapes and ways of life.

Most of Europe's climate types are found within France. Brittany benefits from the warm North Atlantic Drift, and its mild, damp weather contrasts with the varied temperatures of the interior plains such as Alsace. The Mediterranean south has hot, dry summers, and the spiny, deep-rooted plants growing there can resist drought.

Landscape

France's longest river, the Loire, rises in the Massif Central, the high plateaux (level ground) of the centre. Here there are extinct volcanoes that form the cone-shaped peaks of the Auvergne. There are also deep gorges where the River Tarn cuts through dry limestone uplands known as the Causses. Smaller uplands include the forested Vosges in the east and the moorlands of Brittany in the north-west. Elsewhere there are wide plains, most extensive in the Paris Basin and in Aquitaine around the city of Bordeaux. High mountains provide the borders with Italy (the Alps) and Spain (the Pyrenees).

Food and farming

France's large size and variety of physical conditions make it the world's second largest exporter of agricultural goods. A lot of wheat is grown, especially on the large farms of the northern plains, providing flour for the crusty bread the French buy daily. Maize (corn) is grown mainly to feed livestock, and in summer many of the fields are yellow with sunflowers, which provide both food for animals and oil for cooking.

France has some famous breeds of cattle, including the pale-coated Charolais and the rich-brown Limousin, which are exported to many other countries. Dairy cows, most of which feed on the lush pastures of the north-west, produce milk for the cities and for cheeses such as Brie and Camembert, for which France is famous. Roquefort is a cheese made from the milk of sheep.

Vines flourish in many parts of France. The most extensive vineyards are in the south, but some of the best-known wines come from grapes grown on the sunny slopes of Burgundy and (to the north on the River Marne) Champagne. Great skill goes into the blending and maturing of these wines, which are sold throughout the world. The south also produces many other fruits and vegetables, but irrigation water is needed in the dry summer.

Industry

France possesses only limited resources of coal and other fuels. Huge quantities of electricity (70 per cent of France's needs) are generated by nuclear power stations and from hydroelectric dams in the mountains and on rivers such as the Rhône.

Loss of jobs in steel-making and textiles has created employment problems in the older industrial regions of the north-east. New science-based industries flourish in Toulouse, Grenoble and other cities of the south. Concorde, Airbus, the Ariane space rocket and

---

Map

0 ___ 200 km
0 ___ 100 miles

Dunkirk
Calais
Boulogne
BELGIUM
Lille
Valenciennes
Douai
LUX.
English Channel
Cherbourg
Le Havre
Dieppe
Amiens
St-Quentin
GERMANY
Bayeux
Rouen
Oise
Reims
Thionville
Caen
Seine
Marne
Metz
Nancy
Strasbourg
NORMANDY
Versailles
PARIS
CHAMPAGNE
Moselle
Vosges
Brest
St-Malo
Chartres
Seine
Troyes
Mulhouse
Montbéliard
BRITTANY
Rennes
Orléans
Auxerre
BURGUNDY
Dijon
Besançon
Lorient
Le Mans
Loire
Jura
Angers
Tours
Cher
Bourges
St-Nazaire
Nantes
Allier
Loire
Saône
Lake Geneva
SWITZERLAND
Poitiers
Vienne
Montluçon
Rhône
Annecy
4087
La Rochelle
Clermont-Ferrand
Lyons
Mont Blanc
Chambéry
Bay of Biscay
Cognac
Limoges
Auvergne
St-Étienne
Grenoble
ITALY
Angoulême
Massif
Le Puy
Brive
Valence
Bordeaux
Gironde
Garonne
Dordogne
Lot
Central
Rhône
Durance
ALPS
AQUITAINE
Avignon
PROVENCE
MONACO
Bayonne
Adour
Toulouse
Tarn
Nîmes
Aix-en-Provence
Nice
Cannes
Pau
LANGUEDOC
Montpellier
St-Tropez
Lourdes
Carcassonne
Marseille
Toulon
SPAIN
Pyrénées
Perpignan
Mediterranean Sea
ANDORRA

Legend:
— country boundary
◆ capital city
■ ● major cities and towns
— main roads
— main railways
⊕ main airports
▲ high peaks (height in metres)

land height in metres
2000–5000
1000–2000
500–1000
200–500
less than 200
sea level

Corsica
Bastia
Ajaccio

• Almost one-fifth of the population of France live in the city and suburbs of the capital, Paris.

find out more
Canada
Europe

high-speed trains (TGV) are typical products of French technical skills. Tourism is also important in the economy.

▶ FLASHBACK ◀

The Romans occupied what is now France from the 1st century BC to the 5th century AD. Then France was invaded by the Franks, who created a great empire under their king, Charlemagne (747–814). This empire included much of Germany and Italy, but it broke up after Charlemagne's death.

In the later Middle Ages the English kings claimed the French crown and invaded France, but were eventually defeated. In the 17th century France began to build an overseas empire, but in the 18th century it lost its possessions in Canada and India to Britain.

After the French Revolution of 1789, France became a republic. The French general Napoleon Bonaparte conquered most of Europe, but he was finally defeated by the British in 1815.

In the 20th century France was invaded by Germany in both world wars. Since the end

▲ Beaujolais vineyards in the Rhône valley. The wine industry is an important part of France's economy and each year millions of bottles are exported around the world.

of World War II most of France's former colonies have become independent, and France has played a leading part in the European Union.

Geology

The science of geology tries to explain the history of planet Earth – how it was formed, and how it has changed over time. The Earth is still changing all the time. New rocks are being formed, for example when volcanoes erupt and when rivers deposit layers of particles (sediment).

Geologists (scientists who study the Earth) are particularly interested in rocks and minerals, and the way that the Earth's crust (its outermost layer) is made.

There are many different kinds of geologist. *Stratigraphers* study the Earth's history by looking at different rock layers. *Palaeontologists* use fossils to help them study ancient plant and animal life. *Petrologists* study how rocks are made, and *mineralogists* study the minerals that make up the rocks. *Geophysicists* are interested in plate tectonics (the way the continents are moving), the Earth's magnetic field, and in the inside of the Earth. *Volcanologists* study volcanoes, and *seismologists* study earthquakes. *Geomorphologists* are interested in landscape – mountains, valleys, plains, rivers and other features that make up the Earth's surface.

Geologists can use their knowledge to find out where valuable resources are hidden underground. These resources include fuels such as coal, oil and natural gas, the ores of metals such as iron and copper, and many precious and semiprecious stones. Geologists also study the ground before major construction projects – such as new roads and railways – are carried out, to make sure that they can be built safely.

◀ This geologist is examining the mineral content of the rocks in a gold mine in southern Africa.

find out more
Caves
Coal
Continents
Earth
Earthquakes
Erosion
Glaciers
Islands
Lakes
Mining
Mountains
Oil
Rivers and streams
Rocks and minerals
Valleys
Volcanoes

Germany

Germany lies in the middle of Europe between the Alps and Scandinavia. Although not as large as France, Spain or Sweden, it has the biggest population of all European countries (excluding Russia).

Much of Germany consists of the Central Uplands, a mixture of ancient block mountains with low hills and plains. Dark forests crown the hills, and castles look down across orchards and vineyards to fertile plains. In the Northern Lowland the sandy soil is not so fertile. Much of this land is covered with heath and pine forest, strewn with rock boulders left by glaciers of the last ice age. In the far south lie the Alps.

Climate

The climate of Germany is temperate (mild) and allows crops such as wheat, maize (corn) and potatoes to grow well. Cattle graze in the damp and mild north-west and in the foothills of the mountains, but pigs, cattle and poultry are also kept in large battery units near to the cities, especially in the east. One reason for keeping animals indoors is that winters are sometimes very cold, with snow covering the ground for many weeks.

Cities and states

Germany is not dominated by a single huge city, but has a network of large cities. Many of them, including Munich and Dresden, were formerly capitals of independent states such as Bavaria and Saxony that were united into the German empire in the 19th century. These cities inherited splendid palaces and art museums. In western Germany the cities have been well maintained and are prosperous, but in the east the communist government in power until 1989 neglected older buildings. The state provided housing in the form of monotonous prefabricated blocks of apartments on the fringes of the cities.

Bavaria and Saxony are now two of the 16 Länder (federal states) around which the country's federal system of government is built. These states vary greatly in size and population. But they are all important because each has its own constitution, elected parliament and government headed by a minister-president. These governments have responsibility for education, police and local government. They also have local taxation powers.

- In western Germany the Autobahn (motorway) system started by Hitler in the 1930s has been vastly improved and extended. German railways are developing new, high-speed lines which tunnel through hills and climb over valleys to keep an almost dead-level track, even in the mountains.

- Before reunification East Germany relied for most of its electricity output on low-grade brown coal, which caused a high level of air pollution. Its salt, potash, uranium and chemical industries endangered lives of people living nearby, and also poured pollutants into the Weser and Elbe river systems. Since 1990 many of the most polluting plants have been closed down.

Map legend

⎯⎯⎯	country boundary
◆	capital city
■ ●	major cities and towns
⎯⎯	main roads
⎯╫⎯	main railways
⊕	main airports

land height in metres
- 2000–5000
- 1000–2000
- 500–1000
- 200–500
- less than 200
- sea level
- land below sea level

People

The majority of Germans speak German as their first language, but there is a big minority of people who were born outside Germany. The former West Germany had a large number of people who originally came to the country as 'guest workers' to take jobs in factories when Germany was short of labour in the 1960s. The majority of these are from Turkey; the rest are from Bosnia, Croatia, Yugoslavia, Italy, Spain, Greece and Portugal.

German law guarantees admission to anyone claiming German family connections. After the relaxation of frontier controls in the former USSR and eastern Europe from 1989, hundreds of thousands of people arrived from Polish Silesia, Hungary, Romania and the Soviet Union. Germany's liberal immigration laws have also brought an influx of political refugees from countries such as Iran, Lebanon, Sri Lanka and Romania, the latter mainly gypsies. ▶

▲ Berlin today. Older buildings in the eastern part of Germany had been neglected, but today they are being renovated along with the rest of the city.

find out more
Europe
European Union
See also Countries and flags section, page 123

Economy

Germany is the leading economic power in Europe, and one of the world leaders. The former West Germany was famous for high-quality industrial products, such as machine tools, motor vehicles, and its electric and electronic equipment, and chemicals. East Germany had a good reputation as a supplier of machinery, electrical equipment, chemicals and ships to the former USSR and other communist countries. But after the collapse of communist rule in eastern Europe in 1989 and the reunification of

Germany in 1990, very few products from what had been East Germany could compete in a free market. Factories closed and for a while people faced unemployment.

Agriculture is not a very profitable industry in western Germany because of the large number of small family farms. The farms of communist East Germany had been combined into huge co-operative (collective) units. After reunification in 1990 their sales suffered from poor marketing.

▶ FLASHBACK ◀

For many centuries the area that is now Germany was divided into around 400 states. In 1871 the states joined together into a single country, with the king of Prussia (one of the states) as emperor of a united Germany.

Germany became a powerful industrial power. Its rivalry with Britain and France led to World War I (1914–1918), and Germany lost a lot of land after it was defeated. The Nazi dictator Adolf Hitler tried to get this land back in World War II (1939–1945), but the Germans were again defeated. From 1945 to 1990 Germany was divided into the democratic West Germany and the communist East Germany.

Glaciers

A glacier is a moving mass of ice. Glaciers usually form when enough snow builds up an ice layer on the land. They can be seen today in the European Alps and other high mountain ranges, in Alaska and northern Canada, New Zealand, Greenland and Antarctica.

A glacier usually begins high in the mountain. The layers of ice at the bottom where it rests on the ground become soft and slippery, and the glacier begins to move downhill in fits and starts. The ice may move smoothly for a while, until it meets an obstruction such as a bend or a mound of broken rocks.

Glaciers move at different speeds, usually between 1 centimetre and 1 metre per day. The middle part moves faster, and the edges, which rub against the sides of the valleys, may move more slowly. Glaciers can pass right into the sea, where large pieces of ice break away and float off as icebergs. They may retreat if the climate or weather becomes warmer.

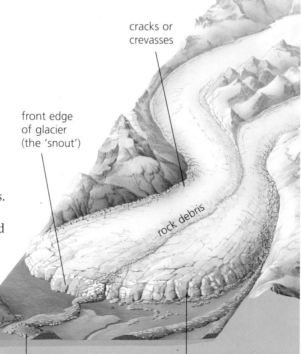

cracks or crevasses

front edge of glacier (the 'snout')

rock debris

rocks and soil are dumped in heaps called moraines

ice cuts away rocks and boulders

find out more
Antarctica
Arctic
Climate
Ice
Valleys

Glacier records
World's largest
Lambert Glacier, Antarctica, 514 km long
World's fastest
Quarayac Glacier, Greenland, 20 m per day

◀ A glacier as it flows through a valley, making it wider and deeper. The valley is changed from a V shape to a U shape.

Grasslands

Grasslands cover more than a fifth of the Earth's land surface. Grass is an important food for many animals, and humans grow and eat grasses like wheat and rice. Grasslands are of many different types, from the desolate steppe lands of Central Asia to the rich farmlands of North America.

• Some parts of the steppes of Russia, Kazakhstan and Mongolia are still roamed by camels and horses. Some of the animals are wild, others are used by nomads, who move about with their animals and live in large round tents made of felt (*yurts* or *gers*).

Grasslands have different names in different parts of the world. There are hot savannahs in East Africa, and veld in southern Africa. In North America there are the fertile prairies, in South America the dry pampas and chacos. The huge areas of grassland in Central Europe and Asia are called steppes, while in western Europe there are meadows and downlands.

Animals

All sorts of animals live on the world's grasslands. Australia's grasslands are home to many of the country's best-known animals, such as kangaroos, emus, kookaburras, and flocks of brightly coloured budgerigars, parrots and cockatoos. Some of the world's largest animals live on the savannahs of East Africa. They include giraffes, elephants and black rhinos.

The North American prairies are home to prairie dogs, small rodents that feed on the grasses. They eat the grass roots as well as the leaves, but they also collect and bury grass seeds, so helping to 'plant' new grasses. The rattlesnake is common in the grasslands of North America. The 'rattle' is in the tip of its tail: the snake rattles when it is disturbed or when coiled ready to strike.

▲ This rolling farmland in Washington State, USA, was once grassland. Much of what used to be prairie is now used to grow cereals such as wheat and maize (corn), which are themselves types of grass.

Most grasslands have a host of tiny animals, which are not usually seen. Earthworms, ants and beetles live in the soil, roots and leaves. Termites build large 'skyscraper' homes of soil in the grasslands, up to 7 metres high.

People and grasslands

Humans have changed grasslands in many parts of the world. Three hundred years ago, there were probably 60 million bison ('buffaloes') roaming the prairies of North America. Settlers from Europe shot bison for their meat and hides, and by the beginning of the 20th century fewer than a thousand were left. During the 20th century the prairies were changed even more dramatically. The grasslands were ploughed up and turned into rich farmland. Grasslands were ploughed for crops in other regions too, such as the steppes of the Ukraine and Russia. In other areas, such as the pampas of Argentina, grasslands are used to graze beef cattle.

find out more
Cereals
Farming
Grasses

◄ Herds of giraffes, wildebeest, zebra and eland graze together on the East African savannah. Grazing in mixed herds enables the animals to help warn each other of danger from predators. Each animal eats different plants or parts of plants. Giraffes, for example, can reach leaves high on the acacia trees, and their tough mouths are not damaged by the trees' huge thorns.

Greenhouse effect

Some of the gases in the Earth's atmosphere act naturally like the glass in a greenhouse. They trap heat from the Sun to help keep the surface of the Earth warm. However, human activities have increased the amounts of these greenhouse gases in the atmosphere and they are now trapping too much heat. Scientists believe that this greenhouse effect is causing the world to become warmer.

The atmosphere is a mixture of gases, but our modern lifestyle is upsetting the natural balance of these gases. Exhaust gases from vehicles and power stations add about 6 billion tonnes of carbon dioxide (the main greenhouse gas) to the atmosphere each year. The destruction of huge areas of forest leaves fewer plants to absorb the gas. Methane, another greenhouse gas, is released by animal waste, swamps, paddy-fields, and oil and gas rigs. Nitrous oxide comes from car exhausts and fertilizers. Chlorofluorocarbons (CFCs) are used in refrigerators, aerosols and foam packaging. They are present only in small quantities in the atmosphere, but they are 10,000 times more effective than carbon dioxide at trapping heat.

Scientists believe that we can slow the greenhouse effect if we produce fewer greenhouse gases. We could burn fewer fossil fuels, like petrol, oil, natural gas and coal, if we develop more efficient heating systems and engines, design buildings which waste less heat, and create transport systems with fewer vehicles.

find out more
Atmosphere
Climate
Energy
Green movement
Pollution

▼ How greenhouse gases trap energy from the Sun.

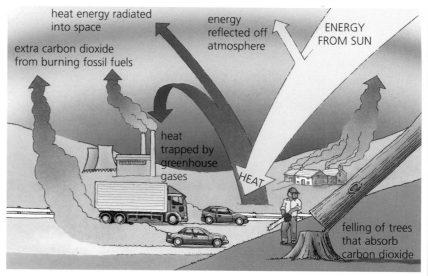

heat energy radiated into space

extra carbon dioxide from burning fossil fuels

energy reflected off atmosphere

ENERGY FROM SUN

heat trapped by greenhouse gases

HEAT

felling of trees that absorb carbon dioxide

Green movement

People who are worried about what humans are doing to the Earth have formed a number of groups to campaign for measures to protect the environment. Together, these groups are known as the green movement.

In many countries, people concerned about green issues have formed political parties. By the end of the 1980s, there was a party known as the Greens or a similar name in almost every country in western and northern Europe. In the 1990s Green parties began to emerge in eastern Europe. In the USA, environmental groups have put forward candidates in elections since the 1980s. Green parties have also developed in such countries as Australia, Canada and New Zealand.

Environmental groups

Many other groups involved in green issues are not political parties. Organizations such as Greenpeace, Friends of the Earth and the Worldwide Fund for Nature raise funds for projects such as the creation of reserves where endangered animals and their habitats can be protected. They also campaign to stop the cutting down of irreplaceable forests, to reduce levels of pollution, to stop dumping of dangerous wastes in the oceans, and on many other environmental issues.

find out more
Energy
Farming
Greenhouse effect
Pollution

▼ Members of Greenpeace trying to stop a beam trawler from putting out its nets. The nets of beam trawlers can cause damage to the sea-bed.

Houses

Houses are made from different materials and come in many shapes and sizes, to suit various climates and ways of life. A bungalow in an Australian suburb is a house, but so is a flat in a high-rise block in Hong Kong.

▲ The nomadic (wandering) people of Mongolia live in tents called gers (yurts). The ger is covered with skin or cloth. Inside it is draped with brightly coloured rugs.

Despite 20th-century improvements in central heating, air-conditioning and insulation, houses last longer and are more pleasant to live in if they are designed to suit the climate. Sloped roofs are best in rainy areas; thick walls and small windows keep rooms cool in hot countries; and verandas or porches are often used as outdoor rooms in countries that have warm summers.

Materials

Houses can now be built from materials brought from distant places by modern transport, but in many countries builders still use local materials. Traditional materials include stone, timber, clay (often made into bricks), straw, reeds or turf.

The Inuit, who live in Arctic regions, use snow blocks for their homes (igloos). Near the Congo River, in Africa, houses are made of woven

▶ A mud-brick house in Yemen, in the Arabian Desert. This style of building is found throughout the Middle East and North Africa.

▶ In some coastal areas of Benin, in Africa, huts are built on stilts to raise them well above the water level. The huts are made of bamboo from the nearby bamboo forests.

bamboo mats. In Saudi Arabia the earth of the desert is pressed together into mud-brick houses. Wood is still used for building in countries that have large forests, such as Canada and the Scandinavian countries.

◀ Wood is used for some of the world's most modern houses. This one, on the USA's east coast, blends well into the surrounding woodland.

▼ Blocks of flats (tenements) that were built up to 400 years ago still stand in Edinburgh's city centre, Scotland.

Style

European-style houses are typically built in rows (terraces), in pairs (semi-detached), or on top of each other in blocks of flats (apartment blocks). This saves land, which is expensive in towns and cities. It also makes the houses cheaper to build and to buy.

The idea of building flats is a very old one. In the ancient Roman town of Ostia, the remains of three-, four- and five-storey blocks of flats can still be seen. By today's standards these flats were quite large – the largest of them had 12 rooms.

With modern building methods, apartment blocks can be built more than 50 storeys high, as in Hong Kong, Kuala Lumpur and other crowded cities of South-east Asia.

Huang He *see* Rivers and streams

Human beings

Today there are over 5.5 billion human beings on Earth. All humans belong to the same animal species – *Homo sapiens sapiens.*

The key to the success of humankind is our intelligence. It has enabled us to use fire, make tools, construct shelters, grow food and clothe our bodies. We have increasingly adapted the environment to our needs. As a result, human beings have spread throughout the world, from forests and deserts to remote islands and the Arctic ice.

About 10,000 years ago small human groups discovered how to grow crops and settled down to farm the land. Since then, human settlements have grown from simple villages to vast cities, where millions of people live and work, and from which money, food and goods are traded across the world.

Rich variety

Tall and short, fat and thin, black and white: although human bodies are all built to the same plan, they are all different. Some of this variety is explained by the fact that human beings have adapted to their environment as they have spread.

As well as physical variety, there is a huge variety in human culture. The food we eat, the music we listen to and the religion we follow are just some of the things that make up our culture. Today, as people are more mobile, cultures are mixing more and more.

◄ Skin colour is the result of how much melanin (dark colouring) your skin contains, and that depends on which part of the world your ancestors came from. Melanin protects the skin from the Sun, so people with dark skin originally came from hot, sunny countries. Pale-skinned people came from colder countries where sunshine is weaker.

find out more
Dress and costume
Farming
Hunter-gatherers
Languages
Migration
Nomads
Population
Settlements

Hunter-gatherers

Hunter-gatherers are people who live by hunting animals, fishing, and gathering wild foods such as fruits, nuts, vegetables and honey.

Hunter-gatherers live in some of the harshest places in the world. The Inuit live in the Arctic, the Bushmen in the Kalahari Desert, the Australian Aborigines in the outback, and the Pygmies in the rainforests of central Africa. Hunter-gatherers live healthy lives where others could not survive at all. This is because of their deep knowledge of their environment, the animals and plants, the weather and the seasons. Hunting and gathering was the way of life of all humankind until about 10,000 years ago. It was only when people discovered how to grow crops that they stopped living in this way.

How hunter-gatherers live

It is mostly the men who hunt and the women who gather, but this is not always the case. Hunter-gatherers are skilled hunters, hunting alone or in groups. They make weapons, nets, traps and tools out of natural materials such as wood, bone, ivory and stone.

Most hunter-gatherers move from place to place so that they can always get food and water. Many live in small groups known as bands. These bands may be just a single family and are rarely bigger than 100 people. They follow the migrations of the wild animals that they hunt, and plan their movements very carefully.

find out more
Arctic
Australia
Farming
Migration
Nomads

◄ The Aeta people of the Philippines belong to the small number of peoples who still live by hunting and gathering. This Aeta man is hunting fish with a bow and arrow.

• Today only about 0.001% of the population of the world are hunter-gatherers.

Ice

Ice is water that is frozen solid. Ice cubes, hail, snow, icicles, frozen puddles and ponds, and glaciers are all composed of the same basic substance – ice. Individual crystals of ice stick together to form larger blocks of ice. Millions of tiny ice crystals measuring only a few millimetres across are packed together tightly to form huge lumps of floating ice called icebergs.

Under a magnifying lens you would see that snowflakes are composed of numbers of six-pointed, star-like crystals. Bigger blocks of ice are also made up of ice crystals, but the crystals are too numerous and too tightly packed together to be seen. Most crystals measure between 1 and 20 millimetres, but the crystals that make up the oldest glaciers in the world have been repeatedly re-formed over a long period, and some now measure about 50 centimetres across.

The expansion of water as it freezes into ice can produce a very powerful force. Freezing water in winter can burst pipes and damage car engines unless they have antifreeze in them. On mountainsides, rainwater seeps into cracks in the rocks. If the water freezes, it expands with such force that it will split the rocks and make pieces fall off.

▼ Icebergs floating in Jokulsarlon Lake, Iceland. The ice has 'calved' from the nearby Vatnajokull glacier, one of the largest in Europe.

If you press ice very hard, it will begin to melt. The best snowballs are made when the snow melts a little if you press it together. If it is much colder than 0 °C (the freezing point of pure water), then the ice and snow will stay frozen and the snow will be too cold to melt when you squeeze it.

Ice-sheets and icebergs

Large areas of ice and snow which permanently cover the land are called ice-sheets. They are all that remain of the great sheets of ice that once covered large parts of the world. The world's main ice-sheets are found in Antarctica and Greenland.

Icebergs are huge lumps of ice that break away from ice-sheets (and glaciers) and float in the sea. Only about a ninth of an iceberg shows above the surface. The part that is hidden under the water may be wider than the part that shows. This is a great danger to shipping. The largest icebergs break away from the edge of Antarctica, such as from the Ross Ice Shelf. This area of floating ice is as large as France. Icebergs in the Arctic are smaller than the Antarctic ones, but they are often taller. Glaciers reach the sea around Greenland, and as the ice begins to float, huge lumps 'calve' or break off.

Icebergs begin to melt as they drift away from the polar regions. Cold currents carry icebergs great distances. The cold Labrador Current can carry Arctic icebergs into the busy North Atlantic shipping routes. The International Ice Patrol warns ships about drifting icebergs.

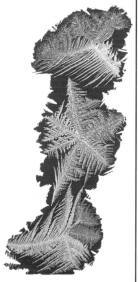

▲ These flower-shaped patterns of frost are really crystals of ice. Frost forms during very cold nights when the air temperature falls below the freezing point of water (0 °C). Moisture in the air freezes into tiny ice crystals where the air is in contact with surfaces such as blades of grass and windows.

Iceberg records
Largest iceberg
Over 31,000 sq km (335 km long and 97 km wide), seen in the South Pacific Ocean in November 1956
Tallest iceberg
167 m high, seen off west Greenland in 1958

find out more
Antarctica
Arctic
Erosion
Glaciers
Greenhouse effect
Mountains
Rain and snow
Water

India

India is a large country in southern Asia with a population of almost 950 million. Only China has more people, but if India's population keeps growing at its current rate, it will overtake China in the 21st century. This land of great natural diversity has been home to many civilizations, religions and peoples over the centuries.

The Himalayan mountain range extends across the north of India. It contains some of the highest peaks in the world. Many great rivers, including the Ganges and the Brahmaputra, flow down from the Himalayas to the northern plains. These contain the most fertile land in the country. Summers here are very hot, but between June and September the wet monsoon wind brings heavy rain and cooler temperatures.

The southern part of India is a huge plateau, called the Deccan plateau. Along the western coast it rises to a rugged mountain range, the Western Ghats.

• India and its neighbouring countries, Pakistan, Bangladesh and Sri Lanka, are known as the Indian subcontinent.

• India is the world's largest democracy. It has a president, who appoints the prime minister, and a parliament with two houses: the House of the People is elected by the whole country; the Council of States is made up of representatives from each of India's 25 states.

• India has 16 major languages and many other minor ones and dialects. Hindi and English are the official languages.

▼ In the 3rd century BC the Indian king Asoka carved his laws on pillars. These were topped with sculptures, like these lions, which became the national emblem of India.

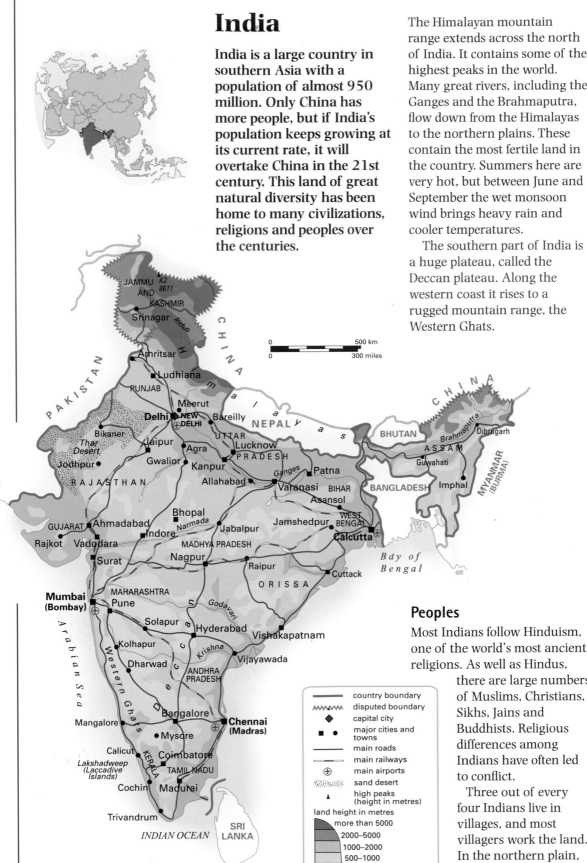

Peoples

Most Indians follow Hinduism, one of the world's most ancient religions. As well as Hindus, there are large numbers of Muslims, Christians, Sikhs, Jains and Buddhists. Religious differences among Indians have often led to conflict.

Three out of every four Indians live in villages, and most villagers work the land. In the northern plain, wheat is the main crop. In the south and east, where it is wetter, rice is the most important crop. Farmers also grow maize (corn), millet, bananas, groundnuts, lentils, sugar cane, pepper, tea, coffee, tobacco and cotton.

In order to feed its rapidly growing population, new types of rice and wheat were introduced in the 1960s to produce bigger crops. This was called the Green Revolution. However, regular droughts and floods still destroy crops.

▲ Cooking on the street in Mysore, southern India. Indian food is famous for its richness and variety, but most Indians have a very simple diet. In the south, this may be rice and dal, a dish made from puréed lentils or split peas.

Mines and factories

India is rich in minerals. It has large deposits of coal, iron ore, bauxite (from which aluminium is made), manganese and zinc. Factories build everything from bicycles and sewing machines to ships and aircraft. In rural areas, small workshops turn out pottery, cloth and other craft goods.

India has its own space industry, and has launched satellites. In such a large country, these are vital for communications. Bangalore, in the south, has an important computer industry. Its workers write software programs that are used throughout the world.

Cities

India has two of the world's largest cities, Mumbai (Bombay) and Calcutta, both with over 10 million inhabitants. Many people travel to the cities from rural areas, because there is not enough work for them to do on the land. In the cities many of them find work, but it is much harder for them to find somewhere to live. To help solve this problem, the government has improved roads and railways, so that villagers can travel to the city each day.

▶ FLASHBACK ◀

One of the world's earliest civilizations flourished around 2500 BC in the Indus valley, and extended east into present-day India. In around 1500 BC Aryan peoples from central Asia arrived in India. The Aryans developed two great religious traditions, Hinduism and Buddhism.

For many centuries India was divided into a number of small kingdoms. For short periods some kings managed to unite most of India under their rule. These kings included the Mauryans (3rd century BC) and the Guptas (AD 320–467).

In the 8th century Arab invaders brought Islam to northern India. More Muslim invaders began to arrive from the 11th century. The greatest of these invaders were the Mughals from central Asia, who arrived in the 16th century and created an empire that lasted until 1858.

At around the same time as the Mughal invasion the first Europeans began to arrive in India. They came as traders but gradually took over more and more of the country. The British were the most successful of the new arrivals. In the 18th century they drove out their French rivals.

The British ruled India less harshly than most conquerors. Nevertheless, the Indians began to demand independence. From 1919 the most important leader of the independence campaign was Mahatma Gandhi. The British eventually agreed to grant independence, and in 1947 the country was divided into the largely Hindu nation of India and the Muslim state of Pakistan.

▲ Children harvesting wheat in Rajasthan, northern India. The monsoon rains do not reach the north-west of India, and a large part of Rajasthan is desert.

find out more
Asia
Bangladesh
Pakistan
See also Countries and flags section, page 123

▼ Huge film posters dominate the streets of Mumbai (Bombay). Mumbai has the largest film industry in the world, producing about 900 films each year.

Indonesia

Indonesia, in South-east Asia, is the world's largest island chain. It is made up of over 13,000 islands, scattered over 8 million square kilometres of ocean. Only 3000 of these islands are inhabited, and 60 per cent of people live on just one island – Java.

The Equator runs through the middle of Indonesia. The climate is hot, and the annual rainfall is over 2000 millimetres in most parts. This hot, wet climate means that farmers can grow rice, which is the country's basic food.

In many of the outer islands, such as Borneo and Sumatra, there are dense rainforests. Unfortunately, much of Indonesia's forest is being cleared for mining, oil exploration, farming and timber. In recent years the economy has grown thanks to the discovery of oil and natural gas, and the building of factories that make shoes, textiles and electronics.

Many different peoples live in Indonesia. In the rainforests some tribes still live traditional lives, either hunting or clearing small plots to grow food, then moving on and letting the forest return. Other people have settled in Indonesia, including Hindus, Buddhists and Muslim traders.

Indonesia was a Dutch colony until 1949. From independence until 1998 Indonesia had only two leaders, Presidents Sukarno and Suharto. President Suharto was forced to stand down in 1998, and democratic elections were held in 1999.

▼ Children playing in Ambon City, Indonesia. Even in quite large cities, Indonesians live in small communities called kampongs, each of which is like a village.

find out more
Asia
See also Countries and flags section, page 123

● Indonesia's rainforests contain a rich mixture of plants and animals, many of which are found nowhere else. Borneo, for example, is the only home of the orang-utan and of the world's largest flowering plant, rafflesia. Gorgeously coloured birds of paradise are found in Irian Jaya.

Industry

● When people make things at home or in a small workshop and sell them through a local market stall or shop, this is called a *cottage industry*. Potters who sell their pottery and knitters who sell their woollen garments through local outlets belong to cottage industries.

● *Industrialized countries* are those that have a lot of manufacturing, or secondary, industry. Now that some countries have a majority of their workforce in tertiary occupations, some people talk of '*post-industrialization*', meaning that these countries are developing service industries to take the place of factories.

Industry is any sort of activity that is done to produce the goods and services that people need. There are many types of industry, including manufacturing, farming, mining, banking and tourism.

An industry is a group of firms or businesses that are all making the same, or similar, products. For example, the world's car-making industry contains a number of individual firms, such as Ford, Volvo, Volkswagen, Renault and Honda. Each of these firms makes cars for sale to the public and aims to make a profit from the sales.

Before the cars are manufactured, however, the firms need to buy raw materials (such as steel and glass), component parts (such as lights and batteries) and energy (such as electricity and gas) from other industries. For any product you buy, you can trace a 'chain of production', which will take you through a number of industries before the product reaches you, the consumer.

The different kinds of industry are divided into three types: primary, secondary and tertiary.

▲ Advances in computer technology have made it possible for more people to work from home. Workers can use personal computers and modems to send data down the telephone lines to their head office.

◀ Workers in a rock quarry in Karnataka, India. In India almost three-quarters of the population work in primary industries. Countries such as India are trying to build up their manufacturing industry. As workers can usually earn higher wages in the new factories than on the land, people are moving to the cities in search of jobs.

Primary industry

Primary industry is the name given to all those industries that take natural resources from the Earth and sea. The mining and quarrying industries extract minerals (such as coal, oil and copper) and stone from the ground. These materials are then taken to be used in factories and power stations and on building projects. Fishing, farming and forestry are also primary industries. Most of the fish, food and timber produced by these industries is then processed by other industries.

Primary industry is not as important now as it once was in the most advanced economies of the world. In Japan and the USA, for instance, primary industries produce only 2 to 3 per cent of the country's Gross Domestic Product (or GDP, the total value of goods and services provided in a country in one year).

In developing countries, however, primary industry may still account for a large proportion of a country's goods and services. For example, more than half of Kenya's exports are agricultural products such as tea and coffee.

Secondary industry

Firms that take raw materials and turn them into products for the public belong to the manufacturing or 'secondary' industries. These businesses make all sorts of products, from matches to space rockets. The construction or building industry is a secondary industry.

Manufacturers talk about the 'market' for their products. This means the number of people who might buy the products. The bigger the market, the more chance there is of making a profit and the more businesses there are likely to be in that particular industry.

Before deciding where to build a factory, the owners will have to ask a number of important questions. The first may be whether the site is in an area targeted for development by government, and therefore eligible for government subsidies (financial help). The people who work in the factory (the labour force) are also important. Are there enough of them, with the necessary skills, within easy reach of the factory? If the raw materials used in production are heavy and expensive to move, will it be a good idea to locate the factory close to the source of raw materials? Transport links are also vital for getting raw materials to the factory and the finished goods to the market. Are there good roads, railways, airports or sea ports close to the factory site? Only when all these questions have been answered can a decision be made about where the factory should be built.

Tertiary industry

Tertiary industry offers people a service. Transporting and selling goods to the public are service activities. So are health care, education, banking, insurance and tourism. They do not make anything, but the services they provide help to improve people's quality of life.

The leisure industry includes skating rinks, hotels, restaurants, swimming pools, cinemas, theatres and wildlife parks. This type of industry has been growing rapidly in recent decades in most of the economies of Europe and North America, and may account for more than half the industrial output of such countries.

find out more

Economics and
  development
Energy
Farming
Fishing
Mining
Pollution
Tourism
Trade
Transport
Wood

● The materials, workforce, energy and money needed to run a factory are called 'inputs' by people in industry. The product made is called the 'output'.

● Mass production is a way of making goods in large numbers in factories by using more machines and fewer people. Goods are cheaper because the cost of buying the machines to make them is spread over more items.

Ireland, Republic of

The Republic of Ireland is a country in north-west Europe. It covers most of the island of Ireland, which is often called the 'Emerald Isle' because its mild and moist climate helps to cover the countryside with lush grass.

Much of the Irish coast faces the Atlantic Ocean. It is a rugged coastline, broken up by numerous bays, inlets, peninsulas and sandy beaches. Most of the country's mountains and moorlands are near the coast, in places such as Wicklow and Waterford in the south-east, Cork and Kerry in the south-west, Clare, Galway and Mayo in the west, and Sligo and Donegal in the north-west. About 15 per cent of the land is covered by peat bogs, and the peat from these is used for heating and as an energy source.

Agriculture and industry

About three-quarters of the country's land is suitable for agriculture. Beef and dairy cattle are raised in large numbers on the lush pastures, and cereals, potatoes and sugar beet are important crops. Much of the country's industry is based on this agriculture, and its dairy and beef products are major exports. Other world-famous Irish products are linen, crystal glass, whiskey and beer. Many new industries have recently been set up, and the production of computer components is particularly important. Tourism is another important industry. Fishing and fish-farming are carried on in small ports around the coast, and the mining industry is growing because of recent discoveries of mineral deposits.

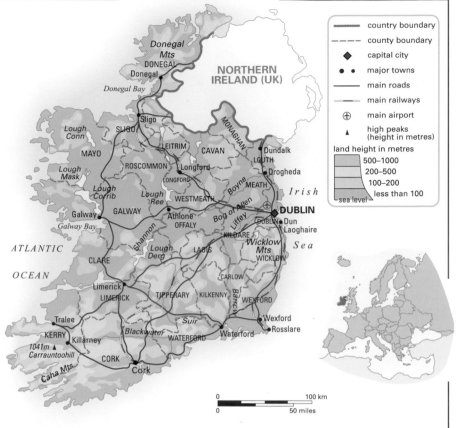

▶ FLASHBACK ◀

Celtic peoples settled in Ireland in around 300 BC, and early Ireland became an important centre of Christianity. In the 12th century the English invaded Ireland, but it was not until the end of the 16th century that they controlled the whole island. The new rulers took much land from the Irish, who remained Catholic, and gave it to English and Scottish Protestants.

For centuries the British ruled Ireland harshly, and there were many revolts. Eventually, in 1921, the British government granted home rule (self-government) to the southern 26 counties, where the majority of people were Catholic. The northern six counties, where there was a Protestant majority, remained as part of the United Kingdom. The south became a republic in 1949.

• The parliament of the Irish Republic is based in Dublin and consists of two houses, the Seanad (Senate) and the Dáil. The head of the government is the Taoiseach (prime minister). The country's president is elected every seven years.

◀ The lush landscape of the Ring of Kerry in Killarney, Ireland.

find out more
Europe
European Union
Northern Ireland
United Kingdom
See also Countries and flags section, page 123

Iron and steel

Iron and steel are used for making buildings, cars, ships, trains and many other things. There are many different kinds of iron and steel. Most of the iron produced is used to make steel. Steel is a mixture of iron and other products.

Iron is a very common metal in nature. One-twentieth of the Earth's crust is made of iron, and the Earth's core is also mostly iron.

Iron is mined from the ground, sometimes in its pure form but mostly as *ore* (rock with metal in it). The commonest iron ore is called haematite. The ore is heated in a blast furnace to make iron, most of which is then turned into steel.

Most of the world's iron ores come from China, Brazil, Australia, Russia, Ukraine, India, the USA, Sweden, Canada, South Africa, Venezuela and Kazakhstan. The biggest makers of steel in the world are Japan, the USA, China, Germany, Italy, South Korea, Brazil, France and the United Kingdom.

Making iron

Iron is made in a *blast furnace* – a tall oven made of steel and lined with fireproof bricks. A mixture of crushed iron ore, coke and limestone is fed into the furnace and heated by a continuous blast of hot air.

The three substances react together inside the furnace to form iron and a waste material called *slag*. When the slag solidifies, it is sold for road-building. Some of the iron solidifies in moulds to form a rather brittle kind of iron. This is called *cast* or *pig iron*. Most of the molten iron is turned into steel.

Steel-making

Steel is made in special furnaces which remove unwanted carbon and other impurities in the iron. A small amount of carbon is left in the iron so that it is hard but not brittle. Other metals are often added to make different kinds of steel, with special properties. Stainless steel, for example, is a mixture of steel and the metal chromium. Unlike ordinary steel, stainless steel does not rust.

◀ Inside the hot-rolling mill at a steel foundry. Red-hot slabs of steel travel backwards and forwards under huge rollers. They are taken out when they have been rolled into steel sheets of the right thickness.

▶ FLASHBACK ◀

Iron was first made in around 2000 BC by heating a mixture of iron ore and charcoal over a fire. While it was still hot, the iron was beaten into shape with a stone. It was used to make tools and weapons, such as knives and axes.

The introduction of the blast furnace to England at the beginning of the 16th century allowed pig iron to be made continuously. The first cheap method of making steel was invented in England in 1856 by Henry Bessemer.

find out more
Earth
Industry
Mining

▼ Making iron in a blast furnace.

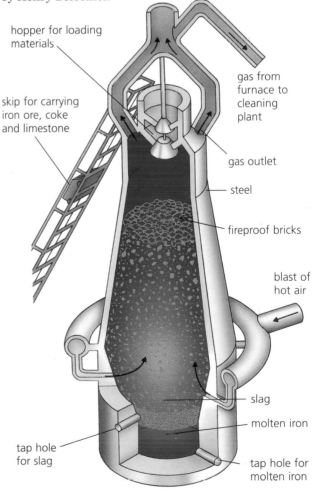

hopper for loading materials

skip for carrying iron ore, coke and limestone

gas from furnace to cleaning plant

gas outlet

steel

fireproof bricks

blast of hot air

tap hole for slag

slag

molten iron

tap hole for molten iron

Islands

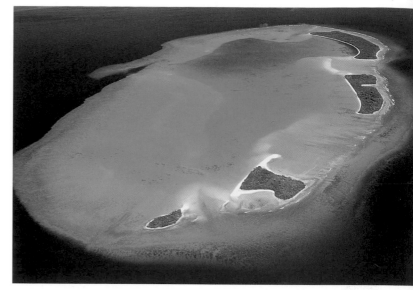

• Some countries, for example Indonesia, are made up of a large group of islands, which is called an *archipelago*.

An island is an area of land that is entirely surrounded by water. Islands are found in lakes or rivers, and also in oceans and seas. They come in many different forms and sizes. The world's largest island is Greenland.

• The white sand found on many beaches in tropical areas is made of broken-up coral.

find out more
Caribbean
Climate
Continents
Indonesia
Migration
Pacific Islands
Volcanoes

Some islands are small landmasses that have become separated from the mainland. Others are formed when the sea level rises after large ice-sheets have melted, for example the British Isles. Lowland areas are flooded, leaving the areas of land in between as islands.

Some mountainous islands are the tops of volcanoes that have erupted on the ocean floor. Hawaii, some of the Caribbean islands and the Aleutian Islands are examples of volcanic islands. Many low-lying islands in warm seas are made of coral. An example is the Maldives in the Indian Ocean. The skeletons

▼ How different kinds of island are formed.

of the tiny coral animals form a solid mass, called a *reef*. Sometimes the coral forms a circular ring called an *atoll*, which encloses an area of water known as a *lagoon*. Atolls tend to form around the submerged rim of a volcano. When a thin layer of soil collects on the atoll and plants begin to grow there, it becomes a coral island.

▲ Kayangel Atoll is part of the Caroline Islands in the Pacific Ocean. This aerial photograph shows a ring of coral reefs just below the water's surface surrounding a deeper lagoon.

Island life

The first plant to grow on many tropical islands is the coconut palm, whose nut is carried long distances by the sea. Other plants may arrive as seeds carried by birds that have been blown off course.

Many islands, such as Madagascar, are home to kinds of plant and animal that are found nowhere else on Earth. On some islands there are no mammals, but there may be reptiles, some of which are very large because they face less competition for food and other resources than they would on the mainland. Giant tortoises were at one time found on many islands.

When sea levels fall, land bridges may form, allowing humans and other animals to cross to new islands. Long ago, Australia was linked to Asia when the Torres Strait between the two continents was exposed.

continental island

rising sea level covers low-lying land

volcanic island

lava is deposited on the ocean floor

the lava builds up above sea level to form an island

coral atoll

a volcanic island, surrounded by a coral reef, is sinking

a lagoon forms between the sinking island and the coral reef

the island sinks below sea level and the reef becomes an atoll

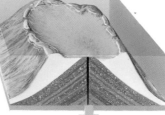
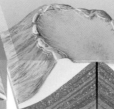

Italy

Italy consists of a long peninsula leading south from the Alps and two large islands, Sicily and Sardinia.

The Alps in the north make a natural barrier between Italy and the rest of Europe. There are several large lakes in the foothills of the Alps. The richest farmland is also in the north, in the wide flat valley of the River Po. Rows of apple and pear trees grow between strips of wheat and maize (corn). There are acres of sugar beet, and rice grows on the wettest lowland. Vines are grown everywhere, making Italy one of the world's biggest producers of wine. The Appennine Mountains stretch right down the centre of the Italian peninsular. In Sicily there are huge orchards of almond trees and lemons.

Italy has several active volcanoes, including Vesuvius and Mount Etna. Earthquakes are also quite common.

- Foreigners are often puzzled by Italy's politics. There are over 20 parties, many of them based in only one region, so governments are usually formed by coalitions (alliances) of politicians.

- Vatican City is the world's smallest independent country. It occupies 0.44 sq km in the Italian capital, Rome, and it is the headquarters of the Roman Catholic Church.

find out more

Europe
European Union
See also Countries and flags section, page 123

▼ Venice was once a great trading centre built on islands in a lagoon. It is now in danger because it is sinking into the lagoon.

Industry

During the 20th century, Italy developed rapidly. It is now the world's fifth largest economy. But this economic growth is uneven. The northern cities are the industrial centres. Turin (Fiat cars), Milan (fashion accessories) and Florence (shoes and fine textiles) are world leaders in design and engineering. But the south and the islands are still farming areas, and quite poor. During the 19th century, thousands of southerners migrated to the USA. Now they travel to the northern cities. The government has invested heavily in roads, dams and irrigation projects to overcome the south's geographical isolation and improve its agriculture.

Tourism is important in many parts of the country. Italy is the fourth most popular tourist destination in the world.

▶ FLASHBACK ◀

Two thousand years ago the Roman empire, based in Italy, included all the lands around the Mediterranean Sea. The Roman empire collapsed in the 5th century AD. For hundreds of years Italy was divided into many small city-states, which often fought each other. Many Italian cities such as Florence and Venice became centres of the arts, learning and trade.

In the 19th century many Italians wanted to make Italy into a single country. By 1870 all parts of Italy were united under an Italian king. Italy was an ally of Britain and France in World War I, but afterwards fell under the control of the fascist dictator Benito Mussolini. In World War II Mussolini sided with Nazi Germany, but he lost power in 1943. After the war the Italians voted to become a republic.

Map legend:
- country boundary
- ◆ capital city
- ■ ● major cities, towns
- main roads
- main railways
- ⊕ main airports
- ▲ high peaks (height in metres)
- land height in metres
  - 2000–5000
  - 1000–2000
  - 500–1000
  - 200–500
  - sea level — less than 200

Japan

Japan is a country of many islands in the north-west Pacific Ocean. It is a wealthy, bustling country, and its industries make goods which sell all over the world. The main island, Honshu, is where most people live.

Thickly wooded hills and mountains occupy two-thirds of Japan. Many short, fast rivers flow from the mountains to the sea. The country has more than 60 active volcanoes and is often shaken by earthquakes.

Japan's climate varies from north to south. In the north winters are cold and snowy, and summers are short. In the south the climate is hot and humid.

People

Because so much of Japan is mountainous, three-quarters of the people live in or near the towns and cities in a narrow coastal plain. Many people live in suburbs and commute to work. Long tunnels and bridges link the main islands.

The traditional arts of Japan are very simple, elegant and formal. The Japanese pioneered bonsai (growing miniature trees). They also perfected origami, or paper folding. The favourite kind of poetry is the haiku, which is just 17 syllables long. Japan is also the home of many martial arts, such as judo, karate and sumo wrestling.

Industry and farming

Japan has become a rich and powerful manufacturing country. It is a leading producer of cars, ships and television sets, and sells a great deal of electronic equipment. But it has to import nearly all its raw materials and its coal and oil.

Japan has large areas of farmland. Farms are often run by families. Rice is the main crop. Most meals are based on rice, and Japanese eat more fish than meat. Although farmers now use machines to plant the young seedlings, a great deal of the work has to be done by hand.

▶ FLASHBACK ◀

Japanese civilization is very old. There have been emperors in

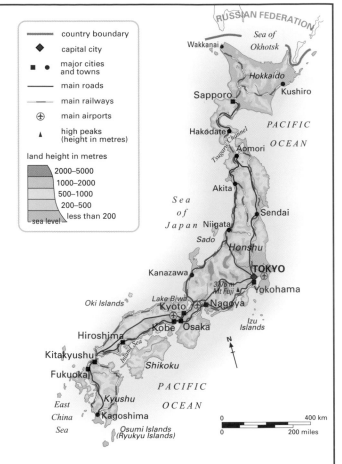

Japan for over 2000 years. For centuries Japan cut itself off from the rest of the world. It only began to open itself up in the late 19th century. After that it quickly built up its industry.

In a series of wars between 1894 and 1937 Japan gained control of Korea, Taiwan and large areas of China. In World War II Japan conquered most of South-east Asia and many Pacific islands. But it eventually surrendered after the USA dropped atom bombs on two Japanese cities. Since then Japan has adopted a democratic government and become one of the world's leading industrial nations.

find out more
Asia
See also Countries and flags section, page 123

◀ The flowering of the cherry blossom in spring is a traditional time for celebration in Japan. Groups of people picnic under the cherry trees. Karaoke (singing along to a song on tape) is also popular.

Lakes

Lakes are areas of water surrounded by land. They occur where water can collect in hollows in the Earth's surface, or behind barriers which may be natural or artificial. The world's largest lake is the Caspian Sea, which receives water from the Volga and Ural rivers.

Crater lakes lie in the natural hollows of old volcanoes. The Eifel district of north-west Germany has hundreds of lakes lying in extinct craters. Lake Bosumtwi in Ghana lies in a crater that was probably made by a meteorite.

Glacial lakes form where ice-sheets and glaciers have left the ground very uneven. They have scraped and hollowed out hard rock or dumped sand, gravel and clay in uneven layers. Such lake districts are found in Finland and in northern Canada. Lakes may fill holes in the glaciated valley floor, as in the Lake District in north-west England.

Rift-valley lakes are long thin lakes such as Lake Malawi, Lake Tanganyika and Lake Turkana in East Africa, and the Dead Sea between Israel and Jordan. When the Earth's crust slipped down between long lines of faults, the water filled part of the floor of the valley.

Artificial lakes are created by humans. People have built earth, stone and huge concrete dams to hold back rivers for water supply, irrigation or hydroelectric power.

find out more
Glaciers
Mountains
Rivers and streams
Valleys

• The world's largest lake is the Caspian Sea in central Asia, with an area of 371,000 sq km. The deepest lake is Lake Baykal in Siberia, Russia, which is 1741 m deep.

▼ Some different kinds of lake.

crater lake

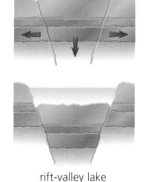
rift-valley lake

glacial lake

Languages

No one is sure how many languages there are in the world, but there are certainly well over 4000. Africa alone has about 1300 languages.

Languages are often similar to one another and can be grouped into families. Most European languages belong to a great Indo-European family of languages. It includes the Celtic languages (including Gaelic and Welsh), Greek, the Romance languages (including Latin, French, Spanish and Italian), the Germanic languages (including German, Dutch and English), the Slavonic languages (including Russian, Polish and Czech), and many of the languages of northern India, Pakistan, Afghanistan and Iran. Other families of languages include Finnish and Hungarian, the Chinese languages and the languages of the Pacific Ocean region. There are four families of African languages.

Languages in use

In some countries it is normal to use a mother tongue (native language) at home and an official language at work. In parts of India and Africa children learn two or three languages. Some languages, including English and French, are used as *international languages*. People from different countries may use them to speak to each other.

Sometimes languages are adapted into special forms. *Pidgins* are simplified languages used by groups of people with no language in common. If a pidgin becomes a native language, it is called a *creole*.

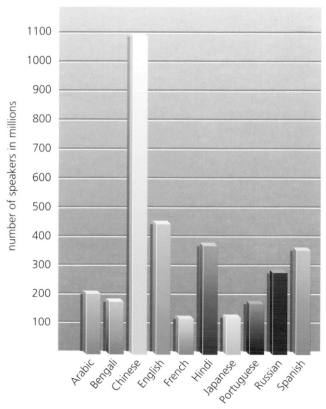

▲ Languages with the most speakers.

Maps

A map is a plan of an area, viewed from above. We use many different kinds of map. Street maps, for example, show you where you are, and how to reach the place you want to go to. By contrast, physical maps tell you about the natural features of an area, whether this is a country or a continent.

Road maps, street maps and railway maps are made simply to show routes. *Theme maps* show special information about places. Geological maps, for example, show which rocks make up the landscape. Economic maps show a wide range of economic information, such as the average income for each inhabitant of a country, how much money countries earn from their exports, and so on. Historical maps show a country or a region at a particular period in the past.

Physical maps show the natural features of an area of land, such as hills and rivers. *Topographic maps* also show these features, together with human features such as towns, roads and country boundaries. Land height is shown by colours. The colour green, for instance, is often used to show low land. *Political maps* include countries and their boundaries, capital cities and sometimes other towns or administrative areas, but do not tell you much about what the land looks like. Colours on these maps are used to mark out the different areas, rather than to give information about land height or the kind of vegetation.

World maps

The most accurate way to look at the size and shape of the Earth's landmasses is to use a globe. However, globes are awkward to carry about and you cannot see the entire Earth's surface at a glance.

A world map is convenient to use but it has to be read with care. It is impossible to flatten the curved surface of the Earth without stretching or cutting part of it. There is always some distortion in the shape or size of the landmasses and oceans on a world map.

Latitude and longitude

Latitude and longitude are imaginary lines that tell you exactly where a place is on the Earth's surface. They help you to find and describe the position of any place on a map. Latitude tells you how far the place is to the north or south of the *Equator*, an imaginary line around the centre of the world dividing it into the northern and southern hemispheres.

Longitude tells you how far a place is to the east or west of a special line called the Prime Meridian, which passes through Greenwich in London, England.

Both latitude and longitude are measured in degrees (°). There are 360° in a complete circle, so longitude runs east and west from 0° to 180°. All the longitude lines meet at the Poles. The latitude of the Equator is 0° and the Poles are 90° north and 90° south. The latitude lines are parallel to the Equator. Each degree of latitude is about 111 kilometres.

The *tropics* are imaginary lines marking the places furthest away from the Equator where the Sun is overhead for part of the year. The Tropic of Cancer is at $23\frac{1}{2}°$ north of the Equator, and the Tropic of Capricorn is at $23\frac{1}{2}°$ south of the Equator. The area between these lines is called the tropics.

Scale

The amount of detail included on a map depends on its scale. Atlas maps are small-scale maps that show large areas with little detail. The maps used by walkers and climbers, however, are large-scale maps that show small areas in a lot of detail. If you are out walking, it is very important to understand scale. What looks like a short distance on the map could turn out to be a very long way.

- Before a map can be made, the positions of all the main features, such as hills, roads and churches, must be found. This is called *surveying*. Map surveys are now carried out using a satellite navigation system called the Global Positioning System (GPS).

- There is a map of the world on pages 120–121.

find out more
Climate
Continents
Weather
See also articles on individual countries and continents

▼ These two world maps are drawn on different *projections*. This means that they have been flattened out in different ways. Map A is an equal area map, which means that the relative areas of the continents are correct. However, the shapes of the continents have been distorted slightly. On map B the shapes of the land areas are more accurate, but their relative sizes are incorrect.

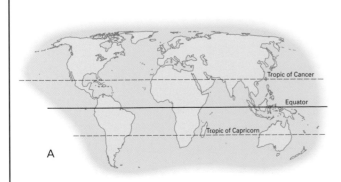

A

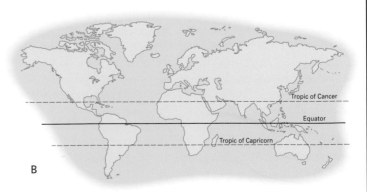

B

Maps

The scale of a map can be shown by a scale line or bar. This is divided up to show what distances on the map mean on the ground. Scale can also be shown in numbers. A scale of 1:50,000 means that one of any unit on the map represents 50,000 of the same unit on the ground. One centimetre along a road on the map would mean 50,000 centimetres along the real road – that is 500 metres or half a kilometre.

Reading maps

Maps do not show everything. You would need an aerial photograph if you wanted to see what a place actually looked like. Maps only show the things that the map maker has decided to include. Supermarkets, for example, are not usually shown, but on many maps churches are included because church spires and towers are good for helping you to find your way around. The landscape features that are shown are marked by simple symbols. Some symbols are like pictures, and others are initial letters (for example, T for telephone). It is always important to refer to the key or legend of the map to find out what the symbols mean.

On some maps the height of the land is shown by lines joining places of the same height above sea level. These imaginary lines, which do not cross each other, are called *contours*. If they seem to join up or stop, they represent a cliff or vertical slope. With practice you can learn to read the pattern of the contours so that you can picture the landscape.

Before using a map outdoors, it is helpful to turn it so that it faces north. This is called setting or orientating the map. You can use a compass to help you.

	capital city
	country boundary
	highest peaks (height in metres)
	ice cap

land height in metres
- 2000–5000
- 1000–2000
- 500–1000
- 200–500
- less than 200
- sea level
- land below sea level

▲▼ Compare the topographic map of the continent of Europe (above) with the satellite image (below) of the same landmass. The colours in the map show different land heights. The white patches in the bottom picture are snow, which can be seen in parts of northern Europe as well as on mountain ranges in the south.

Mediterranean

The Mediterranean Sea stretches over 3000 kilometres from west to east. When we talk about the Mediterranean, we often mean both the sea and the shores surrounding it, where more than 100 million people live.

The Mediterranean region has mild, wet winters and hot, dry summers. The eastern Mediterranean is drier than the west. The coast of North Africa, especially Libya, is desert. It can be very hot here, as it is also in the far south of Italy.

The mountains are wetter and cooler than the coastal plains. In summer, a dry dusty wind often blows from the Sahara. This is the sirocco. In winter comes the mistral, an icy wind from northern Europe, bringing with it a sudden chill.

Shipping and ports

The Mediterranean has been an important sea route since before the civilizations of Greece and Rome. Today, ocean-going tankers bring oil through the Suez Canal and luxury liners take tourists cruising through the islands. Marseille is the largest Mediterranean trading port.

• Over 30 million tourists visit the Mediterranean each year. The Spanish coasts of the Costa del Sol, Costa Brava and Costa Blanca are especially crowded. So too are the Riviera coasts of France and Italy, the Greek islands and Tunisia in North Africa.

find out more
Africa
Europe
Middle East
Oceans and seas

Mexico

Mexico is the most northerly country of the Spanish-speaking Americas. Its landscape changes from dry deserts in the north, through ranges of high mountains and volcanoes, to low tropical jungle in the south-east.

The capital, Mexico City, is 2200 metres above sea level, and although it is usually warm during the day it can be cold at night. Down at sea level in the south-east of Mexico it is warm all the year round. The peninsula known as the Yucatán is very flat and hot and has some fine beaches of white coral sand.

Large oil deposits have been discovered off Mexico's east coast. But Mexico has not become as rich as some oil-producing countries because oil prices fell and foreign debts took most of the money. Today many Mexicans are still very poor. Millions of Mexicans have journeyed to the USA in the 20th century to find better-paid jobs.

• Central and southern Mexico has been the home of a number of ancient civilizations, such as the Maya, the Aztecs and the Olmecs. Today many remains of their buildings and even complete cities can still be seen.

find out more
North America
See also Countries and flags section, page 124

▶ FLASHBACK ◀

Modern Mexico dates from the 16th century, when the Spaniards conquered the Aztecs. The Mexicans gained their independence in 1821, after 11 years of war. For a century after that, dictators ruled the country. The present republic emerged after a civil war lasting from 1911 to 1940.

▼ More than 18 million people live in Mexico City, one of the largest cities on Earth. Beyond Mexico City you can see two of Mexico's highest volcanoes, which are both over 5000 metres high. Their names come from old Aztec words: Iztaccíhuatl and Popocatépetl.

Middle East

Three continents – Europe, Asia and Africa – join in the Middle East. For thousands of years, the Middle East has been a crossroads for travellers and traders. It has also been an area of great conflict.

The Middle East includes the whole of the Arabian Peninsula, Egypt, Israel, Iran, Iraq, Jordan, Lebanon, Syria and Turkey.

Landscape and climate

The region is full of variety. There are large deserts, but also three of the world's great rivers: the Nile, the Tigris and the Euphrates. There are spectacular mountain ranges, but also vast flat stretches of lowland. The climate is hot and dry, although snow can fall on high ground, and desert nights can be cold. In Arabia temperatures soar to 50 °C and people wear lots of loose clothes to protect themselves from the fierce sun.

People and resources

Most people in the Middle East are Arabs, and Arabic is the common language. There are also Iranians, Turks, Kurds and other smaller groups of people. Most live in towns or villages, but some peoples move from place to place with their herds.

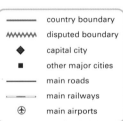

———	country boundary
ᨍᨍᨍᨍ	disputed boundary
◆	capital city
■	other major cities
———	main roads
⎓⎓⎓	main railways
⊕	main airports

The major natural resource of the Middle East is the vast deposits of oil and natural gas. The sale of oil and gas overseas has brought great wealth to some countries and some of the people. Agriculture is also important. Cotton, tobacco, and fruits such as dates, oranges, grapes and olives are grown. Egypt makes a lot of money by taxing ships passing through the Suez Canal.

▶ FLASHBACK ◀

The earliest civilization developed in the Middle East around 5000 BC, in what is now Iraq. Many other ancient civilizations flourished in the region. It was also the birthplace of the three great world religions of Judaism, Christianity and Islam.

When the Jewish country of Israel was founded in 1948, many of the Palestinian Arabs who lived there became refugees. Israel fought a series of wars with its Muslim Arab neighbours, and took more land from the Palestinians. Only in the 1990s did the Palestinians gain some say in their own government. There have also been wars between Iraq and Iran, and between Iraq and an international force led by the USA, following Iraq's invasion of Kuwait in 1990.

◀ The Prophet's Mosque at Medina, Saudi Arabia, is one of the two most sacred sites in the world for Muslims. The prophet Mohammed is buried there.

find out more
Africa
Asia
Deserts
See also individual Middle Eastern countries in Countries and flags section, pages 122–125

Migration

Migration is the movement of people or animals from one area to another. Human migrants mostly move from one place to settle in another, sometimes in a different country. They are called *emigrants* from the country they leave and *immigrants* in the country where they settle. Animals, such as birds, often move in response to the change of seasons.

There have been many migrations throughout human history. The first great migration was that of modern humans, who began to spread out from Africa around 100,000 years ago. We are all descended from these first migrants, who eventually settled in every part of the world.

People migrate for many different reasons. If a population grows too big, and there is not enough food to go round, some people may leave to find new lands to hunt or farm. Sometimes people invade new lands and take them by force. Such invasions can push out other people, who in turn are forced to migrate. For example, in the 4th and 5th centuries AD the Huns from Mongolia swept into eastern Europe. The Germanic tribes who were living there were forced to migrate westward. These 'barbarian' tribes then invaded and destroyed the Roman empire.

Sometimes people have been captured and taken to another country, where they are forced to work as slaves. From the 16th to the 19th century millions of West Africans were taken as slaves to the Americas.

Today, people in many parts of the world have had to flee their

homes to escape bad treatment because of their religion, race or political views. Other people have to leave because of famine or war. Such people are called *refugees*. Sometimes when things improve at home they can return to the land they left, but more often their move is permanent. Other people migrate in search of work and a better life. They often move from the countryside to the city, or even to another, wealthier country.

▲ The Notting Hill Carnival in London, UK. Many people from the former British empire, including the Caribbean, India, Pakistan and Hong Kong, have settled in the UK. These immigrants have brought their own culture and traditions with them, many of which have become part of British culture.

▼ Some of the major human migrations of the last 2000 years.

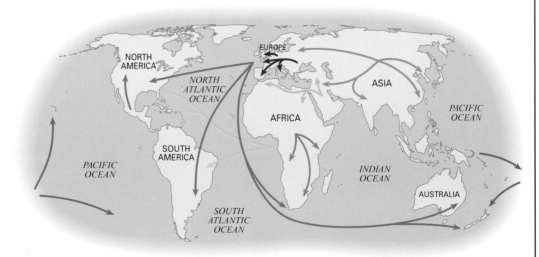

→ Germanic tribes spread into western Europe, 5th century AD
→ Arabs conquer North Africa and Middle East, 7th century AD
→ Polynesians colonize the islands of the eastern Pacific and New Zealand, 300 BC–AD 750
→ southern migration of Bantu peoples in Africa, 2000–1500 years ago
→ Mongol armies push into eastern Europe, Middle East, China and India, 13th–16th centuries
→ Europeans migrate to the Americas (from 16th century), South Africa (from 17th century) and Australia and New Zealand (from 19th century)
→ African slaves taken to the Americas, 16th–19th centuries
→ Latin Americans migrate to the USA, 20th century

Mining

Mining is the process of digging rocks and minerals out of the ground. (A mineral is any substance that can be mined from the ground.) Diamonds, coal and ores (minerals from which we extract metals) are just some of the materials that we mine. Many people think that mining always takes place far underground. In fact, although some mines are very deep, others are near or at the surface of the ground.

• The gold-mines of South Africa are the world's deepest mines, going down over 3 km.

When materials such as coal, iron ore and aluminium ore lie near the surface of the ground, they are dug up by *opencast mining*. In this kind of mining, giant excavators strip off the surface soil. Power shovels and excavators then dig out the materials and load them onto lorries or railway trucks.

Most gold is obtained by *underground mining*. Shafts are dug down to the level of the ore-bearing rock. Tunnels are then dug out from the shaft to that layer. The roofs of the tunnels are often held up with metal props. The ore is removed from the rock with explosives. It is then loaded onto railway wagons, taken to the shaft and lifted to the surface.

Underground coal is mined by tunnelling. Coal is quite soft, so it is often cut by machines. In mines that are not so highly mechanized, a gap is cut beneath the coal, and then the coal is brought down with explosives or by pneumatic drills. In all coalmines, hydraulic props are used to support the roofs of the tunnels while the coal is being cut away.

Other forms of mining

Underwater mining is used to obtain tin ore. This kind of mining is called *placer mining*. Because tin ore is heavy, it tends to settle in the beds of streams or rivers. The ore is extracted by large floating dredges (a kind of scoop). Diamonds and gold, which are also heavy, are sometimes extracted by placer mining.

Stone or rock is dug out of a *quarry* (a pit or hole in the ground). In one type of quarry, large blocks of stone are cut and trimmed by special machines. The rocks quarried in this way include granite, marble, limestone, sandstone and slate. They are used for buildings and ornamental uses such as statues. Another type of quarry produces aggregate (broken stone) for road-making.

Mining dangers

Mining has always been one of the most dangerous jobs. Dusty mine air can damage miners' lungs, and explosives sometimes cause accidents. There is always the risk of poisonous gases, flooding, fire, or the roof of the mine collapsing, trapping the miners deep underground.

▶ Different methods of mining.

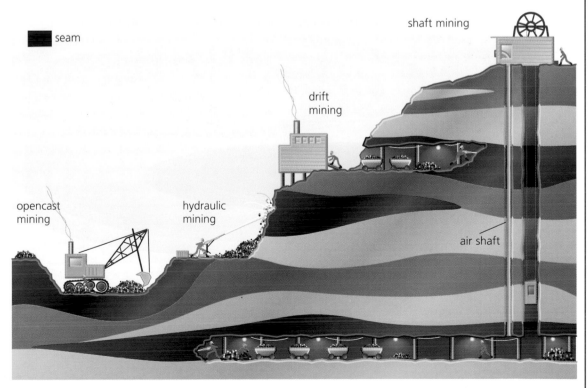

seam

shaft mining

drift mining

opencast mining

hydraulic mining

air shaft

find out more
Coal
Industry
Iron and steel
Oil
Rocks and minerals

Moors and heaths

Moors and heaths are open treeless areas. Some are found where it is too wet or windy, or the soil is too poor and peaty, for trees to grow. Others were formed when people cleared the trees for hunting or to graze sheep or cattle.

Heaths are covered in low-growing heather-like shrubs, while moors are made up of coarse grasses and sedges. If grazing is very heavy, heaths turn into grassy moors. Heaths can become very dry in summer, and fires are common, caused either by lightning or by humans. Without fires or grazing, heaths would soon return to woodland.

Heaths

Heaths are harsh, windswept places. The heathers and their relatives which form the main vegetation are woody shrubs growing close to the ground, with small, bell-shaped flowers. The tiny leaves have a waxy coating to prevent the plant from losing too much water. Heathers provide shelter to many animals. Some related plants, such as cranberry and blueberry, have fleshy berries that provide food for many birds and small mammals. The juicy berries are also popular with people, for making jams and fruit pies.

Heaths are often used for grazing sheep. The tender young heather shoots make good fodder, and farmers often deliberately set fire to the heath from time to time to encourage new growth. Grouse shooting is also a profitable use for moors and heaths.

◀ Moors and heaths are generally bare of trees, but occasional rowan trees (also called mountain ash) are found on this moorland in Lancashire, UK.

Heaths are found on acid soil. When the land was covered by forest, the fallen leaves added nutrients to the soil and made it less acid. Without the trees, the nutrients were soon washed away, leaving very acid soil, poor in nutrients. Because of its acidity, very few bacteria can live in this soil, so plant material does not rot away. Dead bog mosses in the heath pile up and form a spongy material known as *peat*. In some areas, peat is dried and used as fuel.

Moors

Grassy moors are found mainly where the rainfall is very high or where the rock below the surface (usually slate or the similar, but softer, shale) stops rainwater from draining away. The soil is waterlogged most of the time. Waterlogged soils do not have many bacteria to rot down the plant material, so moors also build up peat. The coarse grasses that grow here often form large tussocks (clumps). Water collects in the dips between the tussocks, forming small boggy patches. Insects thrive in boggy moorland pools, and are themselves food for other animals.

find out more
Coal
Grasslands
Wetlands

▼ Heaths and moors are full of bird life. Overhead, birds of prey such as buzzards (shown below), kestrels and peregrines hunt for birds and small mammals.

Mountains

High up in the mountains, you can find some of the most dramatic scenery in the world – jagged snow-capped peaks, deep gorges, large valley glaciers and fast-flowing rivers and streams. Mountains continually challenge the human spirit of adventure, with each generation of climbers seeking new ways to conquer the highest peaks.

As mountains rise above the surrounding land, they are soon attacked by water, wind, rain and ice. The softer rocks are eroded (worn away) to form valleys, and jagged peaks form as the valleys are cut back into the hills. Young and rapidly rising mountains have high, steep-sided peaks and deep valleys and gorges. In time, the

• In the Rocky Mountains, or Rockies, of North America there are mountains with gentle slopes and rounded tops, but others are tall with jagged rocky peaks. Many reach over 4000 metres above sea level.
Highest peak: Mount Elbert, 4402 m

• The Alps in Europe consist of several separate mountain ranges of steep slopes and jagged snow-capped peaks. In places there are huge limestone cliffs and canyons, as well as permanent snowfields and glaciers.
Highest mountain: Mont Blanc, 4808 m

• The Andes is a series of mountain ranges with many peaks over 6700 metres, including some active volcanoes. High plateaux separate some ranges, and in the south, glaciers push down to the Pacific Ocean.
Highest peak: Aconcagua, 6960 m

Mountain records
Highest mountain above sea level
Mount Everest, Himalayas, 8848 m
Largest single mountain mass
Mauna Loa, Hawaii (the total height of the mountain is 9350 m, although only 4170 m are above sea level)
Biggest mountain range on land
Himalaya–Karakoram–Hindu Kush range, 3800 km long, with 14 mountains over 8000 m
Longest underwater mountain range
Indian/East Pacific Ocean Cordillera, 19,000 km long

▼ Mountains are formed in different ways. *Fold mountains* are created when the ocean floor between two moving plates is squeezed upwards. *Block mountains* form when huge blocks of rock are tilted or lifted up along lines of weakness, called faults. When molten lava cannot break through strong rocks above, it forces the rocks to bulge upwards forming a *dome mountain*.

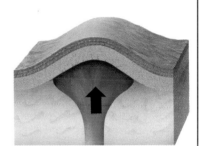

fold mountains: Alps, Europe; Himalayas, Asia; Rocky Mountains, North America; Andes, South America

block mountains: Sierra Nevada Mountains, USA; Black Forest Mountains, Europe; Ruwenzori Mountains, East Africa

dome mountains: Black Hills, South Dakota, USA

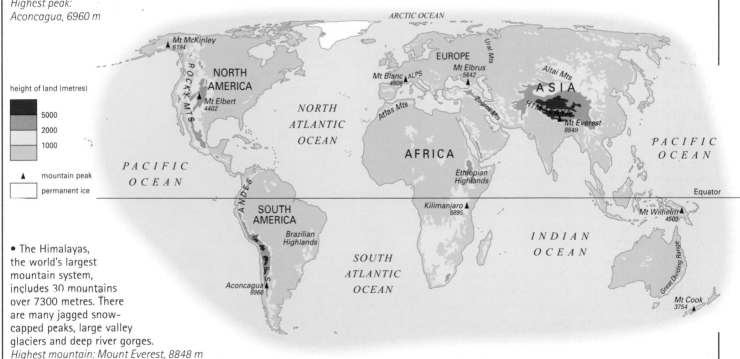

height of land (metres)

5000
2000
1000

▲ mountain peak
permanent ice

• The Himalayas, the world's largest mountain system, includes 30 mountains over 7300 metres. There are many jagged snow-capped peaks, large valley glaciers and deep river gorges.
Highest mountain: Mount Everest, 8848 m

▲ Mount Everest (right), at 8848 m, is the world's highest mountain. It was first climbed in 1953.

find out more
Continents
Erosion
Glaciers
Lakes
Rivers and streams
Rocks and minerals
Volcanoes

mountain peaks and the valley sides are worn away, the hills become lower and more rounded, and the valleys become wider, with slower-flowing, less powerful rivers. In old age, a mountain range may become little more than a gently rolling plain.

Mountain climate

As you climb up a mountain, the temperature falls by 1°C for every 150 metres. There is snow on the top of high mountains even at the Equator. Also, there is less oxygen in the atmosphere the higher up you go. Winds are often extremely strong, and the weather can change very quickly.

Mountains have a dramatic effect on the climate of surrounding areas. As the clouds rise over the mountains, they shed their rain, so the side of a mountain range where the wind blows is often very wet, but the sheltered side (the 'rain shadow') gets very little rain. Parts of the southern Himalayas are very wet because monsoon winds drop rain and snow over the mountains. To the north, the winds become dry and desert conditions exist.

Mountain life

Conditions in mountain areas are harsh and difficult for the people and wildlife trying to survive at such altitudes. People tend to settle in sheltered valleys, by water sources on the mountain slopes, or near deposits of minerals such as zinc, silver, coal and iron ore. Roads and railways follow the valleys. Fast-flowing mountain rivers are often dammed to produce hydroelectric power.

Many mountain people make a living from farming. In the Alps, in Europe, farmers move their dairy cattle to high pastures in spring, and bring them down to the valleys in autumn. Crops may be grown on raised terraces on the slopes. The terrace walls trap rainwater and prevent soil

from being washed away. Other activities in mountain areas include mining, forestry and tourism. Tourists are attracted to mountains by the dramatic scenery. They also come to enjoy walking, climbing, skiing, fishing and hunting.

Mountain plants and animals have to cope with extremes of temperature, hot days and cold nights, and very high winds. Mountain soils are often thin, as soil is washed down the slopes. Above a certain altitude, called the tree-line, trees cannot grow as conditions are too harsh. Lower slopes are often covered with forests. Sheep, goats and other long-haired animals are well suited to harsh climates. In the Himalayas, yaks (mountain cattle with long shaggy hair) are reared for their meat and milk and as a means of transporting people and heavy loads. Many animals, such as mountain hares, grow extra thick coats in winter.

Avalanche danger

An avalanche is a mass of snow which comes loose from a steep mountain slope and hurtles down to the valley below. In any mountainous area with bare slopes and heavy snow, avalanches are a danger, particularly when the snows begin to melt. On some mountains, new forests are planted to reduce the danger, and walls and snow fences help to break up any avalanches. Trained patrols issue forecasts and warnings, especially in popular skiing areas.

◄ An avalanche on Mount McKinley, Alaska, USA. Avalanches are a particular danger after a warm spell. When the snow starts to thaw, one snow layer can slide over another and crash down the mountain slopes.

New Zealand

New Zealand is a country made up of two main islands in the Pacific Ocean. The islands were named in 1642 by the Dutch explorer Abel Tasman. But the Maori people, who had settled the land about 1000 years earlier, call New Zealand 'Aotearoa' ('land of the long white cloud').

New Zealand is in a major earthquake zone. There are many active volcanoes in the North Island, and around the town of Rotorua there are bubbling mud pools, geysers, hot springs and mineral pools to bathe in. The South Island has a spectacular mountain range, with several peaks over 3000 metres high.

Climate and people

New Zealand's mild climate and good soil encourage growth of fruit and vegetables. There is good grazing for animals all year, so livestock farming, particularly of sheep, is an important part of the economy. Outdoor pursuits are popular, especially rugby, sailing, fishing and hiking. New Zealanders value their clean, nuclear-free country, and have campaigned against nuclear tests in the Pacific.

Wildlife

When the Maori first arrived in New Zealand, they found an uninhabited land covered in forest, full of unusual ferns and huge, ancient kauri trees. There were no mammals except for bats, and the most distinctive creatures were flightless birds. Today much of the forest has gone, and some of the birds have been hunted to extinction. Mammals such as rats, introduced from abroad, now compete with the natural wildlife for food and space.

◆	capital city
• •	major cities and towns
—	main roads
▦	main railways
⊕	main airports
▲	high peaks (height in metres)

▶ FLASHBACK ◀

Captain James Cook visited New Zealand in 1769, and soon afterwards traders, missionaries and settlers from Britain began to arrive. There were disputes over land between the new arrivals and the Maori, which led to a series of fierce land wars. By 1870 the Maori had been defeated. As a result, the traditional Maori way of life was almost destroyed.

The invention of refrigeration in 1869 encouraged sheep and dairy farming, as lamb and butter could now be sold abroad. Until the UK joined the European Union in 1973, much New Zealand produce was sold there. Today, however, New Zealand has stronger trading links with Australia and South-east Asia.

find out more

Earthquakes
Pacific Islands
Volcanoes
Wool
See also Countries and flags section, page 124

▼ Milford Sound, in the south-west of the South Island, New Zealand, is a fjord (a steep-sided valley flooded by the sea). It marks the end of the Milford walking track, which is thought to be one of the most beautiful walks in the world.

Nigeria

Nigeria has more people than any other African country, although by area it is only Africa's 14th largest country. It is named after the Niger, Africa's third largest river.

High plains cover most of northern and central Nigeria, with high mountains in the east, on the border with Cameroon. Along the coast in the south are sandy beaches, mangrove forests, and the swampy Niger delta. Inland are grassy plains with some woodland.

About 400 groups of people live in Nigeria, each with its own language. The largest groups are the Muslim Hausa and Fulani peoples in the north, the Yoruba in the south-west, and the Ibo in the south-east.

Two-thirds of Nigerians live in farming villages. In southern Nigeria, women run the markets, work in factories and play a major role in society. By contrast, most women in the north do not work outside their homes.

Nigeria's main export is oil. Money from oil sales has enabled Nigeria to set up many new industries, although much poverty remains.

From 1861 Britain gradually took control of Nigeria, occupying the kingdom of Benin in 1894 and uniting the various regions into a single colony in 1914. Nigeria was granted independence in 1960. From time to time since 1966, its rulers have been army officers. A civil war in the south-east between 1967 and 1970 began in part because of the discovery of oil off Port Harcourt. In the 1990s a period of violent military government strengthened demands for democratic elections.

◄Western clothes are common in the cities, but many Nigerians wear long white or brightly coloured robes, especially on market days, when they meet their relatives and friends.

find out more
Africa
Oil
*See also Countries and
   flags section, page 124*

Nomads

Nomads are groups of people who do not settle down permanently, but keep moving from place to place. Most nomads live within a particular area. They move about in search of food for themselves and their animals, and live in temporary settlements.

In prehistoric times all humans were hunter-gatherers, and led nomadic lives. Hunter-gatherers live in small groups, and spend a few days or weeks in one place, hunting wild animals, fishing and gathering wild foods such as roots, nuts and berries, before moving on. There are still a few peoples who live as hunter-gatherers today.

When people began to farm, around 10,000 years ago,

many settled down in one place to grow crops and raise animals. But in some places, particularly in dry grassland areas, people who raised animals such as goats, sheep, cattle and horses had to move their herds from time to time to find fresh grass. These kinds of nomads are known as *nomadic pastoralists*. Sometimes nomadic

pastoralists move between places depending on whether it is the wet season or the dry season. Sometimes, in mountain areas, they move between lower winter pastures and higher summer pastures. There are still many peoples in the world who follow this way of life, particularly in central Asia, the Middle East and Africa.

find out more
Farming
Grasslands
Hunter-gatherers
Migration
Settlements

◄The nomadic Masai people live in Kenya and Tanzania, in East Africa. They depend almost entirely on meat, milk and blood from their herds of cattle. They take the blood by making a nick in a cow's neck, without killing the animal.

North America

North America is the third largest continent in the world. It is made up of Canada, the United States of America, Greenland, Mexico, and the countries of Central America and the Caribbean. The ancestors of the Native Americans came there over 25,000 years ago from Asia. Five hundred years ago Europeans began to settle there, followed by immigrants from the rest of the world. ◗

• Greenland is the world's largest island. Although situated near North America, it is actually a self-governing part of Denmark. It is a mountainous and rocky island with a polar climate, so it is only sparsely populated. The people are a mixture of Danish and Inuit (Eskimo) origin.

• Central America is a narrow stretch of land, only 82 km wide at the Panama Canal. Spain once ruled the territories now occupied by Guatemala, El Salvador, Honduras, Nicaragua, Costa Rica and Panama. Belize was a British colony.

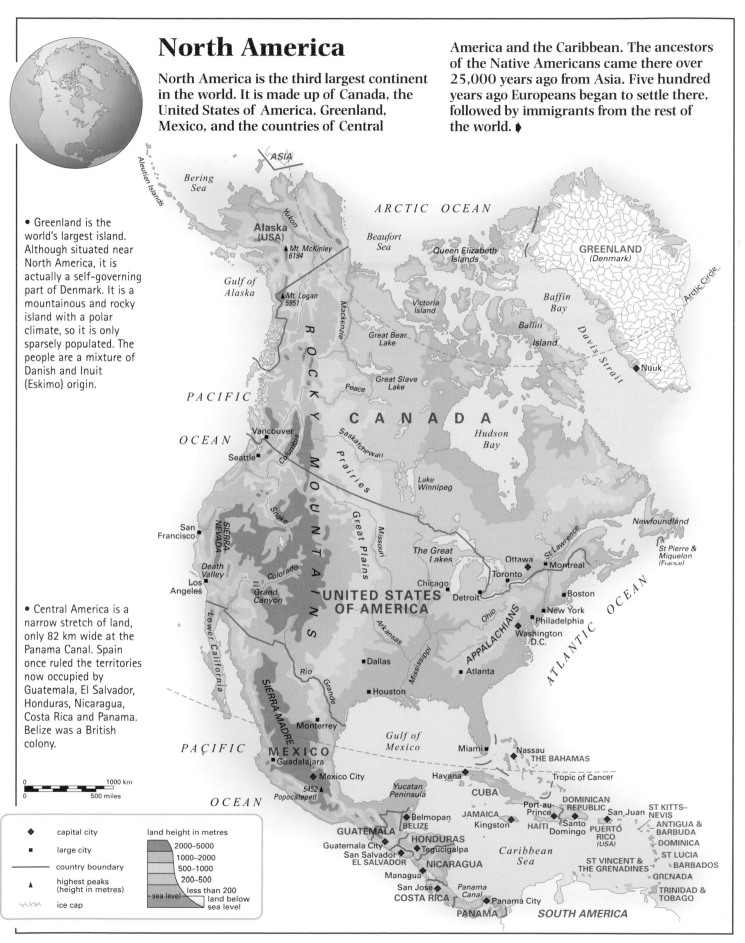

capital city

large city

country boundary

highest peaks (height in metres)

ice cap

land height in metres

2000–5000
1000–2000
500–1000
200–500
sea level — less than 200
land below sea level

▲ Alaska is the largest state of the USA, but it is also the most sparsely populated. This picture shows the icy landscape in the northernmost part of Alaska, which lies within the Arctic Circle.

North America is rich in natural resources, including timber, oil, gas, gold and many metals. These have enabled the continent's societies to become wealthy and successful. Although Native Americans had farms and cities, it was the Europeans who developed the land and resources of North America. They cleared forests and drained land to create farms on fertile soils. The search for timber and minerals, especially gold, helped to open up the continent rapidly in the 19th century as immigrants from Europe crossed the ocean.

Landscape

The west is dominated by several mountain ranges, including the Sierra Nevada of California and the Rocky Mountains or 'Rockies'. This is a series of mountain ranges running like a giant backbone down the west-centre of North America to Mexico. To the east of the Sierra Nevada the Colorado River has cut through this high land to form the Grand Canyon. On the eastern side of the continent lie the Appalachians, low mountains of ridges and valleys. Between this range and the Rockies are huge plains, across which the Mississippi and Missouri rivers run. To the north are great forests and the bleak Arctic. To the south are the Gulf of Mexico and the Caribbean Sea.

Climate

Almost all parts of the continent have warm or hot summers. Only the edge of the Arctic and the high mountains are cool in summer. In winter the northern and central parts of the continent are bitterly cold. There are no mountains to stop icy Arctic air blowing south. The Sierra Nevada do, however, block wet air from the Pacific Ocean. Deserts on the eastern side of these mountains get little rain. Death Valley in California is the hottest and lowest place on the continent. The coastline on the Gulf of Mexico and the Caribbean Sea often suffer from hurricanes.

People

In the USA and Canada descendants of Native American peoples such as the Cree, the Apache and the Navajo became small minorities after Europeans arrived. Some now live on reservations, while others have migrated to the cities. The governments are negotiating with Native Americans over land rights which would enable them to live their own ways of life. In Mexico, Europeans and Native Americans married each other. Their descendants are called *mestizos*. A third of the population belongs to Native American groups, speaking traditional languages.

The people of North America present a mixture of languages and cultures. The largest numbers of early immigrants came from Spain, France and the British Isles. English and Spanish are the most widely spoken languages, and French is spoken in parts of Canada. Black North Americans trace their ancestors back to Africans transported as slaves before 1808. There are also large numbers of Italians, Greeks, Irish, Germans, Chinese and Russians. Recently immigrants have come from Cambodia and other countries in South-east Asia.

FLASHBACK

In 1759 the British defeated the French in Canada, and the whole of Canada came under British rule. The people of what is now the United States of America fought the American Revolution (1775–1783) to achieve their independence from Britain. In 1821 the Mexicans successfully rebelled against their Spanish rulers. Canada became an independent country in 1867.

▶ A totem pole displayed in Stanley Park, Vancouver, on the north-west coast of Canada. Totems are natural objects, particularly animals, which Native Americans adopted as sacred symbols of families or individuals.

find out more
Arctic
Canada
Caribbean
Continents
Grasslands
Mexico
Mountains
South America
United States of America
See also individual North American countries in the Countries and flags section, pages 122–125

Northern Ireland

Northern Ireland occupies the north-east corner of Ireland. It is the smallest of the four areas that form the United Kingdom of Great Britain and Northern Ireland.

► In Belfast many walls are covered with political murals (paintings), like this one in support of the Irish nationalist party Sinn Féin.

find out more
Europe
Ireland, Republic of
United Kingdom

Northern Ireland is a beautiful land of fertile plains and small mountains. Farming is an important industry. Irish linens and tweeds are world-famous and its factories also produce clothing and materials from synthetic fibres. There are also newer industries making aircraft, chemicals, tobacco products and alcohol.

► FLASHBACK ◄
Northern Ireland was formed in 1921 from six of the nine counties of Ulster. Two-thirds of the Northern Irish population were Protestants and one-third was Catholic. The Protestant Unionists wanted to keep Northern Ireland in the UK. Many Catholics were nationalists and wanted it to join the Republic of Ireland.

The period from 1969 was known as the 'troubles', when both nationalist and Unionist groups used shootings and bombings to further their causes. In 1998 a peace plan was agreed that involved establishing closer ties between Northern Ireland and the Republic. At the same time, the plan recognized that Northern Ireland would remain part of the UK so long as a majority of its people wished it to do so.

Oceans and seas

• Parts of the Arctic and Southern Oceans form permanently frozen ice shelves stretching out from the coast. In slightly warmer areas, the sea freezes only in winter, forming pack ice up to 2 m thick.

Oceans and seas cover 71 per cent (over 360 million square kilometres) of the Earth's surface. They contain about 1370 million cubic kilometres of water. The five major oceans – the Pacific, Atlantic, Indian, Arctic and Southern – are connected to each other by open water.

The average depth of water in the oceans is 4000 metres, but in some ocean trenches it may be as much as 11,000 metres deep. This water is constantly moving, driven by winds, waves, tides and currents. Waves, whipped up by the wind,

stir the surface, but do not move the mass of the water. This is done by tides, which shift the water in time with the phases of the Moon. Water circulates between the oceans in currents. The surface currents swirl slowly in a clockwise direction in the northern hemisphere and anticlockwise in the south.

▲ The world's oceans. They contain almost 97% of all the water found on Earth.

The ocean floor

Much of the ocean floor is a flat plain, but in places mountains rise thousands of metres up from the sea-bed. Sometimes they push through the sea's surface as islands. Many of these are active or extinct

North Pole *see* Arctic • **Nuclear power** *see* Energy • **Oases** *see* Deserts • **Oceania** *see* Continents

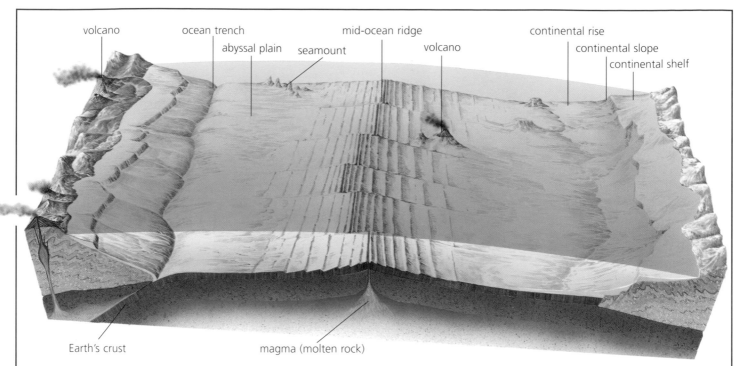

volcano   ocean trench   mid-ocean ridge   continental rise
abyssal plain   seamount   volcano   continental slope
continental shelf

Earth's crust   magma (molten rock)

volcanoes. Running down the centre of the ocean floor in several of the oceans is a ridge of mountains, which is continually being built up by outpourings of lava. As the rock is forced outwards from the ridge by the new lava, the ocean floor spreads.

Much of the ocean floor is covered in sand or mud brought in by rivers. In places, hot springs bubble up, depositing sulphur and other minerals. The remains of microscopic plants and animals from the surface sink down to the bottom to form a layer of tiny particles (sediment). Here, pressure from the water above and from other sediment layers slowly turns the sediment into rock.

Ocean zones

The oceans can be divided into three zones. The sunny surface waters at the top – the *photosynthetic zone* – contain most of the ocean fishes as well as a floating community of billions of microscopic creatures called plankton. Below this zone lie the more dimly lit *twilight zone* and,

reaching down to deep cold waters, the *dark zone*. Fewer life forms, mainly flesh-eating fishes, live in the lower zones.

Most of the ocean is at around the same temperature – about 4 °C. As you go down deeper, the pressure of the water above increases steadily, making it difficult to move quickly. The temperature also falls to around 2 °C in deep water. The amount of light decreases, until at 1000 metres there is no light at all.

People and the sea

Fish from the sea are an important food for many people in the world. For thousands of years people living by the sea have fished for their own food. Today, most of the fish we eat is

caught by large ships a long way from land.

Throughout history people have travelled long distances across the seas and oceans in boats and ships. Until the coming of the railways in the 19th century, most goods were carried by boat, even for quite short distances. Today large quantities of goods are still transported by sea, although most people now travel by plane for long distances, rather than by ship.

Some of the world's richest sources of oil and natural gas are found under the sea-bed. The power of the waves and tides in the oceans are also being developed as possible new sources of alternative energy.

▲ A cross-section of the ocean floor.

find out more
Continents
Earth
Energy
Fishing
Oil
Rivers and streams
Tides
Water

▼ People are beginning to use the power of the sea. In this tidal power station at La Rance in France a dam has been built across the mouth of a river. As the tide goes in and out, the movement of water turns huge turbines, which in turn drive electrical generators.

Oil

Oil is one of the most important substances we use today, and it supplies more of the world's energy than any other fuel. Oil spills from tankers and rigs can cause widespread harm to the oceans and their wildlife. Also, the gases produced when we burn oil are damaging the Earth's atmosphere.

Oil is a fossil fuel, like coal and natural gas. It is the remains of tiny plants and animals which lived in the sea millions of years ago. Oil is found under layers of solid rock, trapped in the holes of porous rock. The geological name for this oil is *petroleum*.

Geologists help oil companies to find places where there is likely to be oil. The companies then drill down through solid rock. If they find oil, it flows up through the drill hole. Oil from the ground is called *crude oil*. The crude oil is carried away by pipeline, tanker ship, rail or road to a refinery. Here it is separated into different substances.

Countries that have a lot of oil can be very rich, particularly if they sell most of their oil to other countries. Many countries in the Middle East produce a lot of oil, and so do the USA and Russia. However, the world's supply of oil may only last for another 30 to 60 years, so it is important to find other sources of energy.

find out more
Energy
Geology
Greenhouse effect
Rocks and minerals

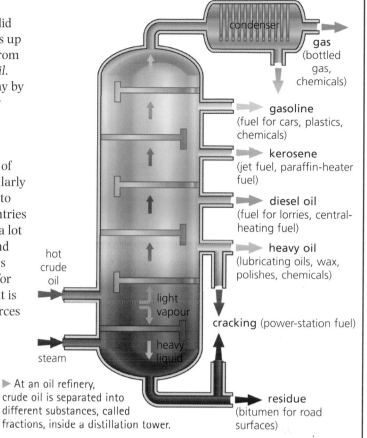

condenser

gas
(bottled gas, chemicals)

gasoline
(fuel for cars, plastics, chemicals)

kerosene
(jet fuel, paraffin-heater fuel)

diesel oil
(fuel for lorries, central-heating fuel)

heavy oil
(lubricating oils, wax, polishes, chemicals)

cracking (power-station fuel)

residue
(bitumen for road surfaces)

hot crude oil

light vapour

heavy liquid

steam

▶ At an oil refinery, crude oil is separated into different substances, called fractions, inside a distillation tower.

Pacific Islands

There are about 10,000 islands in the Pacific Ocean, spread over a very large area. The islands can be divided into three regions: Micronesia, Melanesia and Polynesia.

Each island region has a distinct group of people with its own way of life. Melanesians are dark-skinned and live in the south-west Pacific. Polynesians are lighter skinned, and live in the eastern Pacific. Micronesians live in the western Pacific.

Most of the islands are coral reefs and volcanic peaks. Coconut palms provide copra (dried coconut flesh) and coconut oil, both important exports. Bananas, pineapples and other tropical fruits are also grown.

▶ FLASHBACK ◀
Europeans first came to the islands in the 18th century. They brought new diseases that killed many people, and gradually took more land from the native peoples. During World War II the islands saw battles between the USA and Japan. Several islands have been used to test atomic bombs.

find out more
Australia
Islands
New Zealand
Oceans and seas
See also individual countries in Countries and flags section, pages 122–125

◀ Micronesia includes Guam, Nauru and Kiribati. Melanesia includes Papua New Guinea, the Solomon Islands, New Caledonia and Vanuatu. Polynesia includes Tuvalu, Tonga and Samoa.

• In the 1960s and 1970s many of the islands became independent, but some are still dependent on the USA, France or New Zealand.

Midway Is (USA)
Tropic of Cancer
Wake Island (USA)
NORTHERN MARIANA IS (USA)
Hawaiian Islands (USA)
Johnston Atoll (USA)
PACIFIC OCEAN
Guam (USA)
PALAU Caroline Islands
MARSHALL ISLANDS
International Date Line
FEDERATED STATES OF MICRONESIA
Line Islands
Kiritimati Island (Kiribati)
NAURU KIRIBATI
Equator
PAPUA NEW GUINEA
SOLOMON ISLANDS
TUVALU
Tokelau (New Zealand)
Marquesas Islands
Wallis and Futuna Islands (France)
SAMOA
French Polynesia
Coral Sea
VANUATU
American Samoa
Cook Is. (New Zealand)
Society Islands Tahiti
Tuamotu Archipelago
FIJI
Niue (New Zealand)
AUSTRALIA
New Caledonia (France)
TONGA
Tubuai Islands
Tropic of Capricorn
Pitcairn Island (UK)
Lord Howe Island (Australia)
Norfolk Island (Australia)
PACIFIC OCEAN
Kermadec Island (New Zealand)
Tasman Sea
NEW ZEALAND
Chatham Islands

0   2000 km
0   1000 miles

Pakistan

Pakistan is a country in south-west Asia, with the mighty River Indus at its centre. The Indus flows 2900 kilometres from the plateau of Tibet, passing around the Himalayas, through the Karakoram Mountains and south to the Arabian Sea.

The plains of the Indus make up about one-third of Pakistan. Here, the months of May to August are unpleasantly hot, while in mid-July the monsoon brings 400 to 500 millimetres of rain. Away from the Indus valley, much of the country is either mountainous or very dry. In the northern mountains it is often bitterly cold. The Karakorams have some large glaciers and very little grows there. In south-west Pakistan, Baluchistan is a hot, dry desert. In this region there are large gas fields from which gas is piped to the cities.

People

The Indus valley is where most Pakistanis live. The river's water is used to irrigate the land for crops such as wheat, rice, sugar cane and especially cotton, which is Pakistan's main export. The largest city in Pakistan is Karachi, where over 5 million people live and work.

Pakistan has also developed its own industry. The products it manufactures include cotton textiles, fertilizers, cement and sugar.

Pakistan is an Islamic nation. Almost all Pakistanis are Muslims, and Pakistan's laws are based on Islamic law. But though they share the same religion, there are many different ethnic

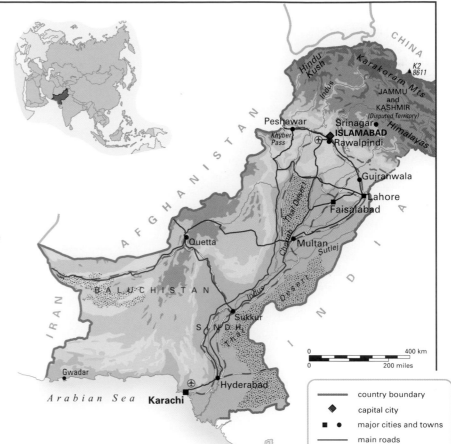

groups within Pakistan, each with its own customs and culture. Punjabis, for example, cook their meat in a clay oven, called a tandoor, while in Baluchistan meat is barbecued over an open fire and eaten as kebabs.

▶ FLASHBACK ◀

From 1858, for almost a hundred years, Pakistan was part of British India. But when in 1947 India gained independence, it was divided into two nations: Muslim Pakistan, and India, which is mostly Hindu. The new state of Pakistan was made up of two parts, West and East, separated by Indian territory. However, in 1974 East Pakistan became an independent nation called Bangladesh. Since Pakistan's independence, democratic government has alternated with periods when the president has been an army officer.

Pakistan and India have been unfriendly to each other since independence. Both claim the northern territory of Kashmir, although each country only occupies a part of it. In 1998 both countries tested their first nuclear weapons.

▼ Cotton is Pakistan's most important crop. These women from the Punjab are drawing out and twisting thick cotton 'rope' into long, thin fibres.

Map legend:
- country boundary
- ◆ capital city
- ■ ● major cities and towns
- main roads
- main railways
- ⊕ main airports
- sand desert
- ▲ high peaks (height in metres)

land height in metres
- more than 5000
- 2000–5000
- 1000–2000
- 500–1000
- 200–500
- less than 200
- sea level

• The highest mountain in Pakistan is in the Karakorams. It is called K2 and is 8611 m high, making it the second highest mountain in the world.

find out more
Bangladesh
India
See also Countries and flags section, page 124

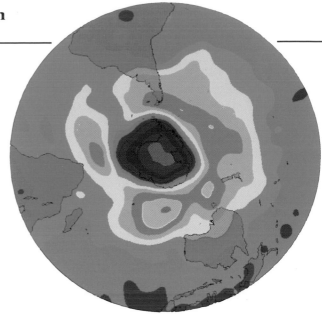

Pollution

We cause pollution when we do damage to our surroundings. Leaving litter is one form of pollution. But chemicals and waste from factories, farms, motor cars and even houses cause much more serious pollution, which can affect the air, water and the land.

Pollution is not something new. Six hundred years ago, the air over London was thick with smoke from coal fires. Over the years, laws have been passed to stop some kinds of pollution. Many countries now have government departments whose job is to limit the damage pollution does.

Air pollution

Factories, power stations and motor vehicles make waste gases, soot and dust, which are all released into the air. The polluted air damages people's lungs. Some kinds of air pollution can even cause brain damage. Waste gases in the air can also cause acid rain, which damages trees, lake and river life, and buildings.

Ozone is a gas produced naturally from oxygen in the upper atmosphere. A thin layer of ozone surrounds the world, and protects us from the harmful ultraviolet rays in sunlight. Ozone is destroyed by pollution from burning fuels and by chemicals called CFCs released from some refrigerators and aerosols. If the ozone layer is badly damaged, more people will get skin cancer.

Water pollution

Acid rain can pollute lakes and rivers. But there are many other kinds of water pollution. Some towns and villages pump untreated sewage into rivers or the sea, while factories sometimes release poisonous chemicals and wastes. These pollutants can kill fishes and other water animals and plants. Farmers use fertilizers and chemical pesticides that can also be washed into rivers and streams after heavy rainfall. The sea can also be polluted by spillages of oil from oil tankers and oil rigs.

Pollution on land

People cause pollution when they thoughtlessly dump their rubbish or litter. Some kinds of rubbish rot away quite quickly, but many plastic materials will never decay.

Radioactive waste from nuclear power stations could cause very serious pollution. Nearly all nuclear waste is safely contained for now, but small amounts do sometimes escape into the air or water. Many scientists are worried about the long-term effects of this type of pollution, because nuclear waste can stay radioactive for thousands of years.

▲ Pollution is causing thinning of the ozone layer, especially over the Poles. This satellite picture taken above the Antarctic shows ozone levels in the upper atmosphere. In the blue, purple and grey area at the centre there is virtually no ozone at all.

▲ In some large cities, the air is so polluted that people wear face masks to filter out dust and soot from the air.

find out more
Climate
Energy
Farming
Greenhouse effect
Green movement
Oil

◀ Water pollution in New Zealand. The wastes from a factory pour out from a pipe directly into the sea, close to a beach.

Population

Today, there are more than 6000 million people in the world. The population of the world has grown steadily since about 1750. Over the past 100 years, and particularly from about 1950 onwards, this growth has been very rapid.

The population is the number of people found in a particular place. We talk about the population of the world, a continent, a country, a city or a village. Governments count the population of their countries using a *census*. The earliest census counts are those of China, which go back over 3000 years. Censuses have been carried out since 1790 in the USA and since 1801 in the United Kingdom. Today, most countries carry out population censuses, many of them on a 10-yearly basis. The population between census counts can be estimated or worked out from records of births and deaths and the numbers of people who have moved.

Population patterns

Scientists who study population figures and patterns are called *demographers*. They try to predict what the world's population will be in the future by studying the present population figures and rates of growth.

The world population first started to increase rapidly during the 18th century, at the beginning of the Industrial Revolution. Most of this increase was in Europe, and in the Americas and Oceania where Europeans settled. Today, a fast growth in population is typical of many countries in Africa, Asia, and Central and South America. These countries are sometimes referred to as 'the South' since many are in southern parts of the world. In Europe and North America, on the other hand, population is now growing slowly or even declining. These countries are sometimes called 'the North'.

The population structure (the number of people in each age group) of these two sets of countries is also different. In the South there are many young people. Half the population may be under 25 or 30 years old. In the North fewer babies are born, but not so many children and young people die, so the numbers in each age group are more equal. In proportion to the total population, there are more elderly people.

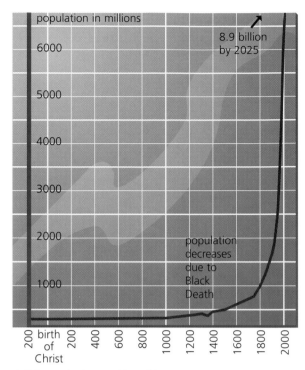

▲ This graph gives an idea of how the population of the world has grown over the past 2000 years.

• The population of China is bigger than that of any other country: nearly 1.2 billion (1200 million) people. During the 1980s Chinese families were told to have just one child.

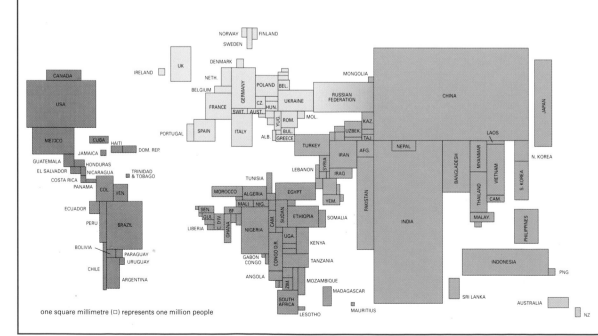

◄ This map of the world shows where people live on the Earth. The size of each country has been drawn to indicate how many people live there, not how much land the country covers.

World population in the 20th century

1900	1550 million
1930	2070 million
1960	3003 million
1990	5300 million
1999	6000 million

• For the population of each country, see pages 122–125.

one square millimetre (□) represents one million people

Rain and snow

Rain and snow are our most important sources of water. Without them, all the world's rivers, lakes and soils would be dry. Very few living things can survive in places where there is no rain or snow. They provide water for humans and other animals. Without rainfall, plants cannot grow properly. However, too much rain and snow can cause flooding that may destroy homes and damage crops.

▼ Much of India receives very heavy rains between the months of July and September. This period is known as the monsoon season. The rains are carried by warm, wet winds that sweep in from the Indian Ocean.

• If a lot of snow falls on a steep slope, it may start to slide downhill and produce dangerous avalanches.

Rain forms when water from the oceans evaporates (changes into a gas) and rises as water vapour. The rising water vapour condenses (cools) to form droplets of water. These droplets collect together to make clouds. You can see condensation for yourself if you watch your warm breath produce a thin layer of water on a cold window.

As clouds rise, they cool down and cannot carry as much water as when they were warm. This cooling causes the small drops of water to grow bigger as more vapour condenses on them. They may grow so heavy that they fall out of the sky as rain.

Drought and floods

Rain falls in most parts of the world, but the amount of rain that falls in a year differs from place to place. Desert regions may have no rain for many years, whereas some tropical areas, for example parts of India, can receive many metres of rain in a single year.

Sometimes a place may have less rainfall than expected, or even no rain at all. When this happens, the water level in nearby rivers and lakes drops. The ground may begin to crack, and the soil becomes dusty and dry. A long dry period

of weather like this is called a drought. During a drought, crops and other plants do not grow properly, and animals and often people may not have enough food to eat.

If too much rain falls over a very short period, rivers may not be able to carry the water back to the oceans and seas quickly enough. When this happens, water levels rise dramatically and floods occur.

Snow and hail

Snow is made up of tiny crystals of ice that stick together. This happens when the temperature is so cold that the water vapour in the air freezes. It forms small, fluffy, hexagonal-shaped ice crystals that fall out of the sky as snow. Snow may not melt for many weeks, and can collect in layers on the ground to become many metres thick. Snow that falls in high mountains or in the very cold polar regions might not melt at all, even during the warmer summer months.

Hail consists of pea-sized balls of ice that fall like rain. They can cause damage to houses, cars and crops. Hail is produced in tall thunderstorm clouds in which the air rises rapidly. The up-draughts of air can be so strong that they carry raindrops to the top of the cloud where the air is cold. The raindrops freeze into hailstones and drop out of the cloud faster than they can melt.

Frost

On very cold mornings you may find a white, sugar-like coating on the grass, on windows and on cars. This is called frost. It forms when the temperature of the air falls below the freezing point of water (0 °C). This causes moisture in the air to freeze onto cold surfaces.

▼ A snow scene in Japan. There are thousands of different shapes of snow crystal, but all have six points.

find out more
Climate
Clouds
Deserts
Ice
Water
Weather
Wind

Rivers and streams

A river travels from its source in the mountains or other highland area to the estuary where it flows into the sea. In the early stages of a river's journey, many small streams join up to form the main river, with other streams feeding in later on. Rivers and streams provide many different habitats for plants and animals. People have always settled along rivers too, taking advantage of the important travel routes they provide as well as using their water for drinking and washing, to water farmland and to make electricity.

People build roads and railways along river valleys, and dams are constructed to supply electricity. Large rivers can be used to transport food, fuel and goods. Dams, waterfalls and water wheels supply electricity for industry and domestic use.

How a river forms

A river is formed when water flows naturally between clearly defined banks. When rain falls or snow melts, some of the water runs off the land, forming trickles of water in folds of the land. These trickles eventually merge together to form streams, in mountain, lowland and woodland areas. The streams which join up to form the main river are called *tributaries*. As it flows towards the sea, a river becomes deeper and broader as more and more tributaries join it.

Rivers cut into the land and create valleys and gorges. Near its source, the river is well above sea-level and is flowing on steep slopes, so it has its greatest cutting power. Rocks, sand and soil (sediment) are swept along by the water, scouring the river-bed and banks. In the USA, the Colorado River has cut a gorge 1.5 kilometres deep called the Grand Canyon. The faster a river flows, the larger the rocks and the greater the load of sediment it can carry. When the river enters a lake or the sea, or when the valley floor becomes less steep, the river's flow is slowed down and it drops some of the sediment it is carrying.

When a river flows over bands of hard then softer rock, there will probably be one or more waterfalls or rapids where the different types of rock meet. The river will plunge off the resistant rock, and wear away the softer rock underneath even faster. The river will undercut the hard rock on top of the falls. Mountain rivers often have lots of waterfalls. The water rushes down steep hillsides, tumbling over boulders and rocky ledges in a series of small falls. Waterfalls are not so common at the coast, though they do happen when a river falls over a cliff into the sea. Spectacular waterfalls occur when a large river plunges into a gorge or falls from a high plateau.

• The Amazon River owes its name to the Amazon warrior women of Greek mythology. When the first European explorers landed in South America, they faced female and male warriors. Some people thought these must be descendants of the ancient Amazons, so the great river was named after them.

• In India the Ganges is considered a sacred river, and thousands of Hindu pilgrims travel each year to holy cities along its banks.

▼ The course of a river from its source in the mountains to its estuary at the sea.

Upper course The river is still small, and quite shallow. Its bed is full of boulders. It has great cutting power.

Middle course The river is fuller and flows more smoothly, often through a wide valley. It winds among the hills, cutting away the banks on the outside of bends.

Lower course The river becomes wide and sluggish, making huge curves called *meanders*. It may take a short cut across a meander, leaving the old bend as a lake (sometimes called an oxbow lake). The river spreads out and deposits sediment. As it enters the sea, it builds out a fan-shaped delta.

▲ The felucca is the traditional boat on the River Nile in Egypt. Rivers were the earliest important routes for trade and travel. Nearly all the major cities of the world are built either on the coast or on a big river. Today, giant barges still carry goods on many large rivers. Sometimes two rivers have been linked by canals. The Rhine and the Rhône have been linked in this way, enabling barges to go directly from the North Sea to the Mediterranean.

River life

Some animals live on the river-bed, others in the open water, among the plants near or on the river bank, or on the bank itself. Herons, kingfishers and otters hunt for fish in the river, and swallows and bats swoop over the water to catch mayflies. The Amazon River alone contains over 2000 different kinds of fish, including piranhas, catfish, electric eels and the giant arapaima. Some river animals such as the Nile crocodile grow very big.

Dead plant and animal material washes into rivers from the land, and leaves and seeds blow into the water. This rotting material provides food for microscopic plants, worms, water snails, shrimps and mussels. These creatures in turn are food for fish, crayfish and turtles, and these animals may be eaten by otters, crocodiles and alligators. In very muddy water, it can be difficult to search for food. Electric catfish and electric eels use tiny pulses of electricity to detect their prey in the water.

River animals must avoid being washed away. Freshwater limpets cling fast to the rocks. Water beetles and mayfly nymphs have flattened bodies for hiding in crevices, and lampreys use sucker-like mouths to cling to rocks.

Floods

Prolonged heavy rains or the sudden melting of snow can cause rivers to overflow, creating a flood. In cold parts of the world, huge areas flood every spring when the winter snows melt. A landslide may dam a river, causing a flood when the dam collapses. Torrential rain is common in many parts of the world, especially in areas that have one short wet season each year. This rain swells the rivers and may flood land far away from the storms. After a flood, the river may settle on a new course.

The Huang He River in China has caused the world's worst floods. In 1931, over 3.5 million people were killed. The Huang He is the world's muddiest river. Its name means 'Yellow River'. A lot of the mud is dumped on the river-bed and at its mouth, which becomes clogged up. Melting snows each spring and heavy rains in summer threaten floods. For thousands of years, dikes have been built to hold back the water, and today the Huang He is controlled by huge sluice-gates.

The area that can be covered in water if a river floods is called its *flood plain*. The silt deposited over flood plains by large rivers provides some of the most fertile soil in the world, and many flood plains are important farmland today. For thousands of years, the Egyptians welcomed the River Nile floods which spread fresh fertile mud over the dried-up land.

find out more
Lakes
Valleys
Water
Wells and springs

Longest rivers by continent

Africa
Nile, 6673 km
Longest river in the world, draining one-tenth of Africa.
Asia
Chang Jiang (Yangtze), 6276 km
Important waterway in China.
Europe
Volga, 3530 km
Frozen in parts during the winter.
North America
Mississippi–Missouri, 6019 km
Main inland waterway of the USA.
Oceania
Murray–Darling, 3718 km
Dries up in winter over much of its course.
South America
Amazon, 6570 km
More water than any other river in the world. Carries about a quarter of all the water that runs off the Earth's surface.

▼ Flooded fields beside the River Severn in Gloucestershire, England. The river has burst its banks, covering the surrounding flood plain with water.

Rocks and minerals

Rocks are the hard, solid parts that make up the Earth. You can find them all around you: in hillsides and mountains, in cliffs along the seashore, in the walls of large buildings, in the broken pieces of stone in the surface of the road. Rocks also lie beneath the oceans and seas, and under the ice in polar regions. Minerals are solid crystal shapes that are the building materials of rocks. Every kind of rock is made up of one or more minerals.

There are three main types of rock. *Igneous* rocks are formed at high temperatures from molten rocky material, either deep within the Earth or at the surface. *Sedimentary* rocks are formed from sand or mud (*sediment*) that has been laid down on land or in ancient rivers, lakes or seas. *Metamorphic* rocks are formed from sedimentary or igneous rocks that have been buried and heated up or put under great pressure.

Igneous rocks

Igneous rocks form from a hot molten mass of rocky material, called *magma*. Magma forces its way up through the Earth's crust from deep below the surface. Sometimes it reaches the surface as the lava (molten rock) which flows from an erupting volcano. When the magma cools, it hardens and forms rock. The kind of igneous rock that forms depends on what the magma is made of, where it cools, and how long it takes to cool. On cooling, the minerals in the magma form crystals. These crystals, like grains of sugar, have particular shapes depending on their chemical composition. The longer it takes the crystals to cool, the larger they become.

Igneous rocks formed deep in the Earth's crust are called *plutonic* rocks. A common type is granite, which consists of the minerals quartz, mica, feldspar and hornblende. Igneous rocks formed nearer the surface have finer grains and contain minerals such as olivine and magnetite but much less quartz. *Volcanic* rocks, which are formed at the surface, include basalt and pumice.

Sedimentary rocks

Soft and moving sands and muds at the bottom of rivers, lakes and seas form sedimentary rocks such as sandstone, mudstone and limestone. These rocks form part of the great cycle of erosion and deposition that takes place all the time. Rocks on land are broken down by the

Mohs' scale of hardness

The hardness of a mineral can be tested by seeing which other minerals it will scratch. Any mineral will scratch one that is softer than itself, but not one that is harder. The Mohs' scale was devised in 1812 by the German Friedrich Mohs (1773–1839).

Softest
1 talc
2 gypsum
3 calcite
4 fluorite
5 apatite
6 feldspar
7 quartz
8 topaz
9 corundum
10 diamond
Hardest

• The igneous rock pumice began as volcanic lava filled with gases. When the gases escaped, they left behind tiny holes that filled with air, making pumice so light that it floats on water.

• Asbestos is a material made up of soft, silky fibres obtained by crushing asbestos rock. It helps to insulate things from intense heat or fire, and is woven into protective clothing for fire-fighters. Asbestos can be very harmful to health, so strict safety rules must be followed wherever it is used.

▶ How different kinds of rock are formed, and, above, an example of each of the three main types.

Granite is an **igneous** rock. It is rich in the mineral quartz. Granite is the most common type of rock in the Earth's crust.

Shale is a soft **sedimentary** rock formed from fine clay. The fossil of an animal has been preserved in the stone.

Schist is a **metamorphic** rock formed from mudstone and limestone. It consists of fine bands of different-coloured minerals.

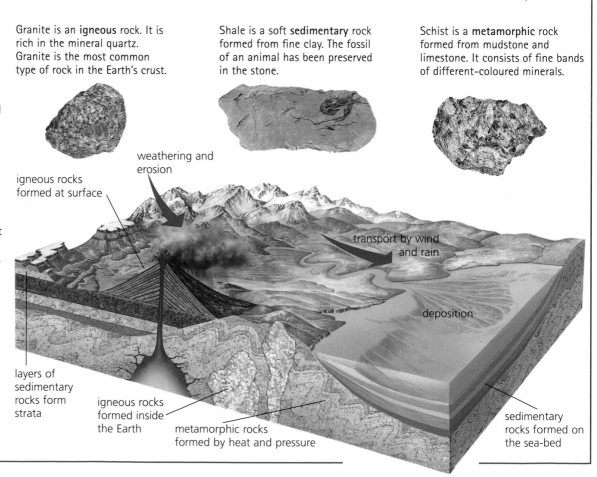

weathering and erosion

igneous rocks formed at surface

transport by wind and rain

deposition

layers of sedimentary rocks form strata

igneous rocks formed inside the Earth

metamorphic rocks formed by heat and pressure

sedimentary rocks formed on the sea-bed

◀ The rocks that form these cliffs at Eleonore Bay, Greenland, have been built up in layers. These rocky layers are known as *strata*.

Large-scale metamorphism can take place when mountains are forming. For example, when major plates of the Earth's crust collide, great pressures are created. Both pressure and heat may alter ocean-floor sediments like mudstone and sandstone to form metamorphic rocks such as slate and schist.

• During metamorphism, the tremendous heat can melt the rock into a liquid. When the liquid cools, impurities come together to form new minerals. A very unusual example of this is the formation of diamonds in coal layers that have been heated by igneous rocks.

action of wind, water, ice and plant roots. Small fragments of sand, silt or clay are then blown away or washed down into rivers or lakes. Over the years, millions of grains may be deposited (laid down) in a single place, building up into thick layers on land or underwater. The largest areas of sediment deposition are in the sea, where sediment is also eroded from the coastline by the action of the sea itself.

Sedimentary rocks also form when material from plants and animals that lived long ago is deposited, usually on the ocean floor. This kind of material is known as 'organic sediment'. On land, the plant material hardened to form beds of peat and coal. In the sea, the skeletons and shells of tiny animals hardened to form rocks such as chalky limestone. A famous example of this rock is the white cliffs of Dover, in southern England.

Two main changes have to take place in order for these sediments to form rock. First, the deeper layers of sediment are pressed down by the weight of sand or mud above, and the water is squeezed out of them. During the second stage, a kind of cement forms. The water that remains around the sediments contains dissolved minerals. As more water is lost, these minerals form crystals that fill the spaces between the rocky grains.

Metamorphic rocks

The word 'metamorphic' means 'later (or changed) form'. Metamorphic rocks have been altered by heat, or by heat and pressure. When magma forces its way up inside the Earth's crust, it heats the surrounding rock. If it passes through sandstone, this may be baked into hard quartzite. Limestone may be baked into marble. This process, which is called *metamorphism*, only affects small amounts of rock that are close to the rising magma.

Minerals

When you look in detail at a piece of rock such as granite, you can make out smaller pieces of individual minerals, often in a variety of colours and shapes. Minerals include such everyday substances as rock salt, asbestos, the graphite used as pencil lead, the talc used to make talcum powder, and the china clay used to make crockery. They also include gold and silver, and the ores of metals such as copper, tin and iron. Minerals that are prized for their beauty and rarity, like diamonds, are known as gems.

Some rocks are made up of only one mineral, while others contain many. Scientists have identified more than 2500 different minerals, but some of these are quite rare. You can identify a mineral by the shape of its crystals as well as by its colour or lustre (the way it reflects light). You can also do a 'streak' test. When minerals are scratched against a rough white surface, many of them leave a distinctive streak of colour. Haematite, the commonest form of iron ore, always produces a red streak.

find out more
Coal
Coasts
Continents
Earth
Erosion
Geology
Mining
Mountains
Oceans and seas
Oil
Rivers and streams
Volcanoes

▼ Erosion by the wind has created these unusual sandstone rock shapes in the Arches National Park, Utah, USA.

Rubber

Rubber is a material used to make products as different as car tyres and surgeon's gloves. Its most important property is that it is elastic: it can be stretched or squeezed out of shape, but returns to its original form.

Natural rubber is made from a liquid called latex, obtained from the trunk of the rubber tree. The rubber tree originally grew in Central and South America. Today it is grown on plantations in hot parts of the world, particularly in South-east Asia. Since World War II synthetic rubber, made from chemicals obtained from oil, has become important. Over two-thirds of all rubber produced is now synthetic.

From tree to factory

Rubber is obtained from trees by a process called 'tapping'. The rubber tapper makes a shallow, diagonal cut in the bark of the tree. The milky latex slowly runs down from the cut into a cup fastened to the tree trunk. The latex is thickened and solidified into doughy sheets, then dried to make raw rubber.

◄ A rubber tapper in Indonesia. Once started, the latex will flow for a few hours, giving about 150 grams of rubber. A tapper can visit about 400 trees each day. Trees can be tapped only every two days, so each tapper looks after about 800 trees.

Raw rubber is hard when cold and sticky when hot. It has to be processed before it is useful. The most important process is *vulcanization*. This involves mixing the rubber with sulphur. The resulting material is stronger and more elastic than raw rubber. Woven fabric or wires are often added to the material to strengthen it.

Over half of all rubber is used for vehicle tyres. Other uses include rubber gloves, hoses, tubing, elastic, tennis balls, and rubber seals to prevent leakage of water or oil in engines and pipelines.

• Rubber balls were made by the Maya people in South America over 900 years ago.

• The vulcanization process was invented in 1839 by Charles Goodyear, when he accidentally spilled some rubber and sulphur on a hot stove.

Russia

Russia is the world's largest country. It is almost the size of the USA and Canada combined. From east to west it is about 8000 kilometres and crosses 11 time zones.

The Ural Mountains separate European and Asian parts of Russia. The largest mountains are on Russia's southern borders and in the Far East along the Kamchatka peninsula, where there are active volcanoes. Three of the world's longest rivers flow through Russia. The River Amur forms the border with China as it flows towards the Sea of Japan.

Mineral wealth

Russia is rich in most of the minerals used by modern society. There are vast deposits of oil, natural gas, coal, copper, iron ore, gold, silver, platinum, lead and nickel. These minerals have helped make the Volga River region one of the world's major centres of industry. Factories get power from

• After the USA, Russia has the longest rail network in the world. It has almost 90,000 km of track. Its railways carry the most freight in the world: 2000 million tonnes a year.

▲ In parts of Russia the climate is very severe. Reindeer are kept in the snowy regions of Siberia in northern Russia. In the capital, Moscow, snow lies on the ground for five months of the year.

hydroelectric power stations on the Don and Volga rivers.

Russia

find out more

Asia
Europe
*See also Countries and
flags section, page 124*

Map legend

- country boundary
- ◆ capital city
- ■ ● major cities and towns
- main roads
- main railways
- ⊕ main airports
- ice cap
- ▲ highest peak (height in metres)

land height in metres

- 2000–5000
- 1000–2000
- 500–1000
- 200–500
- less than 200
- sea level
- land below sea level

▼ Inside a gilded metro (underground) station in St Petersburg, which was built in the 1950s.

People

Russians make up the majority of the population, but there are more than a hundred other nationalities and languages. Most Russians live in the European part of the country. Moscow and St Petersburg are two of Europe's biggest cities. In the far north people have a more traditional way of life. People such as the Nenets, Yakuts and Komi keep reindeer herds or live by fishing. Many farmers live in the west, where the best farmland is. Wheat is a major crop.

▶ FLASHBACK ◀

In the early Middle Ages Kiev was the most powerful state in the region. In 1240 the Mongol-Tartars from central Asia overran Russia. The princes of Moscow finally defeated them in the 16th century, and became tsars (emperors) of Russia.

From the 16th to the 19th centuries Russia expanded its empire to the west into Europe and to the east into central Asia. But the country was slow to modernize. The tsars ruled harshly, and most people remained very poor.

Russia's entry into World War I increased the nation's hardship. The communists led by Lenin seized power in a revolution in 1917. In 1922 they turned the old Russian empire into the Union of Soviet Socialist Republics (USSR). Under the harsh rule of Stalin (1924–1953) there was considerable suffering. During World War II 27 million Soviet people were killed. In 1985 Mikhail Gorbachev became leader and tried to reform the USSR. But he failed, and in 1991 the USSR collapsed. Boris Yeltsin became the first president of the new Russian Federation. Since then there have been many political and economic difficulties.

Commonwealth of Independent States

When the Soviet government voted itself out of existence, the republics became independent. Some of the republics thought it was important to keep in touch with each other. The Commonwealth of Independent States (CIS) was formed in 1991 to include 12 of the 15 republics of the former USSR both in Asia and Europe. Members meet to make agreements in areas such as trade, foreign policy and defence.

Sahara Desert *see* Africa *and* Deserts (map) • **Savannah** *see* Grasslands

find out more
Arctic
Europe
European Union
Forests
Seasons
See also Countries and flags section, pages 122–125

Scandinavia

Scandinavia is a region of northern Europe that includes Norway, Sweden, Denmark, Iceland, the Faeroe Islands and Finland.

The northern part of Scandinavia is in the Arctic Circle, but the cold climate is softened by a warm ocean current called the North Atlantic Drift. The western side consists of rugged mountains, some of which hold glaciers.

Landscapes

Along much of the Norwegian coast, the mountains are indented by long, deep inlets called fjords. Inland, the ancient rock mass is divided by the Baltic Sea and covered in thousands of lakes. Sweden alone has over 95,000 lakes.

While Iceland and the Faeroes are almost treeless, large areas of Norway, Sweden and Finland are covered in forests. Over half of Sweden's land surface is covered with dense forest, mostly pines. Denmark is very flat, and most of the country is farmland. Acid rain is threatening the forests of Scandinavia, while the Baltic Sea suffers from a build-up of industrial and agricultural chemicals.

Iceland was formed by volcanic activity over the last 16 million years. About 30 volcanoes have been active since records began, and the country has thousands of hot springs. Permanent ice covers about one-tenth of the land, much of which is rocky and barren.

▼ Geiranger fjord, on the west coast of Norway. Fjords are long deep inlets that were carved out by glaciers in the last ice age.

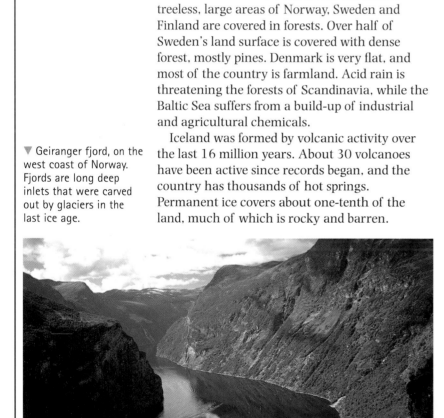

◆ capital city

People

Most Scandinavians speak languages which are related to German and English. However, the languages of the Finns and the Lapps are completely different. The Lapps (or Sami) live in the far north, and live by herding reindeer, hunting and fishing. Most of the Scandinavian countries, apart from Denmark, are thinly populated, and most people in Norway, Sweden and Finland live in the south, where the main cities are.

Fishing, farming and industry

Most of the Scandinavian countries have big fishing fleets, and fishing is the main industry in Iceland. Forestry and related industries such as paper making are important in Norway, Sweden and Finland. Other manufacturing industries include chemicals and engineering. There are many pig and dairy farms in Denmark, and cereals are grown in the south of Sweden and Finland. There is much mineral wealth in Scandinavia, including iron ore, copper and zinc. Norway also gets large amounts of oil and natural gas from the North Sea. Most power comes from hydroelectricity. Iceland also uses the heat from its many hot springs to generate power.

FLASHBACK

Many Scandinavian countries were only formed in the 20th century. Sweden became independent from Denmark in 1523. Finland was ruled by Sweden and then by Russia until 1917. Norway separated from Sweden in 1905, and Iceland became fully independent from Denmark in 1944. The Faeroe Islands are Danish, but have their own government.

Scotland

Scotland is the northern region of the United Kingdom. It was once a separate, independent kingdom, and it still has its own national Church, legal system and educational system.

find out more
Europe
United Kingdom

Scotland usually competes as a separate country in international sport. Some Scots today feel that Scotland should have more independence from the rest of the UK, or even become a separate country again.

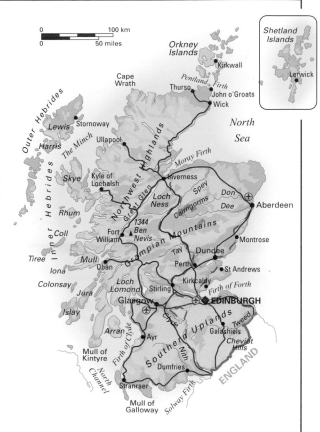

▬▬▬	national boundary
◆	capital city
• •	major cities and towns
──	main roads
══	main railways
⊕	main airports
▲	high peak (height in metres)

land height in metres
- 1000–2000
- 500–1000
- 200–500
- 100–200
- less than 100
- sea level

Highlands

The Highlands in the north are mostly mountainous, with many islands to the west (the Hebrides). Further north are the Orkney and Shetland islands. In the past, many Highland people spoke Gaelic, but it is now heard only in the north-west and in the islands.

The traditional Highland occupations are fishing and farming. Cattle and sheep graze on the hills; and crops are grown in the valleys. Today many small farmers have a second job, often in tourism or another service. Fishing is important round much of Scotland. Fish are often deep-frozen and exported worldwide. Fish farming grew in the 1980s. North Sea oil has provided many jobs. Whisky-making is also important.

▼ Edinburgh is the capital of Scotland and an important financial city. Each summer there is an arts festival, and a splendid military tattoo in the famous castle. Glasgow is Scotland's other chief city. It is an industrial and commercial city, and it is much bigger than Edinburgh.

Lowlands and Southern Uplands

Most of Scotland's people and industry are in the Lowlands. Older industries such as coal-mining, shipbuilding and steel-making have mostly been replaced by newer industries, including chemicals, electronics and light engineering.

The Southern Uplands are more fertile than the Highlands. Crops grow in the Tweed valley and livestock farms are scattered throughout the region. In towns such as Galashiels people use local wool to make knitwear and tweed cloth.

FLASHBACK

For many years the Scots fought to stop the English conquering their country. They finally defeated the English in 1314. But the Scottish kings were weakened in further struggles with the English and with their own nobles. In 1603 James VI of Scotland also became king of England. In 1707 Scotland's separate parliament was abolished, and the country was united with England. From the later 18th century many people in the Highlands were driven off their land to make way for sheep-farming. At the same time the Lowlands became a centre of the Industrial Revolution. In the later 20th century the Scots began to rediscover their old longing for independence, and in 1997 they voted to have their own parliament again.

Seasons

As each season arrives, the length of daylight and the daily weather alter. Summer days are longer and warmer, while winter ones are shorter and cooler. Throughout the year, the different seasons bring changes to the world around us.

• In the night sky, the constellations you can see change day by day. The stars you see in the summer are quite different from the ones you can see in winter.

▲ This time-lapse photograph of the Midnight Sun was taken over northern Norway in midsummer. It shows the position of the Sun in the sky at one-hour intervals. Although the Sun is low in the sky at midnight, it never drops below the horizon.

Midnight Sun

Close to the North and South Poles, there are places where the Sun never sets for days or weeks in midsummer. These places experience the Midnight Sun. In midwinter, the opposite happens and the Sun never rises. This effect happens because the Earth's axis is tilted. The places that get the Midnight Sun lie inside the Arctic and Antarctic circles. The Antarctic has no permanent inhabitants, but people living near and inside the Arctic Circle have to adapt to long periods of continuous daylight or night-time.

find out more
Arctic
Climate
Earth

In spring, after the short days of winter, the amount of daily sunshine increases as the Sun climbs higher in the sky. Summer is the warmest time of the year. The higher the Sun is, the stronger the warming effect of its rays. In autumn, the days shorten again, many trees drop their leaves, and the weather gets cooler as winter approaches.

Near the Equator, the number of hours of daylight does not change much through the year and it stays hot all year round. But the amount of rain that falls varies, so some tropical places have just two seasons: a wet one and a dry one. The seasonal changes are more extreme the further you are from the Equator. Near the Poles, there

are enormous differences between the length of winter and summer days, but it never gets really warm because the Sun is not very high in the sky, even in midsummer.

The changing seasons

The Earth takes one year to travel around the Sun. We have seasons because the Earth's axis (an imaginary line going through the North and South Poles) is tilted to its path round the Sun at an angle of $23\frac{1}{2}°$. From about 21 March to 21 September, the North Pole is tilted towards the Sun and places in the northern hemisphere have spring followed by summer. At the same time, the South Pole faces away from the Sun. From September to March, the North Pole is tilted away from the Sun. Places in the northern hemisphere have autumn and winter while the southern hemisphere has spring and summer.

Each year, on or near 21 March and 23 September, the hours of daylight and darkness everywhere in the world are equal. These days are known as the spring and autumn *equinoxes* (equinox means 'equal night'). At midday on the equinoxes, the Sun is directly overhead at places on the Equator. The days when the number of hours of daylight is greatest and smallest also have a special name. They are called the *solstices* and fall on or about 21 June and 21 December.

▼ Places on Earth receive different amounts of sunlight during the year as the Earth travels around the Sun.

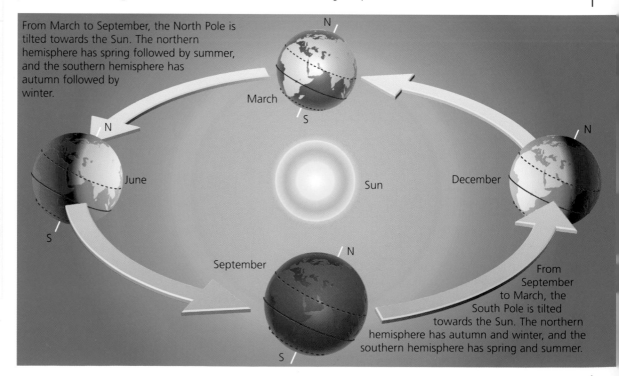

From March to September, the North Pole is tilted towards the Sun. The northern hemisphere has spring followed by summer, and the southern hemisphere has autumn followed by winter.

March

June

September

Sun

December

From September to March, the South Pole is tilted towards the Sun. The northern hemisphere has autumn and winter, and the southern hemisphere has spring and summer.

Sediments *see* Rivers and streams *and* Rocks and minerals

Settlements

▲ A village street in Tibet, a region of south-west China. Tibet is very mountainous and isolated, and it is difficult to grow crops there. But the people who live in villages like this one cannot rely on nearby cities to provide them with goods and services. They must produce almost everything they need themselves.

• In India, three out of every four people live in villages. Many are farmers who have a small piece of land. Some rent land from a landlord in return for cash or part of their harvest. Others have no land of their own and work on a landlord's fields.

• Ancient Rome may have had a population of 1 million, in the 2nd century AD. Now the world has over 280 cities of this size. The largest urban regions – which can include several cities close together – are Tokyo, New York and Mexico City, all of which contain over 18 million people.

Settlements are the places where people live. They vary in size from small villages that can have populations of fewer than 100 people, to vast urban regions with over 20 million inhabitants.

Villages are usually found in rural areas, where about half the world's population lives. The other half lives in towns and cities.

Villages, towns and cities

Villages are traditionally places where farmers live so that they are close to the land they work on. They sometimes keep farm animals such as cows, oxen, pigs, chickens and ducks in the village. In some countries grain and other foods are kept in or near people's homes. Not everyone who lives in a village is a farmer. There may also be shopkeepers or teachers to serve the other inhabitants.

In developed countries, where few people are farmers, villages have changed. The people who live in them often travel to work every day in nearby cities. These *commuters* think that the time spent travelling is worthwhile because country villages are not as noisy or dirty as cities.

Towns are smaller than cities. A city is an important town where lots of people live and work. They are mostly employed in shops, factories and offices. A city may also have some things that small towns do not have. Cathedrals and universities, for example, are usually only found in cities.

Cities and towns that merge together are called *conurbations*. If such a conurbation covers a large region, it is known as a *megalopolis*. The area between Boston and Washington DC in the USA is a megalopolis over 600 kilometres long.

Every country has a *capital city*, where the country's government is usually found. The capital city is often the most important in the country, with the largest population and more businesses, shops and factories than anywhere else. Some countries have built their capitals specially, such as Canberra in Australia and Brasília in Brazil. Such capitals are often smaller than other, more established cities elsewhere in the country.

▶ A shanty town built on a swamp in San Juan, capital city of the Caribbean island of Puerto Rico. In stark contrast, the skyscraper buildings of the city's wealthy financial district rise up in the distance.

Settlement patterns

Settlements are found in different kinds of location. In Europe, for example, some villages are stretched out along a road or a river. Others consist of houses grouped together on a hilltop, originally for defence. In hilly areas villages were often built on the slopes, leaving the level land free for farming.

Cities start as small settlements and grow bigger because they have a particularly favourable site. Some cities, such as Paris, arise at a place where a large river is easy to cross. Others, including Sydney in Australia, have good natural harbours. Many big industrial cities grew up close to places where iron, coal or other natural resources were found. These resources were too bulky to move far and had to be used on the spot.

A country's settlements can be arranged in a pyramid. There are more villages than towns, more towns than cities, and more small cities than big ones. This arrangement is called a settlement *hierarchy*. ◗

◄ The city lights of the USA at night, as photographed by a satellite orbiting the Earth. The lights provide a clear picture of the country's varying population density.

A very small number of people do not live in any kind of permanent settlement. This group includes people such as nomads and hunter-gatherers.

Migration

Cities have grown big because people have migrated (moved) to them from villages and towns. When machines and more efficient methods of farming were invented, fewer people were needed to work the land. At the same time, factories in cities needed workers. This change happened in Europe and North America in the 19th century, and is happening in the developing world now.

Although there are not enough jobs for everyone in a city, people still move there. They have a better chance of finding work in cities than in rural areas. Cities also have better services, such as running water and hospitals, and entertainments, such as big sporting events.

City problems

As cities grow bigger, their disadvantages become greater. If cities expand too quickly, there may not be enough places for everyone to live. In much of the developing world, poor people have to make their own shelters, out of whatever materials they can find. These settlements, crowded with dwellings made of wood or corrugated iron, are called *shanty towns*. When the poor have to build on land that does not belong to them, they create *squatter settlements*. If they can earn some money, they can gradually improve their shanties. Sometimes their governments help by providing materials, electricity and water.

As cities become bigger and more developed, there are more factories and cars, so the pollution and traffic congestion increase. The quality of the air and waterways often worsens, and so does the health of the inhabitants. Since polluted air carries chemicals such as sulphur, which attacks stone, it also damages buildings. This is a major problem in Athens and Rome, where ancient buildings lie close to the city centre. To cope with this problem, cities such as Florence in Italy ban cars from the centre.

FLASHBACK

The first cities grew up in places where it was possible to produce a lot of food. These were usually near rivers which supplied good soils and plentiful water. They developed in different parts of the world: the Middle East, eastern China, the Indus Valley in what is now called Pakistan and India, Central America, and Peru.

Archaeologists are not sure which is the world's oldest city. It might be Çatal Hüyük in Turkey, which is now in ruins. Jericho, on the west bank of the River Jordan, is another candidate, and it is probably the city which has been lived in the longest – since 9000 BC. Byblos, in Lebanon, may have been inhabited for as long as Jericho.

▼ A suburb of Boston, in the USA. Many people now prefer to live on the edges of cities, in areas called *suburbs*, rather than in the crowded city centres. There is usually much more space in the suburbs, and people can live in larger houses with bigger gardens. However, they usually have to travel further to work.

• In some cities most of the residents live in squatter settlements. In Addis Ababa, in Ethiopia, 85% of the population are squatters, and in Bogotá, Colombia, 60% are squatters.

Shops

Shops are where we go to buy the goods and services we need. The business of selling to customers is known as *retailing*, and people who run shops are called retailers.

Small corner shops may be run by just one person or by a family. They may sell everyday items, such as sweets, tobacco, newspapers, magazines and popular grocery items. Some of these independent retailers suffer because larger shops can offer the same goods at lower prices. So smaller shops often join a 'voluntary chain' or 'symbol group', where they can pool their resources to buy in goods more cheaply and to advertise themselves more effectively.

Some smaller shops in shopping centres specialize in one type of goods, such as books, shoes or toys. Most of these shops now belong to a chain, run by a large company. Some large chains have shops in many different countries. *Department stores* are shops which sell a wide variety of items in different sections or departments. Large, self-service food shops are called *supermarkets*. Larger, out-of-town supermarkets, which also sell non-food products, are called *hypermarkets*.

• Co-operative societies are special kinds of companies. Owners of co-operatives share the cost of starting a business, such as a shop. Then they share the profits (after deductions for expenses) among their members in proportion to the amount each spent.

▶ Sainsbury's is now one of the biggest chains of supermarkets, but when this store was opened in Guildford, England, in 1906 customers could sit on chairs while staff took their food orders.

find out more
Industry

Soil

Soil is a combination of rock particles of various sizes and decayed plant and animal matter. Different kinds of rock and different climates produce different types of soils. One square metre of fertile soil can contain over 1000 million living things, yet many are too tiny to see with the naked eye.

Soil is formed when rocks are slowly broken down by the actions of wind, rain and other weather changes. Plants take root among the rock particles. The roots help to bind the particles together, and protect them from rain and wind. When plants and animals living in the soil die, fungi and bacteria break down their remains to produce a dark sticky substance called *humus*. The humus sticks the rock particles together and absorbs water. You can find out about different types of soil by looking at a *soil profile* (a sample taken from the surface down through the soil). Each profile is divided into a series of layers called *horizons*.

The rock particles in soil have air spaces between them. The larger the particles, the bigger the air spaces between them and the faster water drains out of the soil. The air in the soil is important for plants because their roots need oxygen to breathe. The decaying plant and animal remains release minerals which are then absorbed by plant roots.

◀ A soil profile.

• In some parts of the world wind-blown dust accumulates to form a soil called *loess*. In parts of China the loess is as much as 300 m thick.

find out more
Erosion
Grasslands
Rocks and minerals

The *O horizon*, the surface layer, contains many animals and plant roots. It is rich in dark-coloured humus. It is thicker in rich soils than in poor soils.
The *A horizon* still has a lot of humus, but is a paler, greyish colour because many of the minerals have been washed out by rainwater. This process is called leaching.
The *B horizon* contains much less humus, but has some of the minerals washed out of the A horizon. Any iron left here may oxidize, producing a yellow or reddish-brown colour.
The *C horizon* is where weathering takes place, and the parent rock is breaking down.
The *R horizon* is the parent (original) rock.

South Africa

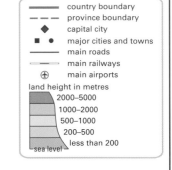

The Republic of South Africa is a country at the southern tip of Africa. It has many natural resources and is the richest country in the continent.

- The descendants of Dutch colonists in South Africa are called Afrikaners.

find out more
Africa
Hunter-gatherers
See also Countries and flags section, page 125

▼ Wild flowers in the Namaqaland Hills, Cape Province. This small region has probably the greatest diversity of flower species in the world.

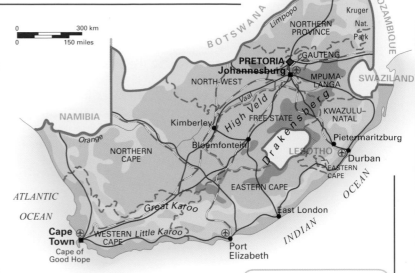

For many years South Africa was ruled by Europeans. Democratic elections were not held until 1994.

A rich landscape

At the heart of South Africa is a huge, grassy plateau called the high veld. To the west, the high veld merges into the Kalahari and Namib deserts. In the east the high veld is bounded by the Drakensberg mountains, while to the south there are lower mountain ranges and the plains of the Great and Little Karoo.

South Africa has a pleasant climate, although nights can be cold on the high veld, and occasionally there is drought. The area in the south-west, around Cape Town, has a Mediterranean climate: hot, dry summers and mild, wet winters.

South Africa has huge reserves of gold, diamonds, chromium, platinum and other minerals of value to industrial nations. It also exports maize (corn), fruit, wine and other foods. It has busy, modern cities with banks, stock exchanges, factories and skyscrapers.

▶ FLASHBACK ◀

The first inhabitants of South Africa were hunter-gatherers, the Bushmen (San) and Hottentots (Khoikhoi). The Bantu peoples, including the Xhosa and the Zulus, arrived later from the north.

The Dutch established a settlement at Cape Town around 1652. This was captured by the British during the Napoleonic wars, and British settlers began to arrive in the 1820s. Many Boers (Dutch farmers) migrated north to found their own republics. The British defeated the Zulus. They also fought two wars with the Boers (1880–1881 and 1899–1902), and took over the

Boer republics. South Africa became a self-governing British territory in 1910.

In the new South Africa non-whites (over 75 per cent of the population) were not allowed to vote. After 1948 the laws that kept whites and non-whites apart were made much stricter. This was the system of apartheid ('apartness'). While most whites lived in luxury, non-whites generally lived in poverty.

The African National Congress (ANC) led opposition to apartheid. Its leader, Nelson Mandela, was imprisoned in 1962. Apartheid was condemned around the world, and many countries refused to trade with South Africa. The white government was forced to reform. In 1990 Mandela was released from prison and apartheid was abolished. When fully democratic elections were held in 1994 and 1999 the ANC won easily.

South America

South America is the fourth largest continent in the world. It extends south from Colombia and covers 13 per cent of the world's total land surface.

• South America is sometimes called Latin America, because the Spanish and Portuguese languages still spoken there grew out of Latin. The phrase Latin America also includes Central America, which is part of the continent of North America.

▼ The village of Maras, in Peru, with the mountains of the Andes in the background. The Andes are a series of mountain ranges which start near the Caribbean Sea in the north, and go through Venezuela, Colombia, Ecuador, Peru and Bolivia. They then run along the border between Chile and Argentina down to Tierra del Fuego in the far south.

Amazonia and the other regions around the Equator are hot all year and very wet. Further south, on the wooded grasslands of the Gran Chaco, there are distinct wet and dry seasons. In the Brazilian Highlands the climate is much less extreme. In north-east Brazil frequent drought has created a landscape of low trees, thorny bushes and cacti, known as *caatinga*. South America stretches much further south than any other continent, so the far south is cool for most of the year. Really cold climates occur only in the extreme south of Argentina and Chile, and high up in the Andes.

Landscape

The Andes are the world's longest mountain range and, after the Himalayas, the second highest. They extend for over 7100 kilometres along the continent's western edge. Snow-capped volcanoes such as the still-active Cotopaxi rise among the mountain peaks. Earthquakes are common.

Between the Andes and the Pacific coast there is an area of desert which stretches for 1600 kilometres from southern Ecuador to northern Chile. The Atacama Desert is the driest place on Earth. Rain has never been recorded in some places.

There are three plateau areas in South America. The Guiana Highlands in the north are deep, forested valleys. They are largely uninhabited. The Brazil Plateau in the east is where most Brazilians live. Its western part forms the savannah grasslands of the Mato Grosso. In the south lies the dry plateau of Patagonia.

The lowlands of the Amazon basin are covered with dense rainforest, with a great variety of species of trees, insects, monkeys and parrots. Away

- French Guiana is an administrative district of France. This means that its people are French citizens.

- America was named after Amerigo Vespucci, an Italian navigator who explored the South American coast.

find out more
Brazil
Caribbean
Grasslands
See also individual South American countries in the Countries and flags section, pages 122–125

▼ Aymará Indians in Bolivia. More than half of all Bolivians are Native Americans. Bolivia was once part of the Inca empire and one of the languages still spoken in Bolivia, Quechua, was spoken by the Inca people.

from the Amazon the forest changes to wooded grassland (the Gran Chaco) and more fertile grasslands (the pampas) in the Paraná–Paraguay basin further south, and to the savannah lands (llanos) of the Orinoco basin in the north.

Countries

Brazil is by far the largest country in South America and contains half the population. Bolivia is the roof of South America. One-third of Bolivia is over 1.5 kilometres high. Argentina and Uruguay share the estuary of Río de la Plata, a great trading route to and from the continent's interior. South America exports many agricultural and mineral products. Chile is the world's leading producer of copper. Brazil produces the most coffee and is a leading exporter of sugar, cocoa, tin and fruit. Peru exports copper, lead and zinc.

People

Modern-day South Americans are descended from Europeans, Africans and Native Americans. Brazilians speak Portuguese. Most other South Americans speak Spanish. Many Native American languages are spoken, especially in the northern Andes and Amazonia. They include Aymará, Guaraní and Quechua.

Today, many Native Americans are moving to the cities, but there they often earn low wages and live in shanty towns. The Native Americans of the tropical forests grow cassava root and vegetables in small clearings. Their villages are scattered to give each family a large area in which to hunt and gather plants. However, the forests are being cleared and people are losing their homes.

In the last 100 years other Europeans have settled in the continent, for example, Italians in Argentina and Japanese on the west coast. Most South Americans live near the coast in cities such as Rio de Janeiro, São Paulo, Buenos Aires and Lima. Roman Catholicism is the most important religion in South America.

FLASHBACK

Before the arrival of European explorers, Native Americans developed large empires in South America. Most were in the northern and central Andes. Great civilizations, such as the Nazcas and Chimus, came and went. The last great empire was that of the Incas, based in what is now Peru.

▲ Huge deposits of metals and minerals, including gold, are found in the Amazon region. In order to exploit these resources, and also to provide farmland and housing, a lot of forest is being destroyed. Scientists are also concerned that the region's vast diversity of plants and animals will be lost.

Shortly after Christopher Columbus discovered the Americas in 1492, the pope divided the newly discovered lands between Spain and Portugal. Portugal was given Brazil, while Spain gained the rest of South America. In 1532 Francisco Pizarro led a group of Spanish adventurers called conquistadores (conquerors) to Peru. They destroyed the Inca empire. Within a few years the Spanish and Portuguese spread their rule over much of the continent. Native Americans and African slaves were forced to work in mines and on plantations, and many died of European diseases.

In the early 19th century the Spanish colonies fought for and won their independence. And in 1825 Portugal recognized the independence of Brazil. Many Europeans settled in South America, and most South Americans today are descendants of European settlers who married Native Americans.

Spain

Spain is the fourth largest country in Europe. It has a varied landscape and is home to a diverse population, a quarter of whom speak a language other than Spanish. It is also a country with an exciting and turbulent history.

Spain is one of the most mountainous countries in Europe. Madrid, at 646 metres above sea level, is Europe's highest capital city. It is near the centre of a high plateau called the Meseta. Rivers such as the Tagus and Duoro have cut deep valleys into this plateau. The Meseta is surrounded by high mountains which keep out the winds from the sea. This is 'dry Spain', with little rain, very cold winters and very hot summers. Northern Spain is 'wet Spain': a green, lush countryside facing the Atlantic Ocean. The southern province of Almería is very hot and dry.

People and industry

Industry is mainly based in northern Spain, and Bilbao is Spain's most important industrial town. The main users of the steel industry are car manufacturers, and cars are Spain's greatest export. Lots of international companies are based in Spain and have factories there, making electrical goods, for example, or printing books.

Much of rural Spain is quite poor. Farming is still important, especially for crops such as oranges and olives which only grow in warmer climates. Wheat and barley grow in the Meseta.

There is a thriving tourist industry on the warm south and east coasts, and in the Balearic Islands in the Mediterranean and the Canary Islands in the Atlantic Ocean, which are also parts of Spain.

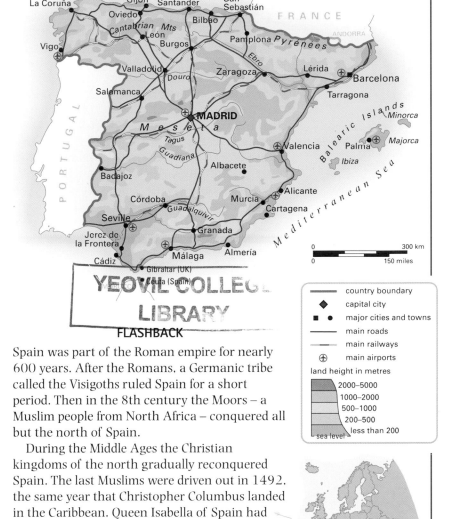

——	country boundary
◆	capital city
■ ●	major cities and towns
——	main roads
══	main railways
⊕	main airports

land height in metres

	2000–5000
	1000–2000
	500–1000
	200–500
sea level	less than 200

FLASHBACK

Spain was part of the Roman empire for nearly 600 years. After the Romans, a Germanic tribe called the Visigoths ruled Spain for a short period. Then in the 8th century the Moors – a Muslim people from North Africa – conquered all but the north of Spain.

During the Middle Ages the Christian kingdoms of the north gradually reconquered Spain. The last Muslims were driven out in 1492, the same year that Christopher Columbus landed in the Caribbean. Queen Isabella of Spain had paid for Columbus's expedition, and the Spanish went on to conquer a vast empire in Central and South America.

By the 16th century Spain was the most powerful and wealthy country in Europe. However, a series of disastrous wars and feeble kings weakened the country. In the 19th century its American colonies gained their independence. In 1931 Spain became a republic, but in 1936 civil war broke out between the left-wing government and the army and its fascist supporters. The fascists won and the dictator General Francisco Franco ruled Spain from 1939 until his death in 1975. After Franco's death Spain became a democracy again.

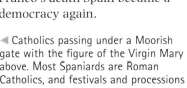

◄ Catholics passing under a Moorish gate with the figure of the Virgin Mary above. Most Spaniards are Roman Catholics, and festivals and processions take place on holy days and saints' days.

• Gibraltar is a tiny country linked to Spain by a narrow strip of lowland 3 km long. Gibraltar has been a British dependency since 1704.

find out more
Europe
South America
See also Countries and flags section, page 125

Textiles

Textiles are all around you. They form the clothes you wear during the day, and the bedding that you sleep in at night. Towels, carpets, curtains and furniture covers are made of textiles. And textiles are used for many other useful things, such as belts, parachutes, tents, sails and bandages.

A textile is a cloth or fabric made from fibres. These might be natural fibres that come from plants or animals, such as cotton, silk, flax and wool. Or they could be synthetic fibres made in factories, such as nylon, polyester and acrylics.

Making textiles

The first step in producing most textiles is to twist the fibres together by *spinning* them, to form a yarn or thread, like the cotton on a reel or the wool in a ball of wool. This is done either by hand or using a machine. Most synthetic fibres are made from chemicals extracted from oil. The fibres are produced by forcing the chemicals through tiny holes in a nozzle called a *spinneret*. As the fibres emerge, they are spun to make yarn.

The yarn may then be dyed before being made into cloth or fabric. This is mainly done by *weaving*, in which lengths of yarn are criss-crossed on a loom, or by *knitting*, in which the yarn is linked in loops. A pattern can be formed by weaving or knitting different-coloured yarns together.

Once made, a textile may next need some kind of treatment – washing or cleaning to remove dirt and impurities, bleaching to whiten it, or waterproofing or fireproofing. Many textiles have patterns printed on their surface. This is done using large rollers which carry a pattern of coloured dyes.

Textile properties

The properties of a finished textile depend partly on the fibres from which it is made. Textiles made from natural fibres are generally softer, absorb moisture better and are more heat-resistant than synthetic fabrics. Synthetic textiles are stronger, harder-wearing and more crease-resistant than natural fabrics. Modern textiles may be made from a mixture of natural and synthetic fibres to give the best combination of properties for a particular product.

Other kinds of textile

Denim: a strong woven cotton cloth used for jeans and other tough garments.
Linen: a fabric made from the flax plant.
Satin: a fabric woven with a smooth surface, so that it appears shiny.
Tweed: a heavy woollen cloth with a rough surface.
Lycra®: shiny fabric made with stretchy synthetic fibres, used to make sportswear.
Gore-Tex®: a 'breathable' waterproof fabric used for outdoor clothing and tents.

find out more
Cotton
Dress and costume
Wool

▶ Weaving involves passing a yarn, called the *weft*, over and under many parallel yarns, called *warp* threads.

1 Each warp thread is attached to a wire loop called a *heddle*.

2 Using the heddles, one set of warp threads is raised and another lowered. The weft is passed through the gap (the *shed*), using a *shuttle*.

3 The warp threads are reversed, so that the lower one is above, and the higher one is below. The weft passes through the shed again.

▼ A Guatemalan woman weaving yarn into cloth using a simple loom.

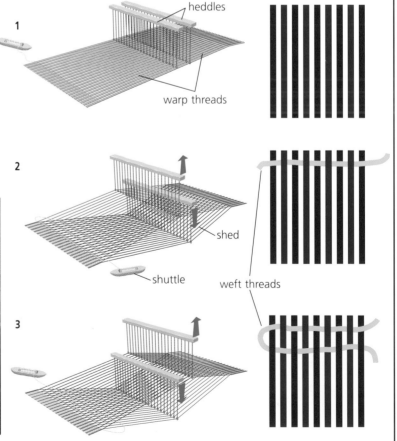

Tides

Tides are the rise and fall of the sea at regular intervals. At high tide, the sea rises high up the beach. At low tide, it falls low down the beach. Tides happen because the Moon's gravity pulls on the Earth and its seas.

▶ The Sun, Moon and Earth line up twice each month. Because the pull of the Sun adds to the pull of the Moon, this makes the sea rise and fall more than at any other time. These very high tides are called spring tides (but they do not only happen in spring). In between, there are neap tides when the change in sea level is smallest.

• High tides send a tidal wave, called a bore, up some rivers. One of the world's highest bores occurs on the Qiantang in China.

find out more
Coasts
Energy
Oceans and seas
Water

Most places have two high tides a day, which take place 50 minutes later each day. The shape of the coastline can affect the tides. In enclosed seas like the Mediterranean the tides are very slight. The highest tidal range in the world is at the Bay of Fundy in Canada. The sea level can rise more than 15 m between low and high tides.

How tides are caused

The seas nearest the Moon are pulled most strongly by its gravity, so they bulge slightly towards the Moon. The seas furthest from the Moon are pulled less than elsewhere, leaving another bulge. There are high tides at the two bulges and low tides in between. As the Earth spins, places move in and out of the bulges and their sea level rises and falls.

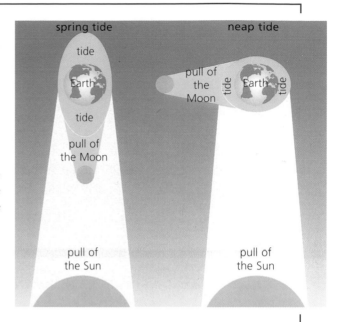

Tidal power

The use of tides as a source of energy to generate electricity is called tidal power. In a tidal-power scheme, a dam is built across the mouth of a river. As the tide comes in and goes out, water rushes in and out of tunnels in the dam. This flow of water turns huge turbines which drive generators.

Tourism

find out more
Industry
Pollution
Transport

Tourists are people who travel within a country or to another country for recreation. Tourists create many jobs in the places they visit, and tourism is now one of the most important industries in many countries.

About three-quarters of all tourists still come from the richest 20 countries, and most of them visit Europe and North America. However, a growing number of people are visiting other parts of the world, for example going on photographic safaris in Africa's game parks or back-packing through remote mountain ranges such as the Himalayas.

Although tourists help create employment, they can also bring problems to the places they visit. Many poorer countries have to spend a lot of money building roads, airports and other facilities for tourist resorts. This may mean that less money is available to spend on more essential services for the country's own inhabitants. Tourists can also cause damage and pollution in the areas they visit. The ancient monuments of Egypt and Greece attract many millions of visitors, but they are suffering damage from the traffic fumes the tourists bring with them.

◀ The beautiful Annapurna Valley is the most popular trekking destination in Nepal. But the booming tourist trade has brought problems as well as profit. In this picture rubbish left by campers pollutes the environment. Forests are being cleared for tourist lodges, and the deforestation leads to landslides and soil erosion. Local life is disrupted by the constant stream of foreign visitors.

Trade

Have you ever swapped something of yours for something else your friend had? If so, you were trading. Trade takes place when people or countries exchange things. When things are swapped directly for other things, we call it barter. Today, most trade involves money.

▲ The New York Stock Exchange on Wall Street is one of the largest and oldest in the world. Stock markets are world markets where shares in companies or commodities (such as oil) can be bought and sold.

The last time you bought a bar of chocolate, yours was just the last in a whole series of trades. Before it was sold to you, the chocolate was probably bought from a bulk supplier (*wholesaler*) by the shopkeeper (*retailer*). In turn, the wholesaler bought it from the manufacturer, who also paid for the people and machines to make the chocolate. Before that, the ingredients had to be bought by the manufacturer and transported to the chocolate factory, probably from another part of the world.

International trade

Goods and services that are sold to foreign customers are known as *exports*, while goods and services bought from another country are *imports*. The trade in exports and imports is called international trade, and it is very important to all countries in the world.

Without international trade, consumers would only be able to buy a limited variety of goods. For example, people in Scandinavia would not be able to enjoy tropical fruits or rice because the climate in Scandinavia is unsuitable for growing such foodstuffs. There are also countries, such as Japan, which have very few energy sources of their own. It is vital for these countries to sell exports so that they can earn the money to buy the coal and oil they need. That is one of the reasons why so many Japanese goods are available in other countries.

Free trade and protection

When all countries specialize in producing the goods and services they are most efficient at producing, they are able to increase the output of goods and services throughout the world. And if there are more goods and services being produced, then the users of these things (*consumers*) will enjoy a higher standard of living. This is the main argument in favour of 'free trade', a situation where no country tries to prevent imports from another country.

Countries sometimes fear that imports of cheaper goods will mean that people making similar goods in the home country will lose their jobs. In the past, this has often led to countries trying to keep imports out. They have used *tariffs*, which are special taxes on imported goods. Tariffs make the imports more expensive, which stops consumers buying them. *Quotas* are also sometimes used. A quota is a limit on the quantity of imports of a particular item that a country will allow. The use of tariffs and quotas is known as *protectionism*, because the import controls are designed to protect the home industries from foreign competition.

find out more
Economics
European Union
Industry
Shops
Transport

• In 1948 trading countries set up the General Agreement on Tariffs and Trade (GATT). At GATT meetings trading nations agreed to make trade as free as possible by reducing tariffs and quotas. GATT has been replaced, since the beginning of 1995, by a new, permanent organization called the World Trade Organization, which has its headquarters in Geneva, Switzerland.

▼ This woman in Sousse, Tunisia, is buying food supplies at a market stall. The produce she is buying was produced and sold, and will probably be consumed, locally. Millions of such small-scale transactions take place every day all over the world.

Transport

Transport involves taking goods or people from one place to another. The vehicles in which they travel – whether they are bicycles, cars, lorries, trains, ships or aeroplanes – are all forms of transport. Transport systems also include roads, railway lines, harbours and airports. Transport is essential to trade, tourism and industry.

People first began to use animals as a form of transport in prehistoric times. In many parts of the world people still ride animals such as horses, donkeys and buffalo, or use them to carry goods or to pull carts. But most people and goods now travel using some form of mechanical transport.

Transporting people

Many people need to travel quite long distances to get to work. This kind of travelling is called *commuting*. Commuters often drive to work in private cars, but as roads become busier and busier, travelling by car gets slower. This is called congestion.

Instead of using cars, some people travel on *public transport* – on buses, trains, underground railways, or trams and trolley-buses (vehicles like buses that run on electricity from overhead wires). Public transport systems may be run by local governments or by private firms.

For travelling longer distances, many people still drive their cars, using the motorways that link big cities, although others use buses or trains. For journeys of more than a few hundred kilometres people mostly now travel by air, which is much quicker, although usually more expensive than going by train.

Transporting goods

Over short distances goods are usually carried in trucks and vans. Many trucks can carry different kinds of goods, but some, such as car-transporters and petrol tankers, are designed to carry only one thing. Trucks can also carry goods on longer journeys, but it is often cheaper to carry bulky goods such as coal by train.

For very long distances, goods are usually carried by sea in cargo ships. Some cargo ships carry many kinds of goods, but there are also specialized cargo ships, such as oil tankers and grain carriers. It is too expensive to transport large amounts of goods in aeroplanes, although letters and packages often go by air.

In recent years many goods have started to travel in containers. Containers are very large metal boxes, all the same size, that can be loaded onto trucks, trains or ships. This means that the goods do not need to be unpacked and packed again when they are moved, for example, from a ship to a truck. There are now many container

◀ A Boeing 777 passenger jet, one of the new generation of air liners.

• Bicycles were invented in the 19th century in Europe. Today they are perhaps the most common means of transport in the world, apart from walking. They are a very efficient way of travelling short distances, and they cause no pollution.

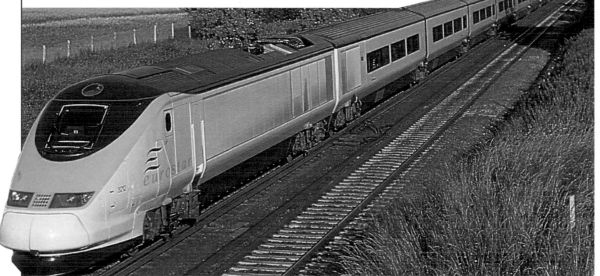

◀ The high-speed Eurostar train carries passengers between Britain and mainland Europe via the Channel Tunnel.

Trees *see* Forests *and* Wood • **Tundra** *see* Arctic • **Typhoons** *see* Weather

An aerial view of the harbour of Salerno Campania in south-west Italy. Many industries, such as shipbuilding, engineering, refineries and food-processing plants, grow up around ports like this because it is cheaper and more convenient to be close for unloading and loading.

Transport firsts

18th century Many canals are built in Britain, and most goods are transported by horse-drawn barges until the coming of the railways.

1804 The first steam railway locomotive is built by Richard Trevithick and runs in an ironworks in Wales.

1825 George Stephenson opens the first passenger railway, which runs between Stockton and Darlington in England. By the end of the 19th century thousands of kilometres of railway line have been built all over the world.

1885–1886 The Germans Gottfried Daimler and Karl Benz build the first vehicles powered by petrol engines.

1903 The American brothers Orville and Wilbur Wright make the first flight in a powered aeroplane.

1907 The American Henry Ford begins to manufacture motor cars in large numbers.

1930s Germany becomes the first country to build a network of motorways.

1952 The world's first jet airliner, the British De Havilland Comet, starts carrying passengers.

1976 The Anglo-French Concorde becomes the first supersonic airliner to enter service.

1981 The French high-speed train, the TGV (*Train à Grande Vitesse*), begins service between Paris and Lyon, travelling at an average speed of 210 km/h.

ports round the world, with cranes designed for lifting containers onto and off special container ships.

Transport and the environment

Many people are worried about the damage that some kinds of transport do to the environment. When there is a lot of traffic on the roads, especially in cities, the fumes from cars, trucks and buses can damage people's health. The noise the vehicles make is also a kind of pollution.

Building new roads to allow the traffic to travel more quickly sometimes only encourages more people to travel by car. Also new roads often destroy the places where wild animals and plants live. Another problem is that cars, buses and trucks run on petrol or diesel fuel, which comes from oil, and the world's supply of oil will not last forever.

New inventions such as electric cars may help the problem, but many people think that the best solution would be for us to stop using cars so much. More people could walk or cycle for short distances, and use public transport more often

for longer journeys. Although buses and trains also use up oil supplies and cause pollution, they can carry many more passengers than a car can. So if more people used public transport there would be far fewer cars on the roads, and much less pollution.

Some cities have already begun to ban private cars altogether from city centres, and in many places some streets are set aside for pedestrians (walkers) only.

find out more
Energy
Greenhouse effect
Pollution
Settlements

This aerial photograph shows a busy intersection on the M62 motorway in northern England. At complex intersections like this one, the roads are usually built on more than one level.

United Kingdom

The United Kingdom is a country in north-west Europe. It is often called simply the UK, but its full name is the United Kingdom of Great Britain and Northern Ireland.

The UK is made up of England, Scotland, Wales and Northern Ireland. The Channel Islands and the Isle of Man are not part of the UK, and they have their own laws and taxes.

Government

The king or queen is the formal head of state but entrusts the running of the country to the government and its ministers. The government is formed by the political party that has the most supporters in the House of Commons in London (Parliament). Members of Parliament, called MPs for short, are elected from areas, or 'constituencies', all over the UK. They make the UK's laws, but each law also has to be approved by another body, the House of Lords. The House of Lords is also in London, and its members are not elected.

In 1997 the people of both Scotland and Wales voted in favour of 'devolution'. This means that the central government in London will share some of its powers with a new Scottish parliament in Edinburgh and a new Welsh assembly in Cardiff.

The UK joined the European Community, now known as the European Union, in 1973. It sends 87 elected representatives to sit in the European Parliament and recognizes certain types of laws passed there.

▼ The Channel Islands. Four main islands make up the Channel Islands, which are in the English Channel: Jersey (below), Guernsey, Alderney and Sark. Many Channel Islanders speak both English and French. A Norman-French dialect is also spoken, and many of the place names are French. The islands have a mild climate and are very popular with tourists.

▶ FLASHBACK ◀

The British Isles were invaded by Celts, Romans, Saxons, Vikings and Normans. Each group of settlers brought their own language and culture.

Wales resisted Norman rule but was eventually conquered and united with England in 1282. In 1603 James VI of Scotland became James I of England. England and Scotland have had a common parliament since 1707. In 1801 Ireland was united with the rest of the British Isles to form the United Kingdom of Great Britain and Ireland. After World War I, southern Ireland broke away to form a separate country, the Republic of Ireland.

• The British Isles became separated from the European mainland about 12,000 years ago, when the sea level rose after the last ice age. Many mainland plants and animals were prevented by the rising sea from reaching the British Isles.

▲ The national flag of the United Kingdom is the Union Flag ('Union Jack'). It was formed by combining the crosses of the patron saints of England (St George), Scotland (St Andrew) and Ireland (St Patrick). The flag was devised in 1801, when no separate recognition was given to the dragon of Wales.

find out more
England
Europe
Northern Ireland
Scotland
Wales
See also Countries and flags section, page 125

United States of America

The USA is the richest and most powerful country in the world. It consists of 50 states, each of which has its own elected government. These can set taxes and pass laws over many of the things that affect people's daily lives. A federal government organizes the whole country and conducts its relations with other countries.

Forty-eight of the states, from California in the west to Maine in the east, make up the main landmass. Alaska, the largest and most northerly state, is separated from the others by Canada. The islands of Hawaii are in the middle of the Pacific Ocean. While Alaska reaches into the Arctic Circle, with freezing winter temperatures, Florida shares the tropical climate of the Caribbean.

Mountains and deserts

Alaska and the western third of the USA are mostly mountainous. The Rocky Mountain range, which runs from Alaska to Mexico, is really a series of mountain ranges separated by plateaux and basins. But while the south-western states like Arizona are hot desert, the north-western states, such as Oregon, are the wettest in the country. Large rivers, such as the Colorado and Snake, have cut deep gorges and canyons through these ranges. In places the rivers have been dammed to provide water for irrigated fields and hydroelectric power for cities.

Plains and rivers

Much of the central and eastern regions of the USA are drained by the Missouri and Ohio rivers,

• Alaska and Hawaii are also in the USA.

⎯⎯⎯	country boundary	▲	high peaks (height in metres)
- - - -	state boundary		land height in metres
◆	capital city		2000–5000
■ ●	major cities and towns		1000–2000
⎯⎯	main roads		500–1000
⎯⎯	main railways		200–500
⊕	main airports	sea level	less than 200 / land below sea level

0 — 500 km
0 — 250 miles

CONN.	Connecticut
DEL.	Delaware
MARY.	Maryland
MASS.	Massachusetts
MISS.	Mississippi
N.H.	New Hampshire
N.J.	New Jersey
PENN.	Pennsylvania
R.I.	Rhode Island
VER.	Vermont
W. VA.	West Virginia

which (along with many others) join the Mississippi River before it enters the sea in the Gulf of Mexico. These rivers provide valuable routes for transporting goods.

Between the Mississippi and the western mountains lie the prairies, vast areas of grassland. Here are found some of the world's most important areas of wheat farming and, where there is less rainfall, cattle ranching.

The east coast is separated from the Mississippi basin by the Appalachian Mountains. These mountains contain deposits of coal which helped US industry develop.

People and cities

The USA has the third largest population of any country. Most Americans are descended from settlers and immigrants who came within the past 400 years, including Africans who were brought as slaves to work the sugar and tobacco plantations of the South. The majority of Americans live in cities. Larger cities such as New York, Chicago and Los Angeles have areas where people have decided to live together because they originally came from the same country, for instance Chinatown in New York.

The country is so big that there are still areas with very few people. Other areas have been kept free of people in order to preserve landscapes, forests and wildlife.

Farms, mines and factories

Almost every kind of agricultural and industrial good is produced in the USA. It is a major world producer of maize (corn), soya beans, tomatoes, oranges, peaches, cheese, beef and chickens. The country has deposits of most of the natural resources useful to modern society. It mines

▲ Central Park becomes a winter playground in the shadow of Manhattan Island skyscrapers in New York.

more coal, copper, gypsum, salt, phosphates and sulphur than any other country. Alaska and the states around the Gulf of Mexico supply most of the country's oil and natural gas.

The world's three largest companies are American: General Motors and Ford (cars) and Exxon (oil). The country makes many goods associated with older, established industries such as chemicals and textiles. But it is also a leader in new industries such as electronics, software and biotechnology.

▶ FLASHBACK ◀

The history of the USA began on 4 July 1776, when the 13 British colonies in North America declared their independence. They went on to defeat the British in the American Revolution (1775–1783). The new country expanded westward throughout the 19th century, and industry and agriculture flourished. Millions of Europeans migrated to the USA, and many Native Americans were forced off their land. Most African Americans were slaves until slavery was abolished at the end of the Civil War in 1865.

In the early years of the 20th century the USA prospered. But in 1929 a terrible economic depression began, which only ended with the start of World War II. The USA entered the war in 1941, and helped to defeat Germany and Japan. After the war the USA led the democratic countries against the communist countries, and used force in Korea and Vietnam. The USA still sends its military forces to other countries to protect its own interests or those of its allies.

• Two of the great plates which make up the Earth's crust, the Pacific and North American plates, meet along the west coast. This means that the region suffers from frequent earthquakes and, less often, volcanoes. The worst earthquakes happen along the San Andreas fault, which runs close to two big cities, San Francisco and Los Angeles.

• Los Angeles is one of the USA's most diverse cities in terms of nationality and language. Out of a population of 8.8 million, one in three was born in another country. Over a quarter speak Spanish.

find out more
Migration
North America
South America
See also Countries and flags section, page 125

▼ The Colorado River has cut a spectacular gorge known as the Grand Canyon. It is 446 km long, and at its deepest point the river is 1870 m below the surrounding landscape. In some places the gorge is 29 km wide.

Valleys

Valleys are formed when rivers or glaciers wear away the rocks of the high ground. As water or ice flows down the mountains, it carves out valleys, leaving ridges of rock on either side and giving the surrounding mountains their shape.

In mountain regions the valleys are the main areas where people live, because the climate is sheltered and the soils are more fertile. Valleys provide routes for roads and railways, and larger rivers can be used for transport.

How valleys are formed

Rivers flowing down steep gradients (slopes) cut deep into the rocks. Where the gradient of the river bed is less, the river flows more slowly and cuts a wider, shallower valley. Glaciers can carve out valleys much more powerfully than rivers. The ice may be hundreds of feet thick, so a great weight presses down on the valley floor. Rocks and boulders on the bottom of the glacier are pushed along by the ice.

Where the river follows a line of weakness in the rocks, such as a fault, it may cut a *gorge*. Some of the most spectacular gorges are the steep-sided canyons of the United States. In desert areas another kind of steep-sided valley forms when occasional heavy rainfall causes 'flash floods'. Because the hard, sun-baked soil cannot soak up the rainfall, powerful floods cut wide, deep channels called *wadis* or *arroyos*.

Valleys may also be drowned, for example where coastlines are sinking or sea levels are rising. When this happens long inlets of the sea called *rias* are formed. Where deep glaciated valleys are drowned, they form *fjords* with very steep sides and extremely deep water.

Life in valleys

The climate in a valley is usually much milder than in the hills around it. The valley sides provide shelter from wind, and often much of the rain or snow falls on the mountains, leaving the valley drier. In some valleys special mountain winds bring warm or cold air at certain times of year. The cold air sinks into the valleys, bringing more frost and fog than in the mountains.

In valleys near a river mouth, the soil is thick and contains sediments brought down by the river. Good crops can be grown in these fertile sediments. In mountain valleys the soils are usually thinner and not very fertile. Sheep farms are more common than crops. On very steep valley slopes, farmers may build terraces to prevent the water and soil rushing away.

Valley records
Largest gorge on land
Grand Canyon on the Colorado River, USA, extends over a distance of 446 km, with an average width of 16 km.
Deepest valley
The Yarlung Zangbo valley in the Himalayas, in eastern Tibet, is 5075 m deep.

find out more
Erosion
Glaciers
Mountains
Rivers and streams

▼ Settlements scattered along the Lauterbrünnen Valley in the Alps, Switzerland. Alpine farmers move their cattle up to high pastures in spring as the snow melts, bringing them back down to the valley floor in winter.

Different kinds of valley

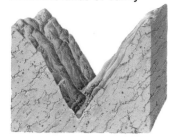

River valleys high up in the mountains have steep sides. They look V-shaped in cross-section. Further down the river course, they become wider and shallower.

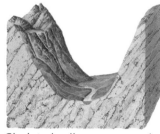

Glaciated valleys are gouged out by ice, rocks and boulders. They are U-shaped in cross-section, with very steep sides and a flat bottom.

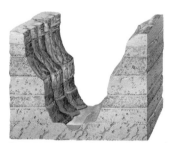

Gorges are very deep valleys with almost vertical sides. One of the best-known examples is the Grand Canyon in the USA.

Rift valleys are formed in two different ways. Either huge blocks of rock rise up to form mountains, leaving a wide valley between them, or the block between drops down to form a valley floor. Two examples are the Rift Valley in Africa and the Rhine rift valley in Germany.

Volcanoes

A volcano is a mountain or hill made of lava which comes from deep beneath the Earth's surface. When a volcano erupts, lava and ash build up to make a cone. Some volcanoes give off clouds of ash and gas when they erupt. Others have streams of red-hot lava pouring down their sides.

The molten rock deep beneath the Earth's crust is called magma. It forces its way up through cracks and weak spots in the Earth's crust and spills out as lava. When a volcano erupts, pieces of broken rock and ash are often thrown out with the lava. Large lumps are called 'volcanic bombs'. As the rock and ash cool, they make layers of solid rock. As magma rises, gases separate out from the molten rock. These gases may collect near the surface and cause a great explosion.

Volcanoes can form on land or on the ocean floor. Some undersea volcanoes grow high enough to reach above sea level and become islands. Mountains can be formed when lava pours out of the ground, then cools and hardens to form hard, solid rock. Mount Fuji in Japan and Vesuvius in Italy are examples of volcanic mountains.

Volcanoes eventually die. A volcano that has not erupted for a long time is said to be *dormant*, although there is always the danger that

it may suddenly erupt. When people think a volcano has finally died, then it is called *extinct*. Gradually, the volcano will be eroded. The softer rocks are worn away first, and in some places the only part left is the hard plug which filled the vent of the volcano.

The birth of a volcano

In Mexico, in 1943, some villagers were worried by earthquakes. Then a crack appeared across a local cornfield and smoke gushed out. The crack widened, and ash and rocks were hurled high into the air. Soon, red-hot lava poured out. After a week, a volcano 150 metres high stood where the cornfield had been, and the villagers had to leave. Mount Parícutin grew to 275 metres in a year, and to 410 metres after nine years.

▲ A thick cloud of smoke, ash and gases rises from Mount Ruapehu, on the North Island of New Zealand. The volcano erupted in September 1995.

• When Vesuvius in southern Italy erupted in the year AD 79, the town of Pompeii was completely buried under volcanic ash. Today, the remains of the town have been dug out.

find out more
Continents
Earth
Earthquakes
Islands
Mountains
Oceans and seas

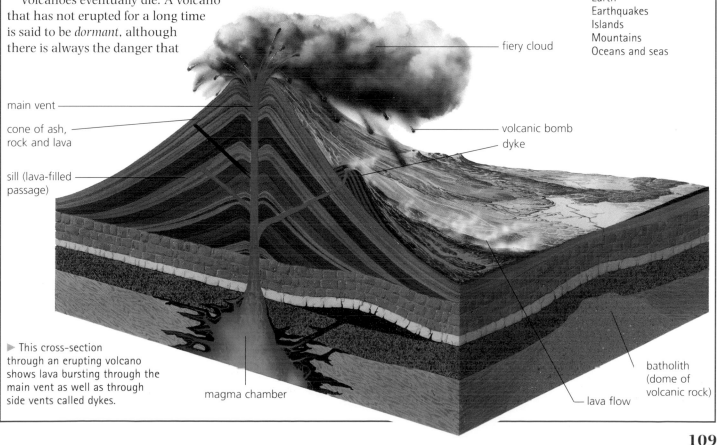

main vent

cone of ash, rock and lava

sill (lava-filled passage)

fiery cloud

volcanic bomb

dyke

batholith (dome of volcanic rock)

▶ This cross-section through an erupting volcano shows lava bursting through the main vent as well as through side vents called dykes.

magma chamber

lava flow

Wales

Wales is a part of the United Kingdom, in north-west Europe. In the Welsh language Wales is known as Cymru.

Much of Wales is mountainous, and there are also many lakes and rivers. Fast-flowing mountain rivers are used for hydroelectricity.

North and central Wales has a small population which lives mainly from farming and tourism. Many of the people speak Welsh. Sheep-farming is common. South Wales is industrial, and it is where most people live. Inland there are narrow valleys, in which houses and chapels cluster around the coalmines. There are few working coalmines now. New factories make cars, refrigerators and televisions.

FLASHBACK

Wales first appeared in recorded history when the Romans attacked it in the 1st century AD. The English conquered Wales at the end of the 13th century, and in 1536 its government was united with England's. The Welsh language was banned for all official business, but it did not die out.

In 1997 the Welsh voted for an assembly to discuss their own affairs.

find out more
Europe
United Kingdom

• Welsh, one of the oldest languages in Europe, might have disappeared if people had not grown to love the language of the Welsh Bible, first translated in 1588.

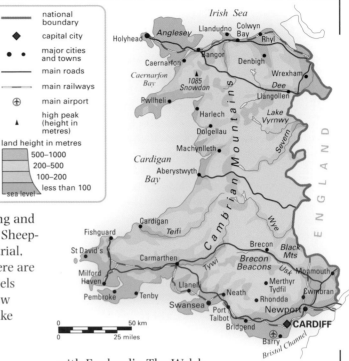

national boundary
capital city
major cities and towns
main roads
main railways
main airport
high peak (height in metres)
land height in metres
500–1000
200–500
100–200
less than 100
sea level

Waste disposal

Every home produces large quantities of tin cans, waste paper, glass and other rubbish. Homes and factories also produce sewage (waste material from toilets). If this waste is not disposed of with care, it can become a hazard, causing disease and pollution.

Rotting rubbish not only looks and smells unpleasant, it also acts as a breeding ground for flies, rats and other carriers of disease. The easiest and cheapest method of disposing of rubbish is *tipping* it into a hole in the ground, such as one left by quarrying or open-cast mining. This kind of tip is called a *landfill* site. It is important that the rainwater running off it does not enter rivers, since it may contain poisonous substances. Tipping can be used to reclaim waste land or marsh land. The reclaimed land cannot be used for building for a long time because it may sink as the buried rubbish rots.

Waste can also be disposed of by *incineration* (burning). This greatly reduces the volume of the waste material, and the ash is clean and germ-free. The heat produced by burning waste can be used to generate electricity. However, the incinerators are expensive and produce some polluting gases. Ground-up waste can be turned into either solid fuel pellets or compost for farmland and gardens.

find out more
Energy
Pollution
Water

▼ Waste water is carried by drains to the sewage works, where it is treated until it is clean enough to be pumped into a river or the sea.

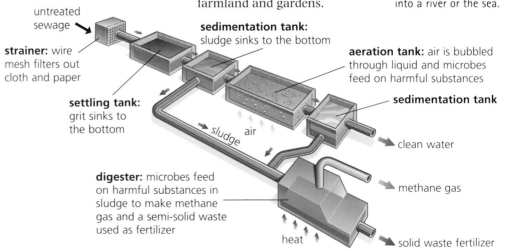

untreated sewage

strainer: wire mesh filters out cloth and paper

settling tank: grit sinks to the bottom

sedimentation tank: sludge sinks to the bottom

aeration tank: air is bubbled through liquid and microbes feed on harmful substances

sedimentation tank

sludge

air

clean water

digester: microbes feed on harmful substances in sludge to make methane gas and a semi-solid waste used as fertilizer

methane gas

heat

solid waste fertilizer

Water

Water covers almost three-quarters of the Earth's surface. The oceans, with an average depth of over 3 kilometres, hold about 97 per cent of the world's water. Frozen water forms the ice-caps at the North and South Poles. In the sky, clouds of water vapour bring rain, and where the rain falls and the rivers flow, plants and animals thrive. We use water in our homes for drinking, cooking, washing, cleaning, and flushing the lavatory. Factories need huge amounts of water for manufacturing things. Without water there would be no life on Earth.

Like many other substances, water is made up of molecules. These are so small that even the smallest raindrop contains billions. Every molecule of water consists of two atoms of hydrogen joined to a single atom of oxygen. Scientists say that the chemical formula for water is H_2O.

- In Europe, an average family of four people uses about 500 litres of water every day. You use 10 litres of water every time you flush a lavatory, and more than seven times that amount to have a bath.

▼ The water cycle. Only about 1% of the world's water is moving round the cycle at any one time.

Water and living things

Two-thirds of your body is water. Most of your blood is water. Your brain, heart, muscles and liver all contain water. Every day your body loses lots of water. About a litre goes down the toilet, and half a litre is lost as sweat and when you breathe out. You need about a litre and a half of water each day to stay alive.

Plants need water to grow. They usually take it in through their roots. They use water and other chemicals to make the substances needed for growth. They also use water to carry substances between their roots and leaves. The pressure of water in their cells helps plants to stay firm.

The water cycle

Water goes round and round in a process called the water cycle. In some parts of the cycle the water is a liquid (rain); in other parts it is a gas (water vapour) or a solid (ice). The warmth of the Sun evaporates water from seas, rivers and lakes, and also from the soil and plants on the land. The water turns into an invisible gas called

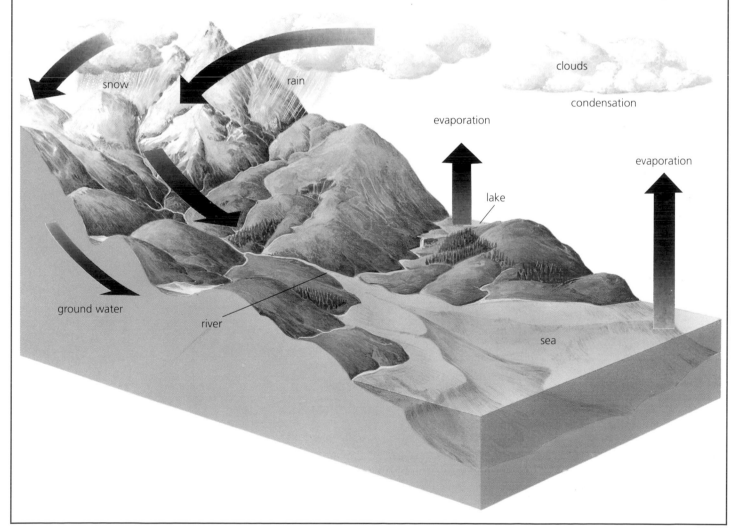

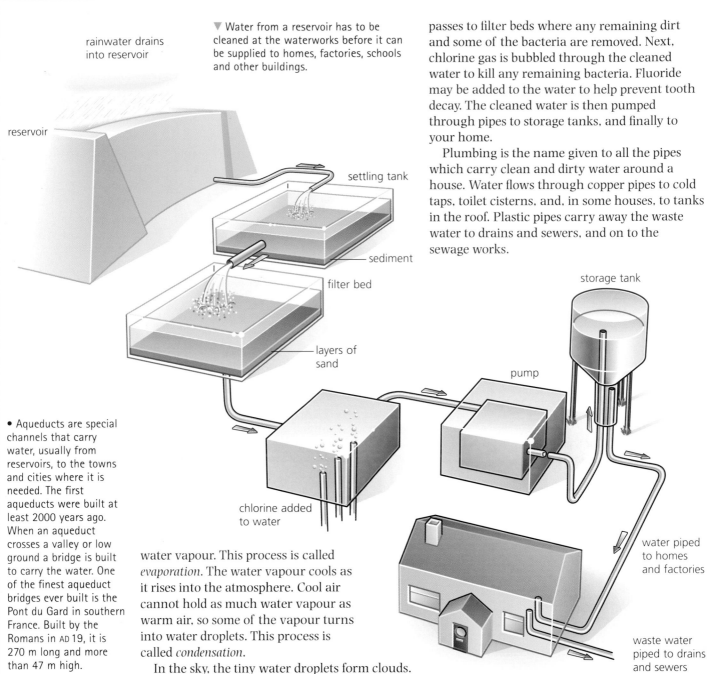

rainwater drains into reservoir

reservoir

▼ Water from a reservoir has to be cleaned at the waterworks before it can be supplied to homes, factories, schools and other buildings.

settling tank

sediment

filter bed

layers of sand

chlorine added to water

storage tank

pump

water piped to homes and factories

waste water piped to drains and sewers

passes to filter beds where any remaining dirt and some of the bacteria are removed. Next, chlorine gas is bubbled through the cleaned water to kill any remaining bacteria. Fluoride may be added to the water to help prevent tooth decay. The cleaned water is then pumped through pipes to storage tanks, and finally to your home.

Plumbing is the name given to all the pipes which carry clean and dirty water around a house. Water flows through copper pipes to cold taps, toilet cisterns, and, in some houses, to tanks in the roof. Plastic pipes carry away the waste water to drains and sewers, and on to the sewage works.

• Aqueducts are special channels that carry water, usually from reservoirs, to the towns and cities where it is needed. The first aqueducts were built at least 2000 years ago. When an aqueduct crosses a valley or low ground a bridge is built to carry the water. One of the finest aqueduct bridges ever built is the Pont du Gard in southern France. Built by the Romans in AD 19, it is 270 m long and more than 47 m high.

water vapour. This process is called *evaporation*. The water vapour cools as it rises into the atmosphere. Cool air cannot hold as much water vapour as warm air, so some of the vapour turns into water droplets. This process is called *condensation*.

In the sky, the tiny water droplets form clouds. If these droplets combine to form larger droplets, they will fall to Earth as rain, hail or snow. Much of the water that falls on the land flows to the sea in streams and rivers. Some soaks into the ground and some stays as ice. The water eventually finds its way into rivers and seas, where the water cycle begins again.

Water supplies

The water we use in our homes is rainwater from reservoirs, wells or rivers. Before this water can be pumped to your home, it must be cleaned at the waterworks. First, particles of sand, mud and grit sink and settle in a tank, and then the water

Hard and soft water

On its long journey to your home, rainwater washes over rocks and flows along rivers, dissolving gases from the air and many different substances from the rocks. Where there are chalk and limestone rocks, these dissolve in the rain and join with the dissolved gas, carbon dioxide, to form a substance called calcium bicarbonate. This and other similar chemicals produce 'hard' water. It is difficult to make a good lather with soap in hard water. Water that does not have these particular substances is called 'soft', but it still contains lots of different chemicals.

Weather

Rain, clouds, sunshine, wind: the conditions in the atmosphere and their day-to-day changes make up the weather. The weather affects our daily lives, and so we need to know in advance what it will be like. Weather forecasts aim to provide us with accurate details about weather conditions in the next 24 hours and for longer periods.

- The word 'meteorology' comes from two Greek words meaning 'study of what is high in the air'. (The word 'meteor' originally meant anything unusual that appeared in the sky.)

- It is likely that the weather affects people's moods. The warm, dusty sirocco wind of the Mediterranean and the mistral wind which blows down the Rhône Valley in France are famous for making people irritable.

Will it be safe to climb the mountain tomorrow? Do we need to grit the roads tonight? Will it be dry enough to harvest the crop this week? Everyone needs to know what the weather will be like in order to plan ahead. Information about future weather conditions saves money and can also save lives. Scientists who study the Earth's atmosphere and the weather are called *meteorologists*.

Weather recording

Reliable weather forecasting depends on a good supply of information about weather conditions all over the Earth. Thousands of separate pieces of weather information are collected several times a day from weather stations on land, from ships, from aeroplanes,

▲ A satellite view of Hurricane Fran approaching the US mainland from the Caribbean in September 1996. The hurricane brought winds up to 190 km per hour. The day after this picture was taken the hurricane came ashore, killing 34 people.

from weather balloons up in the atmosphere and from satellites orbiting the Earth.

Weather observations are made at ground level by recording instruments located in weather stations. These stations need to be on open sites, away from buildings and trees which could influence the accuracy of readings. Observations must be precise and presented in a standard way so they can be compared with those taken at other sites and times. Some recordings are made by instruments carried up into the atmosphere by special weather balloons. The instruments can measure temperature, air pressure and wind speed, and transmit their readings back to Earth by radio.

Up in space, weather satellites photograph cloud patterns and movements, and the Earth's surface. Some carry instruments that can measure the heat given off by clouds and the Earth. Weather satellites of NOAA (National Oceanographic and Atmospheric Administration) in the USA provide most of the cloud pictures that we see on TV weather forecasts.

Weather forecasting

Forecasters have to know what is happening over the whole planet, because today's weather in America could affect the weather in Europe a week later. The data collected from all the different forms of weather recording are fed into a giant communications network called the Global Telecommunications System. The information is sent round the world at great speed by satellite, radio and cable. Weather forecasters in

▼ Some weather-recording instruments.

Rainfall is measured in a **rain gauge**. The amount of rain that falls in a day is measured in a cylinder marked in millimetres.

An **anemometer** measures the speed of the wind in metres per second.

A **barograph** measures air pressure. When the air pressure changes, the top of the metal box (centre) bends and the movement is recorded on a rotating drum.

every country take from the system the data they need to make their own local forecast.

The information is first mapped on a 'synoptic chart', which shows the overall weather situation. Forecasters then make their predictions using their knowledge of how the atmosphere behaves, and with the help of computers which show what happened the last time when there were similar conditions. The forecasts must then be turned into maps and descriptions of what the weather will be like for the next 24 hours, for newspapers, television and radio.

Forecasts are becoming more accurate as time goes by, especially for short periods ahead. However, long-range forecasting is still difficult.

Cyclones and anticyclones

Cyclones and anticyclones affect the weather. A cyclone is an area of low air pressure, which means the air is rising. Cyclones often bring strong winds, stormy weather and even snow. They form over the sea, but as they move over large land areas cyclones gradually lose energy and fade out. Cyclones usually move faster than anticyclones. If you look at the weather maps for three or four days in a row, you can often follow the path of a cyclone.

Cyclones have different names in different parts of the world. In Britain they are usually called *depressions*. In tropical and subtropical areas a cyclone with very strong winds is called a *hurricane* or a *typhoon*. A tropical cyclone seen from a satellite is a great swirling mass of clouds. Its violent winds can do great damage as they roar across the oceans and islands.

In an anticyclone the air pressure is high because the air is sinking. Anticyclones bring more settled weather. In an anticyclone, high air pressure remains stable over a wide area. For example, a very large anticyclone stays over the vast area of Siberia in Russia every winter. It hardly changes its position from October to March, during which time the weather in Siberia is bitterly cold. Other parts of the world also have anticyclones in certain seasons. The weather map over the Sahara Desert often shows an anticyclone in the winter months.

• Many sayings about the weather are based on what the sky looks like. 'Red sky at night, shepherds' delight' is not always true, but 'Red sky in the morning, shepherds' warning' is usually reliable.

find out more
Atmosphere
Climate
Clouds
Energy
Greenhouse effect
Rain and snow
Seasons
Water
Wind

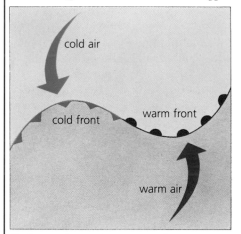

Before a depression: warm air meets cold air to form a warm front and a cold front.

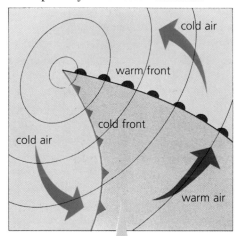

During a depression: the cold front pushes the warm air upwards. Large clouds form and heavy rain falls.

After a depression: the cold front catches up with the warm front. The different air masses mix, forming an occluded front.

◀ A depression has two *fronts* (the lines where two different masses of air meet). The warm front is the forward edge of warm air pushing against cold air. The cold front is the following edge of cold air pushing against warm air.

Wells and springs

A water well is a deep hole dug or drilled in the ground to obtain water. Many people still get their water supply from wells, particularly in rural areas. A spring is the name given to any natural flow of water out of the ground. Long ago, villages frequently grew up around large springs.

Some of the rain that falls on the land sinks into the ground. The water soaks easily through rocks such as sandstone or chalk. These rocks are said to be permeable. But some materials, such as clay, stop the water sinking any further, and are said to be impermeable. The water that goes into the ground sinks until it reaches either a layer of impermeable material, or a rock that cannot soak up any more water. The level in the ground below which water collects is called the *water table*. If a hole is dug deep enough to reach below the water table, water will seep from the surrounding rocks into the well. The water is then drawn or pumped up to the surface.

Springs are often found where permeable rocks lie above impermeable ones, particularly at the foot of steep slopes. Many of the largest rivers begin their lives as springs.

Sometimes a layer of water-holding rock is sandwiched between two layers of impermeable rock.

London is built over rocks like these. At one time, if a well was dug down to the water table under London, the pressure underground was so high that the water came out of the well like a fountain. A well like this is called an *artesian well*.

• Long ago, people believed that many wells were holy or lucky. The Celts of western Europe frequently built altars and made sacrifices at wells, while the Romans dedicated their wells to goddesses.

◀ Water from this village well in India is drawn up in buckets attached to a moving chain. The chain is driven round by a wheel moved by the oxen.

find out more
Oil
Rocks and minerals
Water

Wetlands

• People are slowly learning the usefulness of wetlands. In some places, beds of reeds are being planted to act as a natural filter for sewage, instead of building expensive treatment works.

find out more
Coasts
Lakes
Moors and heaths
Rivers and streams

Wetlands are damp, boggy areas where water lies on the surface, forming lakes or pools, or where plants have grown out into open water to form marshes or swamps. Wetlands support huge numbers of plants and animals, and their value to humans is enormous. For example, two-thirds of the fish caught around the world began their life in wetlands.

Wetlands are always changing. Once wetland plants begin to grow, they gradually build up and stabilize the ground, until eventually plants that grow on dry land can move in. In the same way, salt-marshes along coasts gradually extend out to sea. Wetlands disappear naturally as they become silted up, but at the same time new wetlands form in other places.

Types of wetland
There are many different kinds of wetland. Some are formed naturally, while others result from human activities.

Where rivers meander slowly over large flat flood plains, the slow-moving water drops the fine particles of soil and rock (sediment) into the water, and mudbanks gradually build up. River bends may get separated off, and form marshy

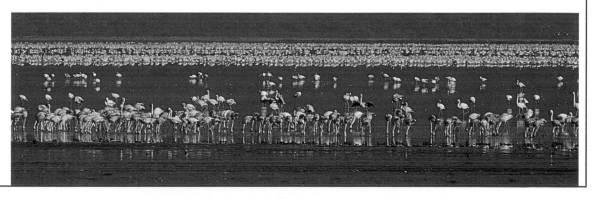

▶ Lesser flamingos on Lake Nakuru, a salty lake in Kenya, East Africa. Millions of birds come to the lake because the shallow water is full of the tiny insects, worms and crustaceans that they feed on.

An American alligator in the Everglades, a huge area of marshland in southern Florida, USA.

The importance of wetlands

Wetlands are enormously rich food sources. Many small animals live in the soft ground, and provide food for shrews, frogs, toads and long-legged shore birds such as sandpipers and curlews. Insects thrive in wetlands, attracting insect-eating warblers and flycatchers. Seed-eating birds come to wetlands for the seed heads of the reeds and rushes, and large mammals come for water. Because of the water and rich feeding available, wetlands are important stopover places for millions of migrating birds.

Wetlands are valuable for humans as well as animals and plants. They soak up water during storms and let it drain away gradually. This reduces the effect of floods downstream. Peatlands 'lock up' carbon dioxide released by burning coal and oil, and so help reduce global warming. Mangrove swamps help to protect tropical coastlines, by forming a natural barrier against severe storms and hurricanes. They are also important to the fishing industry, as many commercially caught fish breed in them.

In some places, wetlands ensure that the water supply for local cities is good enough to drink. The mud acts like a water filter, removing impurities from the water that passes through.

Saving wetlands

In recent years, humans have been destroying wetlands at an alarming rate. It is estimated that half the wetlands that once existed have been lost, and many more are under threat. Many wetlands have been drained so that the land they occupy can be built on or farmed. Other areas have been filled in as rubbish dumps. Many wetlands have become polluted, as the rivers that feed them have picked up pesticides and other chemicals. Some peatlands are being destroyed by large peat-fired power stations, which use up the peat much faster than it can be replaced. Peat is also used by gardeners, which adds to the destruction of wild peatlands.

Conservationists and scientists are persuading governments to set aside wetlands for wildlife, because of their valuable role in protecting the environment. But simply leaving wetlands alone is not enough. Many would gradually silt up and disappear. Their water supply must be carefully controlled to prevent this, and to stop the water draining away to surrounding areas.

▶ Mudskippers are small fishes that live in mangrove swamps, scuttling over the mud on their front fins. They can stay out of water for long periods, breathing a mixture of air and water stored in their gill chambers.

pools or lakes. Mud also builds up on the shores of estuaries, where rivers meet the sea. At the mouth of the largest rivers, this mud forms vast fan-shaped deltas. Plants which can cope with occasional flooding by salty sea water grow here, forming *salt-marshes*, which are home to many wading birds and other animals.

The coasts of some tropical seas are fringed with *mangrove swamps*. Mangroves are trees adapted to live in wet, salty places. Their roots stick up into the air from the mud. The plants take in oxygen from the air through these roots, because there is very little oxygen in the wet mud. Mangrove swamps are home to many different animals such as fiddler crabs, fishes, crocodiles, alligators and birds such as storks, ibises and herons.

Large areas of the cooler parts of the world are covered in *peatlands*. These are formed by remarkable plants called bog mosses, which are able to grow in waterlogged areas. As they grow, bog mosses trap water amongst their leaves, like a natural sponge. In the waterlogged soil of the peatlands, plant material does not rot away. Bog mosses pile up and form a spongy material known as peat. Peatlands are important areas for many breeding birds and insects.

Some wetlands are made by human activity. Disused gravel pits fill with water, and marshes develop around the edges of reservoirs. Many of these make valuable nature reserves. In warm countries, flooded paddy fields, made for growing rice, are home to fishes, egrets and herons.

Wind

Wind is flowing air. You can feel it on the ground and high up in the air. The wind can be very destructive, in the form of hurricanes and tornadoes. It can also be put to work for us, powering sailing ships, windmills and modern aerogenerators which produce electricity.

▲ A tornado looks like a violent, twisting funnel of cloud which stretches down from a storm cloud to the Earth. The wind twists up within the tunnel at speeds of up to 650 km/h.

• In southern France, a cold northerly wind called the mistral often blows for several days at a time during March and April.

• In North America a warm dry wind called the chinook blows down the eastern slopes of the Rocky Mountains. It causes the temperature to rise quickly, often making snow thaw rapidly. The word Chinook means 'snow eater' in a local Native American language.

find out more
Climate
Rain and snow
Weather

When the Sun warms the ground, the air above it rises up and cooler air flows in to take the place of the air which has risen. This flowing air is what we call wind.

Many winds have names. Among the most constant winds are the 'trade winds'. These winds blow towards the Equator and blow most of the year round. They got their name in the times when much world trade was done by sailing ships. Ships always tried to avoid other areas in tropical oceans where winds hardly ever blow. These are called the 'doldrums'.

Hurricanes and tornadoes

Hurricanes are violent storms with winds that can blow at 250 to 350 km/h and bring torrential rain. They pick up moisture over an area of warm sea and hurtle towards the land. Such storms are called hurricanes in the Atlantic, but in the Pacific and Indian Oceans they are often called *cyclones* or *typhoons*. The swirling mass of winds spirals upwards around the 'eye' at the centre of the storm. The eye of the hurricane is a fairly calm area, but the strongest winds occur immediately around it.

Hurricane winds can uproot trees, destroy buildings, and even lift up boats and cars and throw them around. Along with the heavy rains and destructive winds, hurricanes bring very high tides. Today, hurricanes can be tracked on satellite photos. Each one is given a name, and warnings are issued in good time so that people can leave the area if necessary.

A tornado is quite different from a hurricane. It is a smaller, faster and more violent wind. A tornado (sometimes called a *whirlwind* or *twister*) is a terrifying wind which destroys everything in its path. It rushes across the land, sucking up dust, sand, and even people and animals like a giant vacuum cleaner into its twisting centre.

Wind power
For centuries, windmills have used the power of the wind for grinding corn and pumping water. In the Netherlands and the fens of eastern England, windmills were used to drain water from low-lying land. They are still used in many parts of the world for pumping water from wells and drainage ditches. Today, *aerogenerators* are using the wind's energy to generate electricity. Unlike oil and gas, the wind is an energy source which will never run out and does not cause any pollution.

Most aerogenerators have a tall, slim tower with huge propeller-like blades mounted on top. The blades can be over 20 metres long. As they spin in the wind, they turn a generator which produces electricity. Aerogenerators are placed on exposed sites on high ground to catch the maximum force of the wind. Large groups of them form 'wind farms' like this one at Altamont Pass in California, USA.

Wood

Wood is the material that makes up the trunks of trees and shrubs. People use wood for making all kinds of things, and for building. Perhaps the greatest advantage of wood over other materials is that trees are a renewable resource – as long as we go on planting new trees, we can go on using wood for ever.

The business of planting trees, looking after forests, and felling (cutting down) trees is called *forestry*. It is a bit like a farmer sowing seeds and later harvesting the crops – except that trees take much longer to grow. Most wood grown in northern countries is from coniferous trees, such as pine and spruce. In some places people are cutting down conifers in wild forests without replanting them. This is also happening in tropical forests, and some of the most valuable wood from tropical forests, such as teak and mahogany, is becoming very rare.

   At the sawmill, large saws slice many logs into planks. Other logs are sliced into thin sheets, called veneers. These veneers may then be used to make plywood, which is stronger and cheaper to produce than solid woods of the same thickness. Any waste wood left over at the sawmill can be made into chipboard, which is often used for kitchen fittings and furniture. A lot of wood is also turned into pulp for making paper.

◀ Foresters at work in British Columbia, Canada. Foresters use power saws to fell trees, and large machines to trim the branches off the tree trunk.

• Wood from coniferous trees such as pine is called *softwood timber*. This is used for cheaper furniture, making paper, and many other things. Wood from broadleaved trees, such as beech, oak and mahogany, is called *hardwood timber*. It is used for high-quality furniture, and special items such as boats and musical instruments.

find out more
Forests

Wool

Wool comes from sheep, goats, llamas and some other animals. It is soft and resists dirt, static and tearing. Wool protects against both the cold and the heat. We use it to make strong, lasting fabrics for rugs, blankets and items of warm clothing such as coats, sweaters and gloves.

Wool has some unusual qualities which make it a very useful fibre. Wool is said to breathe because it stays in balance with the surrounding moisture even when no longer alive and growing. It absorbs and evaporates moisture.

   Two kinds of yarn are made from wool for weaving and knitting. *Woollens* are spun from fibres which vary in length and are jumbled up together.

Worsteds are spun from wool that is combed to make a smoother, more even yarn.

   Many countries have sheep and produce wool, but four countries dominate the world trade in wool: Australia, New Zealand, South Africa and Argentina. They export more than half their wool to countries in the northern hemisphere.

▶ FLASHBACK ◀

Prehistoric people wore sheepskins, but also made yarn and fabric from the fleece. From ancient to medieval times women spent time spinning, but weaving was considered more difficult and was left to men.

   Two hundred years ago cloth manufacture was revolutionized by the introduction of machines which could do work that had previously been done by hand.

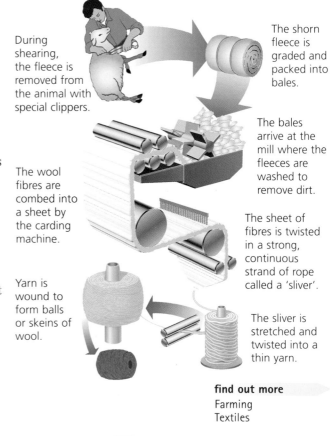

During shearing, the fleece is removed from the animal with special clippers.

The wool fibres are combed into a sheet by the carding machine.

Yarn is wound to form balls or skeins of wool.

The shorn fleece is graded and packed into bales.

The bales arrive at the mill where the fleeces are washed to remove dirt.

The sheet of fibres is twisted in a strong, continuous strand of rope called a 'sliver'.

The sliver is stretched and twisted into a thin yarn.

find out more
Farming
Textiles

DATA FILE

Countries of the world

The Countries of the world section includes maps and statistics that provide data about the world. You can use it to find out where a country that you are reading about in the encyclopedia is. You can also use it to find out some basic facts about each country.

The section opens with a small map of the world, which shows how the Earth is divided up into different time zones. This is followed by a large world map, which shows all the sovereign countries of the world. (A sovereign country is a territory with its own government.)

    The world map is followed by a list of all the sovereign countries, with their flags and some statistics. Countries that have entries in the A–Z section of the Encyclopedia are marked with an asterisk.

Time zones

Because the Earth spins, places across the world have day and night at different times. But if everyone used different local times it would be very confusing. Because of this the world is divided up into 24 'time zones', each of about 15° longitude.

Key

Numbers indicate how many hours ahead or behind Greenwich Mean Time (GMT) a place is.

- even no. of hours different from GMT
- odd no. of hours different from GMT
- $\frac{1}{2}$-hour difference from adjacent zone
- less than $\frac{1}{2}$-hour difference from adjacent zone

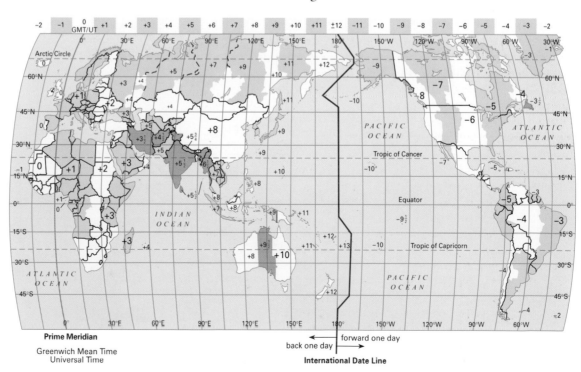

Countries and flags

A country is often defined as a *sovereign state* – a territory with its own people, its own government and its own laws. There are at present 189 sovereign states in the world, almost all of which are members of the United Nations. The exact number is always changing. Sometimes countries break up into separate states, while others unite. All these countries, apart from the tiny European countries of Liechtenstein, San Marino and Vatican City, appear on the map on the right. In addition, there are many islands and other territories that are part of other countries, which may control their affairs and make their laws. These are known as *dependencies* or *colonies*. Some of these territories also appear on the map, but their names are printed in small letters, not capitals.

All independent (sovereign) countries are listed, with their flags, on the following pages. There are articles in the main part of the encyclopedia on some of these. Those that have their own entry are indicated by an asterisk (*). Each of these country entries includes a locator map to show you the part of the world where it is situated. Many also contain a detailed map of the country. There are entries for each of the continents, which also include maps. There are also entries on certain regions, such as Scandinavia and the Middle East, again including maps. More information on maps is given in the article on **Maps**.

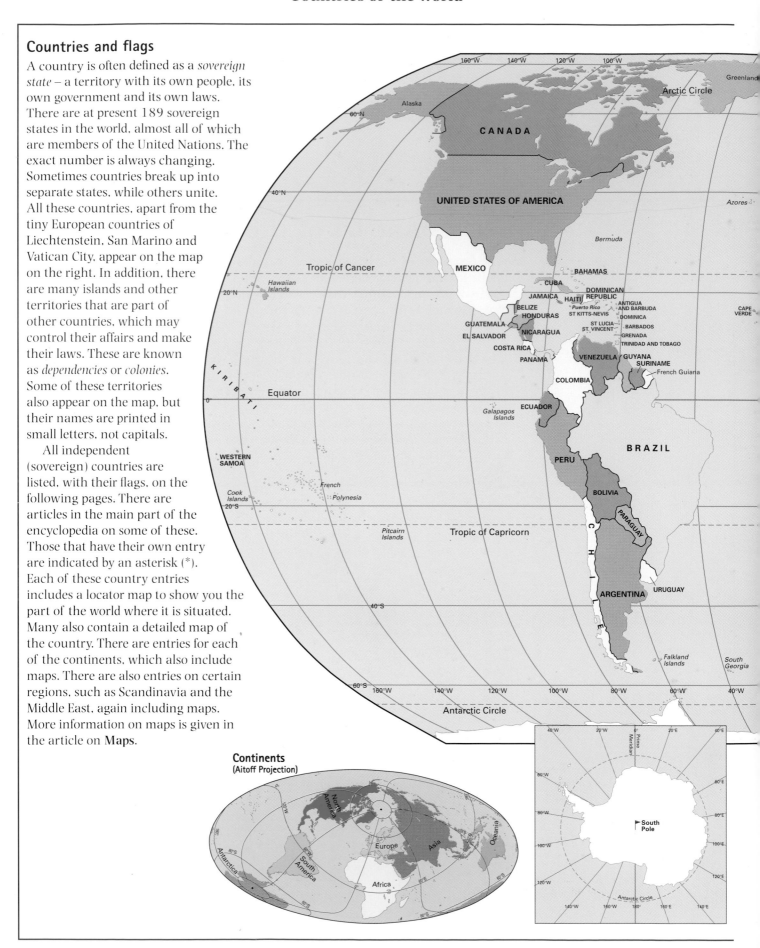

Continents
(Aitoff Projection)

Countries of the world

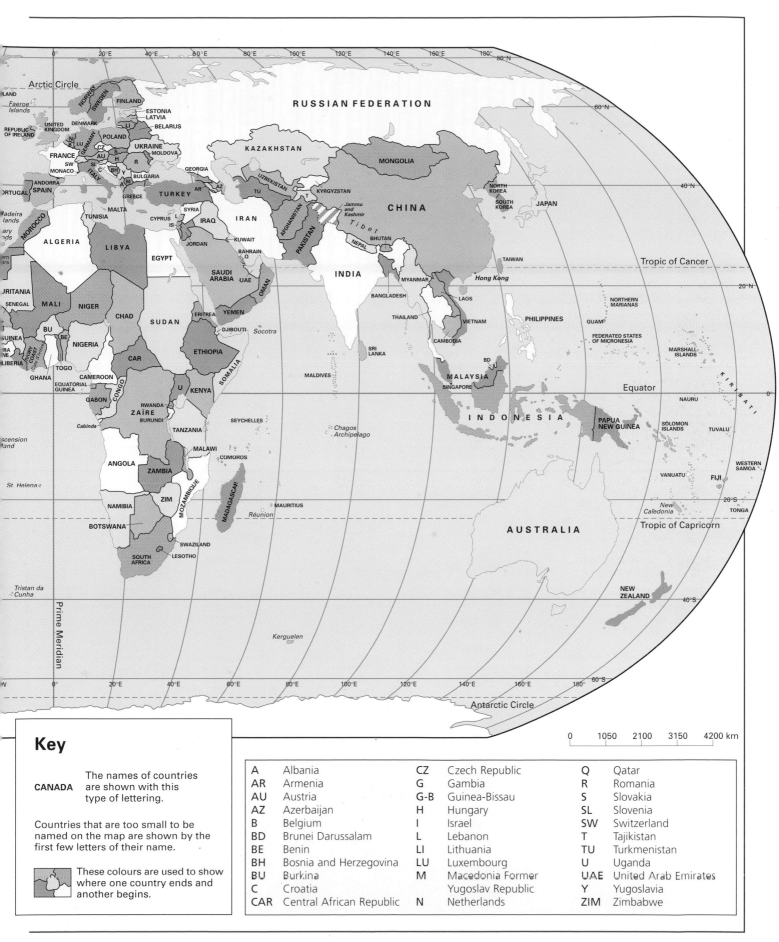

Key

CANADA The names of countries are shown with this type of lettering.

Countries that are too small to be named on the map are shown by the first few letters of their name.

These colours are used to show where one country ends and another begins.

A	Albania	CZ	Czech Republic	Q	Qatar
AR	Armenia	G	Gambia	R	Romania
AU	Austria	G-B	Guinea-Bissau	S	Slovakia
AZ	Azerbaijan	H	Hungary	SL	Slovenia
B	Belgium	I	Israel	SW	Switzerland
BD	Brunei Darussalam	L	Lebanon	T	Tajikistan
BE	Benin	LI	Lithuania	TU	Turkmenistan
BH	Bosnia and Herzegovina	LU	Luxembourg	U	Uganda
BU	Burkina	M	Macedonia Former	UAE	United Arab Emirates
C	Croatia		Yugoslav Republic	Y	Yugoslavia
CAR	Central African Republic	N	Netherlands	ZIM	Zimbabwe

Countries of the world

Afghanistan
Capital Kabul
Population 20,500,000
Area 652,090 sq km

Albania
Capital Tiranë
Population 3,420,000
Area 28,748 sq km

Algeria
Capital Algiers
Population 28,580,000
Area 2,381,741 sq km

Andorra
Capital Andorra la Vella
Population 62,500
Area 465 sq km

Angola
Capital Luanda
Population 11,500,000
Area 1,246,700 sq km

Antigua and Barbuda
Capital St John's
Population 63,900
Area 442 sq km

Argentina
Capital Buenos Aires
Population 34,770,000
Area 2,766,889 sq km

Armenia
Capital Yerevan
Population 3,700,000
Area 29,800 sq km

*Australia
Capital Canberra
Population 18,300,000
Area 7,682,300 sq km

Austria
Capital Vienna
Population 8,050,000
Area 83,853 sq km

Azerbaijan
Capital Baku
Population 7,500,000
Area 86,600 sq km

Bahamas
Capital Nassau
Population 275,000
Area 13,935 sq km

Bahrain
Capital Manama
Population 586,109
Area 688 sq km

*Bangladesh
Capital Dhaka
Population 118,700,000
Area 143,999 sq km

Barbados
Capital Bridgetown
Population 264,300
Area 430 sq km

Belarus
Capital Minsk
Population 10,400,000
Area 207,600 sq km

Belgium
Capital Brussels
Population 10,140,000
Area 30,513 sq km

Belize
Capital Belmopan
Population 209,500
Area 22,963 sq km

Benin
Capital Porto Novo
Population 5,460,000
Area 112,622 sq km

Bhutan
Capital Thimphu
Population 600,000
Area 46,500 sq km

Bolivia
Capital La Paz
Population 8,070,000
Area 1,098,600 sq km

Bosnia and Herzegovina
Capital Sarajevo
Population 4,370,000
Area 51,129 sq km

Botswana
Capital Gaborone
Population 1,400,000
Area 581,730 sq km

*Brazil
Capital Brasília
Population 155,800,000
Area 8,511,965 sq km

Brunei Darussalam
Capital Bandar Seri Begawan
Population 276,300
Area 5765 sq km

Bulgaria
Capital Sofia
Population 8,430,000
Area 110,911 sq km

Burkina
Capital Ouagadougou
Population 10,000,000
Area 274,200 sq km

Burundi
Capital Bujumbura
Population 5,360,000
Area 27,834 sq km

Cambodia
Capital Phnom Penh
Population 9,860,000
Area 181,035 sq km

Cameroon
Capital Yaoundé
Population 12,200,000
Area 465,054 sq km

*Canada
Capital Ottawa
Population 29,960,000
Area 9,970,610 sq km

Cape Verde
Capital Praia, on São Tiago
Population 420,000
Area 4033 sq km

Central African Republic
Capital Bangui
Population 3,070,000
Area 622,984 sq km

Chad
Capital N'Djamena
Population 6,280,000
Area 1,284,000 sq km

Chile
Capital Santiago
Population 14,660,000
Area 756,945 sq km

*China
Capital Beijing
Population 1,119,000,000
Area 9,596,961 sq km

Colombia
Capital Bogotá
Population 34,500,000
Area 1,138,914 sq km

Comoros
Capital Moroni, on Njazidja
Population 490,000
Area 1862 sq km

Congo, Democratic Republic of
Capital Kinshasa
Population 45,260,000
Area 2,344,885 sq km

Congo, Republic of
Capital Brazzaville
Population 2,940,000
Area 342,000 sq km

Costa Rica
Capital San José
Population 3,370,000
Area 51,100 sq km

Croatia
Capital Zagreb
Population 4,840,000
Area 56,538 sq km

Cuba
Capital La Habana (Havana)
Population 10,980,000
Area 110,861 sq km

Cyprus
Capital Nicosia
Population 729,800
Area 9,251 sq km

Czech Republic
Capital Prague
Population 10,330,000
Area 78,664 sq km

Denmark
Capital Copenhagen
Population 5,300,000
Area 43,075 sq km

Djibouti
Capital Djibouti
Population 586,000
Area 23,200 sq km

*Countries marked with an asterisk have their own entry in the main part of the encyclopedia.

Countries of the world

 Dominica
Capital Roseau
Population 74,200
Area 750 sq km

 Dominican Republic
Capital Santo Domingo
Population 7,770,000
Area 48,442 sq km

 Ecuador
Capital Quito
Population 11,700,000
Area 283,561 sq km

 Egypt
Capital Cairo
Population 60,240,000
Area 1,002,000 sq km

 El Salvador
Capital San Salvador
Population 5,050,000
Area 21,393 sq km

 Equatorial Guinea
Capital Malabo
Population 420,000
Area 28,051 sq km

 Eritrea
Capital Asmara
Population 3,530,000
Area 93,679 sq km

 Estonia
Capital Tallinn
Population 1,600,000
Area 45,100 sq km

 Ethiopia
Capital Addis Ababa
Population 55,000,000
Area 1,104,300 sq km

 Fiji
Capital Suva
Population 803,500
Area 18,274 sq km

 Finland
Capital Helsinki
Population 5,120,000
Area 338,142 sq km

 *France
Capital Paris
Population 58,000,000
Area 547,026 sq km

 Gabon
Capital Libreville
Population 1,010,000
Area 267,667 sq km

 Gambia
Capital Banjul
Population 1,090,000
Area 11,295 sq km

 Georgia
Capital Tbilisi (Tiflis)
Population 5,430,000
Area 69,700 sq km

 *Germany
Capital Berlin (formal)
Population 81,540,000
Area 356,945 sq km

 Ghana
Capital Accra
Population 16,470,000
Area 238,537 sq km

 Greece
Capital Athens
Population 10,400,000
Area 131,957 sq km

 Grenada
Capital St George's
Population 96,000
Area 344 sq km

 Guatemala
Capital Guatemala City
Population 10,620,000
Area 108,889 sq km

 Guinea
Capital Conakry
Population 6,500,000
Area 245,857 sq km

 Guinea-Bissau
Capital Bissau
Population 1,060,000
Area 36,125 sq km

 Guyana
Capital Georgetown
Population 730,000
Area 215,000 sq km

 Haiti
Capital Port-au-Prince
Population 6,760,000
Area 27,750 sq km

 Honduras
Capital Tegucigalpa
Population 5,290,000
Area 112,088 sq km

 Hungary
Capital Budapest
Population 10,210,000
Area 93,032 sq km

 Iceland
Capital Reykjavik
Population 267,800
Area 103,000 sq km

 *India
Capital New Delhi
Population 913,200,000
Area 3,287,590 sq km

 *Indonesia
Capital Jakarta
Population 191,360,000
Area 1,904,569 sq km

 Iran
Capital Tehran
Population 63,200,000
Area 1,648,000 sq km

 Iraq
Capital Baghdad
Population 19,410,000
Area 434,925 sq km

 *Ireland, Republic of
Capital Dublin
Population 3,620,000
Area 70,283 sq km

 Israel
Capital Jerusalem
Population 5,710,000
Area 20,700 sq km

 *Italy
Capital Rome
Population 57,270,000
Area 301,225 sq km

 Ivory Coast (Côte d'Ivoire)
Capital Yamoussoukro
Population 13,720,000
Area 322,463 sq km

 Jamaica
Capital Kingston
Population 2,500,000
Area 10,991 sq km

 *Japan
Capital Tokyo
Population 125,570,000
Area 377,708 sq km

 Jordan
Capital Amman
Population 4,100,000
Area 91,860 sq km

 Kazakhstan
Capital Alma-Ata
Population 16,500,000
Area 2,717,300 sq km

 Kenya
Capital Nairobi
Population 26,440,000
Area 582,600 sq km

 Kiribati
Capital Bairiki
Population 80,000
Area 811 sq km

 Kuwait
Capital Kuwait City
Population 2,020,000
Area 17,819 sq km

 Kyrgyzstan
Capital Biskek
Population 4,460,000
Area 198,500 sq km

 Laos
Capital Vientiane
Population 4,580,000
Area 236,800 sq km

 Latvia
Capital Riga
Population 2,490,000
Area 64,500 sq km

 Lebanon
Capital Beirut
Population 2,840,000
Area 10,400 sq km

 Lesotho
Capital Maseru
Population 2,110,000
Area 30,355 sq km

 Liberia
Capital Monrovia
Population 2,830,000
Area 111,370 sq km

Countries of the world

 Libya
Capital Tripoli
Population 5,590,000
Area 1,759,540 sq km

 Liechtenstein
Capital Vaduz
Population 30,923
Area 160 sq km

 Lithuania
Capital Vilnius
Population 3,710,000
Area 65,200 sq km

 Luxembourg
Capital Luxembourg
Population 412,800
Area 2586 sq km

 Macedonia (FYROM)
Capital Skopje
Population 1,950,000
Area 25,713 sq km

 Madagascar
Capital Antananarivo
Population 13,500,000
Area 587,041 sq km

 Malawi
Capital Lilongwe
Population 11,000,000
Area 118,484 sq km

 Malaysia
Capital Kuala Lumpur
Population 21,300,000
Area 330,434 sq km

 Maldives
Capital Malé
Population 253,300
Area 298 sq km

 Mali
Capital Bamako
Population 9,200,000
Area 1,240,000 sq km

 Malta
Capital Valletta
Population 376,330
Area 316 sq km

 Mauritania
Capital Nouakchott
Population 2,330,000
Area 1,030,700 sq km

 Mauritius
Capital Port Louis
Population 1,130,000
Area 2045 sq km

 ***Mexico**
Capital Mexico City
Population 91,120,000
Area 1,972,547 sq km

 Moldova
Capital Kishinev
Population 4,400,000
Area 33,700 sq km

 Monaco
Capital Monaco
Population 29,970
Area 1.95 sq km

 Mongolia
Capital Ulan Bator
Population 2,300,000
Area 1,565,000 sq km

 Morocco
Capital Rabat
Population 26,100,000
Area 446,550 sq km

 Mozambique
Capital Maputo
Population 16,000,000
Area 799,380 sq km

 Myanmar (Burma)
Capital Rangoon (Yangon)
Population 44,740,000
Area 676,552 sq km

 Namibia
Capital Windhoek
Population 1,510,000
Area 823,172 sq km

 Nauru
Capital Yaren
Population 8,100
Area 21 sq km

 Nepal
Capital Kathmandu
Population 19,280,000
Area 140,747 sq km

 Netherlands
Capital Amsterdam
Population 15,420,000
Area 40,844 sq km

 ***New Zealand**
Capital Wellington
Population 3,660,000
Area 268,046 sq km

 Nicaragua
Capital Managua
Population 4,400,000
Area 130,000 sq km

 Niger
Capital Niamey
Population 9,460,000
Area 1,267,00 sq km

 ***Nigeria**
Capital Abuja
Population 97,220,000
Area 923,768 sq km

 North Korea
Capital Pyongyang
Population 23,260,000
Area 121,250 sq km

 Norway
Capital Oslo
Population 4,400,000
Area 386,638 sq km

 Oman
Capital Muscat
Population 2,140,000
Area 300,000 sq km

 ***Pakistan**
Capital Islamabad
Population 130,200,000
Area 796,095 sq km

 Palau
Capital Koror
Population 18,000
Area 1632 sq km

 Panama
Capital Panama City
Population 2,330,000
Area 77,082 sq km

 Papua New Guinea
Capital Port Moresby
Population 3,850,000
Area 461,691 sq km

 Paraguay
Capital Asunción
Population 4,900,000
Area 406,800 sq km

 Peru
Capital Lima
Population 23,850,000
Area 1,285,215 sq km

 Philippines
Capital Manila
Population 69,800,000
Area 300,000 sq km

 Poland
Capital Warsaw
Population 38,610,000
Area 312,683 sq km

 Portugal
Capital Lisbon
Population 9,900,000
Area 92,082 sq km

 Qatar
Capital Doha
Population 539,000
Area 11,437 sq km

 Romania
Capital Bucharest
Population 22,730,500
Area 237,500 sq km

 ***Russia**
Capital Moscow
Population 147,500,000
Area 17,075,000 sq km

 Rwanda
Capital Kigali
Population 7,460,000
Area 26,338 sq km

 St Kitts–Nevis
Capital Basseterre
Population 45,100
Area 261 sq km

 St Lucia
Capital Castries
Population 140,900
Area 617 sq km

 St Vincent & Grenadines
Capital Kingstown
Population 109,000
Area 344 sq km

*Countries marked with an
asterisk have their own entry in
the main part of the encyclopedia.

Countries of the world

 Samoa
Capital Apia
Population 163,000
Area 2831 sq km

 San Marino
Capital San Marino
Population 24,003
Area 61 sq km

 São Tomé and Principe
Capital São Tomé
Population 131,000
Area 1001 sq km

 Saudi Arabia
Capital Riyadh
Population 16,900,000
Area 2,200,000 sq km

 Senegal
Capital Dakar
Population 7,970,000
Area 196,192 sq km

 Seychelles
Capital Victoria, on Mahé
Population 73,850
Area 455 sq km

 Sierra Leone
Capital Freetown
Population 4,460,000
Area 71,740 sq km

 Singapore
Capital Singapore City
Population 2,990,000
Area 618 sq km

 Slovakia
Capital Bratislava
Population 5,370,000
Area 49,035 sq km

 Slovenia
Capital Ljubljana
Population 1,980,000
Area 20,251 sq km

 Solomon Islands
Capital Honiara
Population 349,500
Area 28,370 sq km

 Somalia
Capital Mogadishu
Population 9,200,000
Area 637,657 sq km

 ***South Africa**
Capital Pretoria (administrative)
Population 41,540,000
Area 1,221,031 sq km

 South Korea
Capital Seoul
Population 44,610,000
Area 98,992 sq km

 ***Spain**
Capital Madrid
Population 40,460,000
Area 504,750 sq km

 Sri Lanka
Capital Colombo
Population 17,900,000
Area 65,610 sq km

 Sudan
Capital Khartoum
Population 28,900,000
Area 2,505,800 sq km

 Suriname
Capital Paramaribo
Population 407,000
Area 163,265 sq km

 Swaziland
Capital Mbabane
Population 850,630
Area 17,400 sq km

 Sweden
Capital Stockholm
Population 8,840,000
Area 449,964 sq km

 Switzerland
Capital Bern
Population 7,020,000
Area 41,293 sq km

 Syria
Capital Damascus
Population 14,620,000
Area 185,180 sq km

 Taiwan
Capital Taipei
Population 21,500,000
Area 36,174 sq km

 Tajikistan
Capital Dushanbe
Population 5,700,000
Area 143,100 sq km

 Tanzania
Capital Dodoma
Population 29,700,000
Area 945,050 sq km

 Thailand
Capital Bangkok
Population 58,340,000
Area 514,820 sq km

 Togo
Capital Lomé
Population 3,500,000
Area 56,785 sq km

 Tonga
Capital Nuku'alofa
Population 103,000
Area 749,900 sq km

 Trinidad and Tobago
Capital Port of Spain
Population 1,270,000
Area 5130 sq km

 Tunisia
Capital Tunis
Population 8,800,000
Area 164,150 sq km

 Turkey
Capital Ankara
Population 62,530,000
Area 779,452 sq km

 Turkmenistan
Capital Ashkhabad
Population 4,500,000
Area 488,100 sq km

 Tuvalu
Capital Fongafale
Population 10,900
Area 24 sq km

 Uganda
Capital Kampala
Population 16,670,000
Area 236,036 sq km

 Ukraine
Capital Kiev
Population 52,140,000
Area 603,700 sq km

 United Arab Emirates
Capital Abu Dhabi
Population 2,400,000
Area 83,600 sq km

 ***United Kingdom**
Capital London
Population 58,780,000
Area 244,046 sq km

 ***United States of America**
Capital Washington, DC
Population 265,620,000
Area 9,372,614 sq km

 Uruguay
Capital Montevideo
Population 3,200,000
Area 186,925 sq km

 Uzbekistan
Capital Tashkent
Population 22,200,000
Area 447,000 sq km

 Vanuatu
Capital Vila
Population 160,000
Area 12,190 sq km

 Vatican City
Population 1000
Area 0.44 sq km

 Venezuela
Capital Caracas
Population 20,410,000
Area 912,050 sq km

 Vietnam
Capital Hanoi
Population 74,000,000
Area 329,556 sq km

 Yemen
Capital Sana'a
Population 15,800,000
Area 528,000 sq km

 Yugoslavia
Capital Belgrade
Population 10,540,000
Area 102,350 sq km

 Zambia
Capital Lusaka
Population 8,940,000
Area 752,620 sq km

 Zimbabwe
Capital Harare
Population 11,500,000
Area 390,580 sq km

Index

If an index entry is printed in **bold**, it means that there is an article under that name in the A–Z section of the encyclopedia. When an entry has more than one page number, the most important one may be printed in **bold**. Page numbers in *italic* mean that there is an illustration relating to the entry on that page.